Rogan

HarperCollins*Publishers*
1 London Bridge Street
London SE1 9GF

www.harpercollins.co.uk

First published by HarperCollins*Publishers* 2018

1 3 5 7 9 10 8 6 4 2

Photographs © Cristian Barnett 2018,
apart from page 33 © nnattalli/Shutterstock.com
Photographs on pages 170, 171, 216 and 217, reproduced courtesy of the Flying Fish Company

Jacket image © Valentina Razumova/Shutterstock.com

Food stylist: Nicole Herft
Prop stylist: Lydia Brun
Design and art direction: James Empringham

Simon Rogan asserts the moral right to be identified as the author of this work

A catalogue record of this book is available from the British Library

HB ISBN 978-0-00-823272-6
EB ISBN 978-0-00-823273-3

Printed and bound by GPS Group

MIX
Paper from
responsible sources
FSC™ C007454

This book is produced from independently certified FSC paper to ensure
responsible forest management.
For more information visit: www.harpercollins.co.uk/green

Rogan

THE COOKBOOK

PHOTOGRAPHY BY

CRISTIAN BARNETT

CONTENTS

INTRODUCTION

The rolling hills of Cumbria might not seem the obvious place for a city boy from Southampton to settle down, and once I thought so too, but now, sixteen years after setting up my restaurants and farm at Cartmel, I feel totally at home there. It is a place that has allowed me to fulfil my dreams, and to create the sort of food I have always wanted to, using ingredients produced to my specifications.

My passion for cooking began as a child, and by my teens I was working in the kitchens of some of the best restaurants in the world for the finest, most inspirational chefs. I was lucky to get such a fantastic training, but the basis of my cooking is not just about the combination of flavours, textures and colours on the plate; what matters most is the origins of the foods I am using. While working in other chefs' kitchens I always knew that what I really wanted was to cook my way, using the freshest, most seasonal ingredients that I could find, whose provenance I knew.

Opening my own restaurant was, of course, my ultimate goal, but for me the vision didn't end there. With taste and flavour at the forefront of my mind, my main aim then, as it is now, was to have a restaurant that used foodstuffs from its own world-leading, natural and sustainable growing operation. What I'd been dreaming of for so long was an organic farm designed by chefs, run by chefs for chefs.

My food philosophy has always been about connecting the restaurant and the food we serve to the local area and the seasons, but this also goes deeper. I believe, whether we are cooking at home or in a professional kitchen, we can't truly understand our food if we don't know where it has come from. The origins of our ingredients is crucial, not just for our enjoyment of it and our health, but also for the sake of our planet. We need to do more to protect the Earth; we are on the verge of a climate disaster and if we don't make changes fast, gastronomy will not be sustainable, and may not even exist as we know it today. It's not all doom and gloom, though; rather than be overwhelmed by anxiety over climate change, we should see this as the time to adopt a new approach, to create a positive future for the generations to come.

The way we eat now has shifted more in the last five years than in the last 10,000; we were once such simple creatures, working with the seasons and taking only what we needed from the land, but with the quest for cheap food and high profits we have created a world where any ingredient is available all of the time.

In the supermarkets, there are no seasons – you can buy tomatoes year round which are grown on the other side of the world, picked when green and ripened using ethylene gas. What you get looks like a tomato, but really it is just an idea of a tomato, lacking the flavours, textures and colours of the home-grown product.

This isn't only true of the foods that are imported from around the globe; the majority of non-organic locally sourced vegetables you find in supermarkets are grown 'conventionally' – meaning they have been sprayed with seriously dangerous, toxic chemicals to ensure 'perfect' blemish-free crops and high yields. Chemical pesticides, herbicides and fertilisers are big business, and many farmers are wholly reliant on them. Thus the majority of commercial vegetables are actually bad for our health. To me, this just isn't right.

This food revolution shouldn't just be confined to fruit and vegetables, it is also relevant to the vitally important question of how we rear livestock. Fundamentally, although I do eat meat and would never call myself a vegetarian, I think we should eat less meat and try to change our

mindsets so that meat and fish don't dominate the plate. I cook meat in the restaurants, but often only as the protein element of a dish, which plays a supporting role to fresh vegetables and herbs.

I'm not anti-animal husbandry per se, but the commercial farming of livestock has a huge impact on both the environment and the health and happiness of the animals themselves, which in turn has an effect on the flavour of the meat produced. Most of the processed foods that we consume every single day have a connection to chemically produced corn, wheat and soy bean fields, and these three commodities are also fed en masse to the world's cattle population.

Cows are not designed to eat these products, they are designed to eat grass and forage from woodlands, but instead they are pumped full of dangerous grains to fatten and finish them very quickly, then topped up with hormones and antibiotics to cope with the stress of such an unnatural diet. We are effectively producing meat that is damaging to our health.

Feeding these animals in this way has a very clear impact on the planet, as a staggering 45 per cent of the world's land mass has been cleared for animal agriculture and to cultivate the grains to feed them. Producing meat and dairy products also puts pressure on water supplies – animals consume 30 per cent of the world's water (humans consume 19.6 billion litres of water and 9.5 billion kg of food per day, cows 170.3 billion litres of water and 61.3 billion kg of food per day) and are fed water-intensive grains. In addition, waste and fertiliser run-off is the leading cause of water pollution and ocean dead zones, destroying habitats and causing species extinction on land and in waterways.

And the impact of commercially rearing livestock doesn't end there. Raising cattle in intensive systems produces more greenhouse gases than the world's transportation system combined. Livestock produce methane, which is 86 times more destructive than carbon dioxide emissions from vehicles. Animal agriculture produces both of these

gases, along with nitrous oxide, which accounts for 51 per cent of 'human-caused' climate change.

To me, none of this makes sense. Nature provides such abundance when it is nurtured and respected, and in these days of overconsumption on a global scale, I believe we need to step back and appreciate what our local area offers us. And now is the time to make those major changes that are needed within our food system.

This wider environmental context was, and still is, very much a part of my vision and approach to food. As with everything we cook, I need to know that it has been produced in an environmentally sensitive way. If we purchase ingredients from outside of the farm, I want to know their history, and that they have been produced in a sustainable, organic way.

So, at the start of the new millenium, frustrated at the way in which I was cooking, I started to actively search for suitable premises to open up my own restaurant. Originally I looked in the area around my home on the south coast, but after months of searching and visiting sites, I drew a blank – nothing was quite right. Then, suddenly, I got a phone call from an old friend, telling me about a site ... in a village in Cumbria. Once I'd worked out where Cartmel actually was, and got my head round the fact that it was hundreds of miles from where I'd envisaged being based, I agreed to take a look.

Having been lured up north by the promise of an 800-year-old former smithy in a picturesque Cumbrian village, I left the south coast on a wet Friday morning and arrived at Cartmel that afternoon. The building, in the process of being converted into a restaurant, was tucked away in the corner of a sleepy, twelfth-century village famed for its medieval priory, the smallest horse-racing track in Britain and sticky toffee pudding, set amongst the rolling hills and valleys of the Lake District. Although it was in the process of renovation, I could see its potential. I had been sold a vision – and I bought it. Here was a restaurant that could be everything I dreamed of.

The original idea behind the restaurant, of course, was to be able to cultivate our own fruits and vegetables, so that we could then get these delicious, lovingly nurtured products from farm to plate in minutes, fresh from our own organic soil, rather than be dependent on suppliers shipping in produce from distant shores or across the length of the country.

So once the building had been acquired, stage two of the plan was finding an organic farm near the restaurant who could grow this for us. Being 100 per cent self-sufficient was not the intention – we knew the limitations of our abilities, being chefs, not farmers – but we wanted what we served to our guests to be locally produced and seasonal. The surrounding woodlands, the nearby coast, all the many local artisans – the cheese makers, farmers and brewers – meant that in the Lake District I could create a business that was just that, one that connected and worked in total harmony with its environment.

We worked with the farm for a while, before we had the opportunity to take over the land. Soon, though, we had outgrown the site and found ourselves needing more space – and to be closer to the restaurants. So in autumn 2011 we took possession of a huge, flat grazing field on the outskirts of Cartmel. It was ideal for our purposes; very fertile, located in the bottom of valley with a beck running alongside for natural irrigation, and sheltered from winds by trees and hedgerows.

It took a lot of time and back-breaking work to get the land into shape for what we needed – we had to source a lot of good-quality soil to improve what was there – but it was worth it, because it is such a vital part of what we do in all our restaurants. Our Farm, as it is called, works hard for us, providing us with what we need for the kitchens on a daily basis, but also enough to preserve for the out-of-season months as well as to experiment with.

We grow our own not just because we fundamentally believe in strengthening the link between produce, its development, the environment and what we eat, but from a chef's perspective, working with fresh ingredients gives us ultimate control in the kitchen – we are able to enjoy the most diverse seasonal produce picked fresh for the plate.

And not only can we grow what we want, need and love, and be able to use it fresh when we need it, we also know that everything that comes into our kitchen has been grown naturally, free from chemical farming and without the carbon footprint that comes with imported goods.

The early days (make that early years!) were a steep learning curve, and we're still learning – even now we spend a lot of time researching how other people manage their organic growing operations around the world, and we have a go at putting the best ideas into practice on our own land. Some work, some don't; these are the vagaries of our soil and our location in a valley in the north of England, but we learn and we move on, designing our growing systems to reflect our beliefs about food and to serve the needs and demands of the restaurant. And that is the joy of having our land, as it allows us to experiment. When you are able to grow whatever you want, you can try different crops, which is how we have discovered some incredible new tastes, flavours and surprising combinations. My work often takes me to far-flung places around the world, where I love to wander through the markets, taking in the sights, smells and colours of interesting and exotic foods, and it's even more fascinating to watch what the locals do with them. I often come back from these trips with seeds for these unusual plants, which I have a go at planting at home. While most of the stuff we grow is indigenous (and it's indigenous for a reason, because that's what grows best!), if we can get an exotic seedling to grow and flourish in our soil without the need for expensive and unnatural special attention such as lighting and heating, I'll give it a go. The beauty is in knowing that I can take a rare herb, vegetable or fruit from anywhere in the world and try to grow it in Cumbria, then without any point of reference it becomes a new food experience for our guests. Apple marigold

is one great example of this; originally from South America, we grow it at Our Farm because it brings something unique to our dishes both sweet and savoury, and because, despite its origins, it thrives in our climate.

So sometimes these seeds work out, sometimes they don't. We don't push it – over the years, amongst the successes there have been many failures, but that's Nature letting us know that it just isn't right for us. If it doesn't work, we let it go. It goes against everything we believe in to provide enhanced conditions for the sake of growing something – we have polytunnels but they are not artificially heated, and we won't bring in extra equipment for the sake of cultivating an exotic species.

We grow many varieties of vegetables, fruits, herbs, young plants and shoots, and they are all carefully chosen for maximum flavour and nutrient content.

We are always aware of new foods making their mark on the culinary scene, but we don't follow fads – what we grow, we grow because it works for us. We won't fall into line with a trend, or sacrifice our principle or ethos for any movement or accolade.

This is true for all our crops, and so perhaps intentionally and perhaps because of circumstance (our colder climate), we cultivate our crops slowly. However, although slow means lower yields than commercial growers, it does allow our crops to develop their flavours properly. We are not forcing plants to overproduce, we are attempting to get the best possible flavour from individual plants.

And perhaps this has been the most important lesson that we have learned over the years, that in order to get the amazing flavours we want on the plate and to nurture the best-quality ingredients, we must feed and respect the soil in which they are grown and work with nature. The best dishes have the best ingredients. It is an obsession of mine. Flavour is all-important. And that's our ethos; it's all about growing the perfect

carrot rather than cooking it perfectly. Over my career I have used many of the fancy techniques or equipment that you find in many top restaurants, but since I have had access to the very best ingredients we can produce, my style of cuisine has become far simpler – both in method and execution. With the right ingredients, you don't need lots of technology and gadgets to produce amazing food. It is this simplicity that is the keystone of my recipes, and the foundation of everything we serve in our restaurants.

These amazing shoots and herbs can be simply dressed in a light vinaigrette and served up having only been growing in the ground half an hour before. You can't beat that freshness, that flavour, that message.

The success of our restaurants in Cartmel and London is the result of team effort. The land in the Lake District is called Our Farm because everyone who works with me has a stake in it. It is a vital cog in the business; every member of the team – whether in the kitchens or front of house – must spend one month on the land before they can work in the restaurant. Most chefs who join us have little or no experience with growing, and they can be a little overwhelmed at the sight of the rows and rows of beds and polytunnels, but once they've had this hands-on experience with the ingredients they have optimum respect for them and understand completely what they are working with. There's no set pattern to what we grow, and this is reflected in our menu, so the chefs need this knowledge to be able to think on their feet and be able to combine flavours quickly and effectively. You can go up to the farm in the morning and then later in the afternoon and in that time a bunch of flowers will have opened up, ready to use. It is that violently seasonal – you have to be there four or five times a day before you can make a final decision because stuff just appears from nowhere, and to use it at its freshest you have to be there, on site, ready to pick it. You need to know every single millimetre of the land to know what is going on – and to be

able to realise its potential. I'll admit that at times this might seem a real pain to the chefs, and undeniably it means more work, but it is such a beautiful and simple concept.

Having the input from the chefs is also crucial because it means we can grow according to how they want to use the ingredients, cultivating leaves to the perfect size, nurturing live shoots in trays that can be delivered to the restaurant still in their soil ready to be snipped fresh for each plate. This is where growing our own is truly invaluable; because we mostly use micro veg – such as baby leaves, pencil leeks and tiny sweet radishes – we have the opportunity to produce bespoke ingredients for maximum flavour and texture.

We use vegetables at micro size not just because of the way they look on the plate, but also because at this point in their growth they are very small, delicate, perfectly textured and at their flavoursome peak.

As we grow our crops slowly, it is really important to use every corner of the site. The polytunnels and beds at Our Farm are hard-working; from spring through to early autumn every available inch of space is crammed with seedlings or plants – we even have pallets hanging from the tunnels' struts in order to maximise growing space. These tunnels allow us to extend our growing season in a more natural way, to get a head start in spring and protect the plants from the British weather. If we need extra heat in the winter, we use the traditional method of using hot compost heaps to keep the roots of plants warm. In addition, we will place cloches, cold frames and hot beds around the site to keep the more tender plants warm in frosty conditions, and we have areas which are left untilled, to encourage the growth of edible wild plants, which we also harvest. The orchard beyond the beds is carefully planted not only to provide fruit, but to act as a natural windbreak against the wind that sometimes races through the valley.

Spring and summer are our key growing periods, when we need to get cracking to produce as much as possible. Often when we get to August we have so much stuff we can't get it all on the menu, there's no space for it all. Winter is the only time when the soil is visible and we can at last draw breath, after a long year the last of the crops are harvested in autumn and stored to supply the restaurant through the winter. This is when we go back to our roots, embracing good old-fashioned preserving techniques.

All the traditional methods are employed to prevent wastage from our summer excesses – pickling, drying, fermenting, smoking, freezing, clamping (storing root vegetables in boxes filled with sand). Many of these processes even enhance the flavours of our ingredients; clamping vegetables encourages the carbohydrates to turn to sugar, creating a tastier, sweeter veg, while pickling and preserving allows us to add other flavourings and produce a whole different taste.

Our crops work hard for us – we study each plant at every stage of its growth, discovering new ways of using different parts of even the simplest varieties. When you've taken all that time to grow and nurture a plant you want to use every part of it. What's left over and can't be used gets composted – along with vegetable waste, animal manure, charcoal from the wood-burning oven. What we take out of the land we must put back, in order to maintain our mutually beneficial and respectful relationship with it.

Here again we can control what goes back into our soil, as we know that we are not introducing any chemicals into our compost and therefore the earth, so we can ensure it is healthy.

To me, this sums up so much of what we are trying to achieve in Cartmel. Experimentation is so much a part of what we do in the restaurants and the test kitchen; we are constantly trying to innovate and push the boundaries of what we can achieve, using all our natural resources to create new dishes and combinations.

In the sixteen years that we having been growing and cooking in Cartmel, we have made improvements year on year, learning from every mistake and every success. Weather and pests permitting, we now know what grows well, what doesn't, and how we can get the best from what we are growing. But that doesn't mean we're going to stop there; the size of the farm has tripled since we first started and we now have chickens, pigs, sheep and cattle grazing the land around the tunnels and in the orchard, to produce a closed system where the animal waste is returned to the land, completing the circle of nature. This year we have our bees to provide honey and bee pollen – not to mention the benefits to our plants to have pollinators on site and doing our bit to help a dwindling bee population in this country.

For us, growing and rearing our own means being responsible for our levels of consumption – using what we have and not demanding more – and making best use of our natural resources.

We are proud of the unique way in which we stock our restaurants, and we are delighted to be at the forefront of a movement where chefs either produce their own ingredients or seek out local farmers to do it for them, with an awareness of the provenance of the food they are serving and a passion for their ingredients.

In the spirit of spreading the message and sharing our passion, this book was born. This isn't a L'Enclume cookbook; you won't find in these pages the recipes for some of the more complex dishes that we serve there, but these are variations of many favourites from our menu that have the essence of the flavours of our food. It isn't an everyday cookbook, the recipes here are perhaps best used for inspiration and ideas for trying out new and exciting combinations, flavours and ingredients.

Of course, my cooking tends to use some more unusual ingredients or varieties because I'm lucky enough to be able to grow, source or forage for them in my local area. I know that some

of these are hard to find for many, particularly if you are based in a city, so the recipes here mostly include ingredients that you can get hold of without too much trouble. Not everyone has access to woodlands on the doorstep for foraging in, coastal fish markets or 12 acres of land, I know, but we do all have access to good local markets and suppliers where we can buy organic fruit and vegetables, or meat, poultry or fish, knowing its provenance, and even local cheeses.

My journey from Southampton to Cartmel has been a long, and at times agonising one, but I would do it all again. For me, and the chefs who work with me, the idea of seasonality and fresh ingredients isn't a gimmick, it's our passion, it underlies everything we do. I am fortunate to have a restaurant and a team who have helped me to achieve great accolades in the culinary world, but I would cheerfully sacrifice any of these to uphold my principles about food production and the environment. It matters. It is our responsibility to future generations to nurture what we have now, and to leave them that legacy.

With this book I hope to share with you another way to eat – our way to eat – which will inspire you to demand more from your food. Think seasonal, think local, think organic, and if all else fails, think about the origins of your ingredients.

HERBS

Simply created as a celebration of all the flavoursome and delicious herbs and baby vegetables that we produce, this is a showcase for the produce from Our Farm, demonstrating exactly what we are all about, so it seemed only right to call this dish after the land where we grow – Aynesome.

AYNESOME VEGETABLE INFUSION

To make the broth, preheat the oven to 200°C/180°C Fan/Gas Mark 6. Place the onions cut side down on a baking tray and bake for 40 minutes until golden. After 5 minutes, put the peppers, cut side down on another baking tray and bake in the oven for 30–35 minutes until soft and starting to char, then add the tomatoes on another baking tray for the last 20 minutes of cooking. If the onions or peppers are beginning to brown too much, move them to a lower shelf or cover them with foil to avoid the stock becoming too dark.

Once cooked, put the vegetables into separate large, heavy-based saucepans and add 2 litres of water to each, adding the rosemary to the tomatoes, bay leaves to the peppers and thyme to the onions. Bring the pans to the boil over a medium heat, then cover with lids, turn the heat down as low as possible and cook for a further hour. Strain each liquid through a fine sieve into a measuring jug, making a note of how much stock you have – aim for 1 litre per pan – then stir them together in a large, clean saucepan.

For every 500ml of vegetable broth, blend 15g tapioca flour and 30ml water to a paste. Add to the warm liquid and whisk over a low heat for 5–10 minutes until it has thickened to a broth consistency (do not let it boil).

While the stock is thickening, arrange the Aynesome vegetables evenly into four bowls and sprinkle over some Thai basil leaves and brassica flowers. Pour over the hot thickened broth and serve immediately.

NOTE: This recipe yields around 1 litre of each broth, which is more than you need. Keep the leftover broth in the fridge for up to a week.

SERVES 4, AS A STARTER

Vegetable broth
3 large onions, halved
6 red peppers, halved and deseeded
6 plum tomatoes, halved
2 sprigs of rosemary
2 bay leaves
2 sprigs of thyme
tapioca flour, for thickening

Aynesome vegetables
a few sprigs of bronze fennel tops
6 mixed colour cherry tomatoes, peeled
    (see page 34) and halved
4 baby pigeon cabbage leaves
2 courgette flowers, halved
2 baby turnips, halved
5mm-thick slice of kohlrabi, cut into
    4 small discs using an apple corer
4 tiny baby radishes
32 broad beans, shelled
2 baby courgettes, 1 green, 1 yellow, each
    cut into 8
8 cooked simane onion petals (see page
    74)

Thai basil leaves and brassica flowers, to
    serve

If you grow your own courgettes, use a few different-coloured varieties for maximum visual effect. We use whatever we have growing, but particular favourites are green Passandra F1 and yellow Easy Pick Gold. (This dish is a great way to use up a glut, too!) The grilled courgettes are served with butter sauce flecked with marjoram, which adds a sweet spiciness. Add this right at the end, though, as these subtle flavours can be lost during cooking. The soft-boiled quails' eggs from our birds add a little extravagant luxury here.

GRILLED COURGETTES AND QUAILS' EGGS WITH MARJORAM BUTTER

To make the purée, melt the butter in a large, heavy-based saucepan over a medium–high heat, then add the courgettes and sweat them for 5–6 minutes until tender and soft. Add the cream and cook for about 2 minutes to reduce the liquid, until the cream is almost split. Transfer to a blender and blitz until smooth. Season with salt and leave to one side.

Preheat a barbecue or grill to high.

To make the marjoram butter sauce, warm a large saucepan over a medium heat, add the oil and sweat the onion, stirring regularly, for 5–7 minutes until translucent. Deglaze the pan with the vinegar and wine, add half the marjoram and cook for 3–4 minutes until reduced to a syrup. Pass the syrup through a fine sieve into a medium saucepan, set the pan over a medium heat and add the cream, stirring well. Bring to the boil then reduce to a simmer. Gradually add the butter pieces, whisking constantly and adding more when the previous piece has melted and is incorporated into the sauce. Remove from the heat and season with salt.

Halve the courgettes, cutting any larger bits into chunks, coat in the oil and season with a pinch of salt. Cook on the barbecue or grill until charred and tender.

To cook the quails' eggs, pour 45ml of the white wine vinegar into a wide bowl and carefully crack in all of the eggs, slightly spaced apart. Allow the eggs to sit in the vinegar for 2 minutes. Meanwhile, bring a medium saucepan of water to the boil and add the remaining vinegar. Turn down the heat and reduce to a simmer. Swiftly but carefully remove the eggs from the vinegar one at a time with a slotted spoon, transfer straight into the simmering water and cook all the eggs together for 1 minute 20 seconds. Remove and season with salt. They will look like little hard-boiled eggs because the vinegar sets the white around the yolk.

Spoon the courgette purée on to plates, then divide the grilled courgettes among the plates, distributing the shapes and sizes evenly. Finish the sauce with the remaining chopped marjoram and drizzle over. Carefully halve the eggs and add to each plate.

SERVES 4, AS A STARTER

Grilled courgettes
selection of mixed-size different-coloured
    courgettes, such as Partner, Passandra,
    Alena F1
2 tbsp sunflower oil

Courgette purée
75g unsalted butter
300g large green courgettes, thinly sliced
100ml double cream

Marjoram butter sauce
2 tbsp sunflower oil
140g white onion, finely diced
50ml white wine vinegar
150ml white wine
10g marjoram leaves
160ml double cream
300g unsalted butter, cut into small
    pieces

Quails' eggs
50ml white wine vinegar
12 quails' eggs

salt, for seasoning

We grow heritage potatoes at Our Farm, because they have a deeper flavour than most ordinary new potatoes, but a good organic baby potato will do just as well here. The maltodextrin for the onions is optional; it adds a white speckling to the black powder that, visually, gives it more depth and the appearance of real ash, but you can leave it out if you can't get hold of it. Lovage is a staple in my mind and its pungent, musky overtones of anise, lemon and mint are perfect for livening up potato dishes – but be warned, a little goes a long way!

HERITAGE POTATOES WITH LOVAGE AND ONION ASH

Preheat the oven to 200°C/180°C Fan/Gas Mark 6. To make the onion ash, cut the unpeeled onions in half and place on a baking sheet lined with baking parchment. Bake for 1½ hours until black. Leaving the onions in the oven, reduce the heat to 110°C/90°C Fan/Gas Mark ¼ and dry them out for about 3 hours.

Meanwhile, confit the potatoes. Put all the ingredients in a medium, heavy-based saucepan over a low heat and cook slowly for about 2 hours until the potatoes are tender.

Meanwhile, make the purée. Cook the shallots in the oil and butter in a large, heavy-based saucepan over a low heat for 35–40 minutes, stirring regularly. When the shallots have turned a deep golden colour, strain them, pouring off and reserving the 'onion oil'. Blitz the drained shallots with the milk in a blender until smooth. Pass through a fine sieve, season with salt and leave to one side.

Blend the blackened dried onions and maltodextrin, if using, into a powder, then stir in the 'onion oil' to make the ash a little clumpy. Put to one side.

To make the emulsion, bring a large saucepan of water to the boil and blanch the parsley and lovage leaves for 1 minute. Scoop them out with a slotted spoon and refresh in a bowl of iced water. Drain, squeeze out the excess water and blitz the herbs with the oil in a blender until smooth. Pass the herb oil through a muslin-lined sieve. Blitz the soft-boiled eggs in a clean blender on medium speed, adding the lovage oil slowly until the emulsion has a mayonnaise consistency; season with salt.

Spoon dots of shallot purée on to a serving dish and sit the drained warm potatoes on top. Spoon a small amount of lovage emulsion on each potato and scatter over the onion ash.

SERVES 6–8, AS A SIDE

Onion ash
1kg large white onions
50g maltodextrin (optional)

Confit potatoes
500g heritage baby potatoes, such as
    baby red King Edwards
300ml rapeseed oil
10g salt
2 bay leaves
1 tsp white peppercorns
4 garlic cloves, crushed

Caramelised shallot purée
350g shallots, sliced
1 tbsp sunflower oil
50g unsalted butter
70ml whole milk
salt, for seasoning

Lovage emulsion
100g flat-leaf parsley leaves
100g lovage leaves
300ml sunflower oil
2 soft-boiled eggs (cooked for 4 minutes)

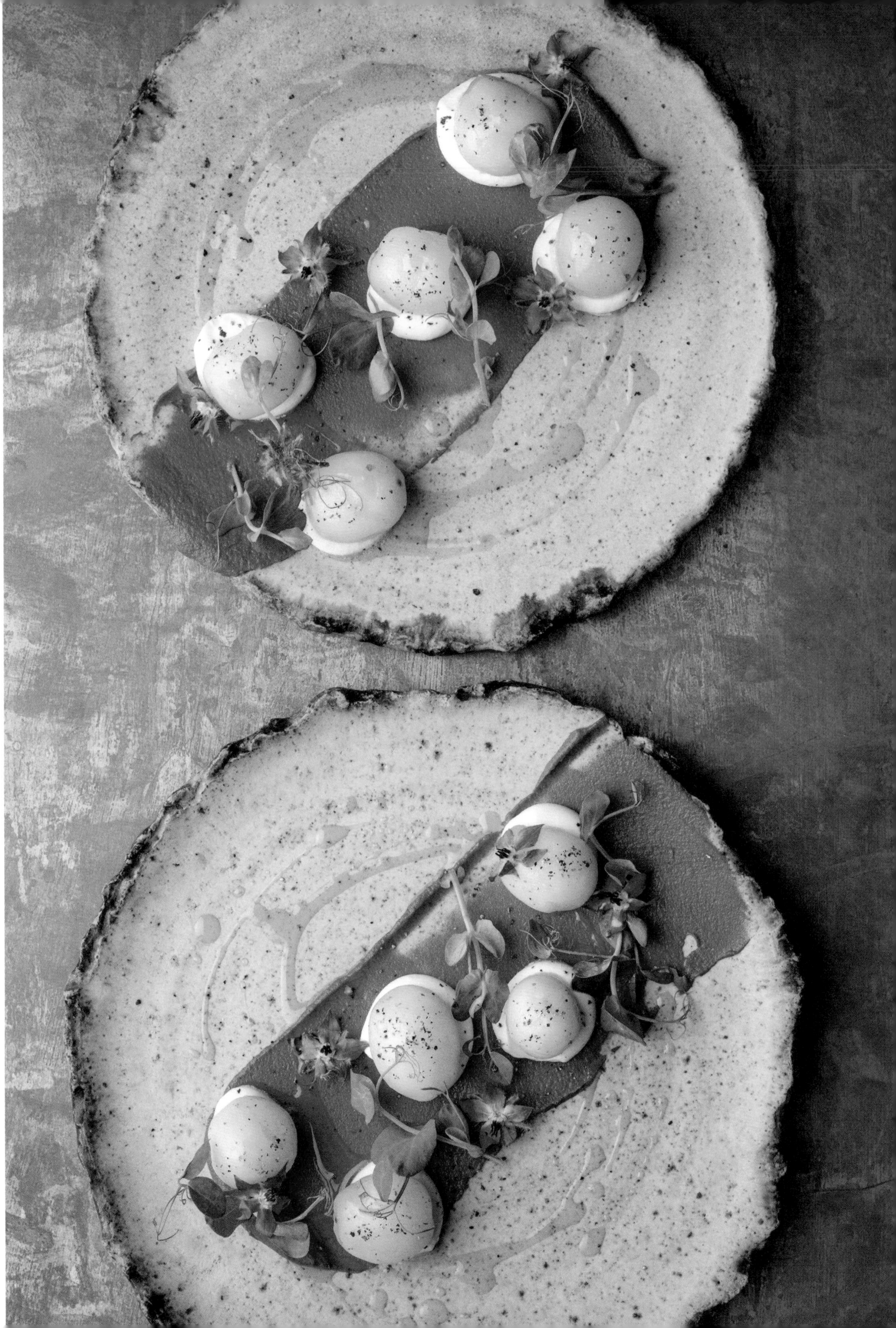

In June you will see ox-eye daisies everywhere – along roadside verges as well as in domestic gardens. These yellow-centred white flowers grow like weeds, so there's no problem with foraging a few flowerheads for this dish. The flower buds are pleasingly aromatic and perfect for flavouring savoury vegetable dishes. Cultured cream is fermented crème fraîche, so including this helps you to stock up on good bacteria in your digestive system. The cultures take 4 days to activate, so you need to plan ahead, and make sure you use live culture crème fraîche to ensure proper fermentation.

BABY POTATOES WITH OX-EYE DAISY SPREAD AND CULTURED CREAM

To start the cultured cream, warm the cream in a small, heavy-based saucepan over a low heat until it reaches 34°C (check with a thermometer). When the temperature is reached, remove the pan from the heat and stir in the crème fraîche. Transfer the mixture to an airtight container and leave for 3 days at room temperature, then transfer to the fridge for 1 day.

Heat a large, heavy-based saucepan over a medium heat. Cook the carrot, beetroot, onion and garlic in the pan with the butter and a pinch of salt, stirring regularly, for 10–12 minutes until tender. Sprinkle in the flour, stir it into the vegetables and cook for a further minute. Add the rest of the ingredients, along with 20ml water, and cook for a further 5 minutes, stirring at regular intervals. When almost all the liquid in the mixture has evaporated, remove from the heat and blitz with a hand-held blender until smooth. Pass through a fine sieve. Keep warm.

Put the baby potatoes in a medium saucepan with the salt and cover with cold water. Cook over a medium heat for 10–12 minutes, or until tender, then drain.

Smear ox-eye daisy spread on each plate, add dollops of cultured cream and set the warm potatoes on top. Season with Maldon sea salt and freshly ground black pepper, sprinkle with pea shoots and borage flowers and drizzle with rapeseed oil.

SERVES 6, AS A STARTER

Cultured cream
250g double cream
40g crème fraîche

Ox-eye daisy spread
1 carrot, chopped
1 beetroot, chopped
1 onion, chopped
2 garlic cloves, chopped
50g unsalted butter
1 tbsp plain flour
2 handfuls of ox-eye daisy
1 handful of mugwort
1 tsp ground ginger
juice of 1 lemon
1 tbsp tomato purée

Baby potatoes
350g baby potatoes
1 tbsp salt

Maldon sea salt and freshly ground black pepper, for seasoning
pea shoots, borage flowers, rapeseed oil, to serve

In Cumbria this is traditionally eaten at Easter and is better known as Lent pudding. It is eaten at this time of year because supposedly this combination of fresh spring herbs cleanses the system of the fats eaten during the winter. The flavours are fresh and aromatic; acidic dock and herby, vegetal nettles are accentuated by the garlicky hit from the ramson emulsion. This recipe is a forager's dream; nettle, dandelion and dock leaves grow across the country throughout most of the year, but ramsons, also known as wild garlic, have a short season in late spring, so make plenty of emulsion then, as we do, when ramsons are available and freeze it for use over the next few months.

DOCK PUDDING WITH RAMSON EMULSION

First, make the dock pudding. Cook the pearl barley in 1 litre of water in a medium saucepan over a medium heat for 25 minutes until soft and tender. When cooked, rinse under cold running water to cool, then leave to drain.

Bring a large pan of salted water to the boil and blanch the cabbage leaves for 2 minutes, then remove them with a slotted spoon and refresh them in a bowl of iced water. Drain and squeeze out the excess water. Repeat with the nettle, dandelion and dock leaves, blanching them for 1 minute each. Slice all the blanched leaves thinly and leave to one side.

Warm the oil in a large, heavy-based saucepan over a medium heat, add the onion and leek and sweat for 3–5 minutes, or until translucent. Add the cooked pearl barley, blanched leaves and porridge oats, stir well and cook for a further 2 minutes. Remove from the heat. Grate the hard-boiled eggs and add them to the mixture. Taste, season with salt and leave to one side to cool, then roll the mixture into golf ball-sized balls and chill.

To coat the dock pudding, blitz the breadcrumbs and dried leaves together in a blender to form a powder and put in a shallow dish. Put the beaten eggs in another shallow dish, and the flour in a third dish. Roll and coat the dock pudding balls first in the flour, then the egg and finally the breadcrumbs.

To make the ramson emulsion, blitz the parsley, ramsons and sunflower oil in a blender until smooth. Strain through a muslin-lined sieve and put straight into the fridge to chill. In a clean blender, blitz the soft-boiled eggs on medium speed. Add the green oil slowly until the emulsion has a mayonnaise consistency. Strain through a fine sieve to create a smoother texture and season with salt.

Deep-fry the dock pudding balls in batches in a pan of oil heated to 180°C until crisp and lightly golden, removing with a slotted spoon and leaving them to drain on kitchen paper. Serve with the ramson emulsion.

SERVES 4, AS A STARTER

Dock pudding
200g pearl barley
6 Savoy cabbage leaves
10g nettle leaves
5g dandelion leaves
5g dock leaves
2 tbsp sunflower oil
½ onion, diced
1 leek, thinly sliced
75g porridge oats
2 hard-boiled eggs (cooked for 8 minutes)

Dock pudding crumb
250g panko breadcrumbs
5g dock leaves, dried
5g ramson leaves, dried
4 eggs, beaten
200g plain flour

Ramson emulsion
100g flat-leaf parsley leaves
20g ramson leaves
200ml sunflower oil
2 soft-boiled eggs (cooked for 4 minutes)

salt, for seasoning
vegetable oil, for deep-frying

Bone marrow is a much-neglected cut of beef shin, which is a shame because it gives a big protein hit and has an intense umami flavour. I've included rosehips here for their wonderfully fragrant aroma, and because I often forage for them near my home, so I'm always trying new ways to use them. For the best flavour, infuse the hips in the syrup for 24 hours. This recipe produces a lot of syrup, but it stores well and can be added to granola and yoghurt, drizzled over ice cream or tossed through summer berries.

HALF-DRIED TOMATOES WITH ROSEHIP, MINT AND BONE MARROW CRUMB

For the rosehip syrup, put all the ingredients in a large, heavy-based saucepan with 375ml water and bring to the boil over a medium heat, then reduce the heat and simmer for 15 minutes. Remove from the heat and leave to cool. Cover, transfer to the fridge and allow to infuse for 24 hours. Pass through a muslin-lined sieve, discard the pulp and leave to one side.

Preheat the oven to 80°C/60°C Fan (if you have a gas oven, set it to the lowest setting and leave the door slightly ajar). Bring a large pan of water to the boil and blanch the tomatoes for 30 seconds. Remove with a slotted spoon and plunge them into iced water to stop the cooking process. Once cool enough to handle, peel away the skin. Place the tomatoes as a single layer on a baking tray, dress with the oil and salt and dehydrate in the oven for 5 hours until jammy and slightly dry. Remove from the oven and leave to one side.

Cook the bone marrow in a small, heavy-based saucepan over a low heat to release the fat. Strain the fat and discard the solids. In a medium pan over a medium heat, toast the breadcrumbs in the bone marrow fat for a few minutes, stirring continuously until evenly brown. Drain on kitchen paper and leave to cool. When cool, fold in the chives.

While the marrow crumb is cooling, bring a large saucepan of water to the boil and blanch the mint for 1 minute. Remove the leaves with a slotted spoon and refresh in a bowl of iced water. Drain, squeeze out the excess water and blitz the mint with the oil in a blender. Strain the mint oil through a muslin-lined sieve into a bowl. Put the maltodextrin in a small bowl, then add the oil a teaspoon at a time to create a crumb.

Pour a small amount of syrup into each bowl (the leftover syrup will keep for 1 week) and put the semi-dried tomatoes on top. Add small piles of the mint maltodextrin and marrow breadcrumbs, sprinkle each serving with texsel greens and drizzle with rapeseed oil.

SERVES 4, AS A STARTER

Rosehip syrup
500g rosehips
125g caster sugar
peel of 1 orange
juice of 1 lemon

Semi-dried tomatoes
500g mixed-colour cherry tomatoes (we use Sweet Olive, Golden Grape)
20ml rapeseed oil
a generous pinch of salt

Bone marrow crumb
200g bone marrow
50g panko breadcrumbs
1 tbsp finely chopped chives

Mint maltodextrin
75g mint leaves
100ml sunflower oil
30g maltodextrin

texsel greens and rapeseed oil, to serve

At Our Farm we grow a wonderful variety of cabbage called Kalibos. It is red with a firm heart and has a high sugar content, which gives it a delicious sweetness. Seeds are widely available if you fancy growing these yourself (it's well worth the effort), but if not, use any young red cabbage – you might need to cook the leaves a little longer, depending on how tender they are. Perilla is a sweet, yet strongly aromatic herb which adds notes of anise, basil, cumin and citrus to the wonderful early autumn ingredients on this plate.

KALIBOS CABBAGE WITH MUSSELS AND PARSNIP SAUCE

Thinly slice 1kg of the parsnips. In a large, heavy-based saucepan over a low heat, warm the sliced parsnips and milk together, removing the pan from the heat before the milk boils. Leave to cool and infuse for 3 hours.

Strain the milk through a fine sieve and discard the parsnip. Thinly slice 200g of the remaining raw parsnip and cook in the butter in a medium, heavy-based saucepan over a medium heat for 15–20 minutes, or until soft. Add the parsnip-infused milk to the pan, bring to the boil and immediately remove from the heat. Blitz until smooth with a hand-held blender. Pass through a fine sieve and leave to one side.

Separate the cabbage into individual leaves, discarding the larger, coarse outer ones. Combine the apple juice, vinegar and cabbage juice in a large saucepan and bring to the boil. Blanch the cabbage leaves in the boiling liquid for 1–2 minutes until tender. Remove from the liquid with a slotted spoon and drain on kitchen paper. Pour off 100ml of the blanching liquid and leave to one side. Add the perilla to the rest of the blanching liquid and reduce to a syrup over a low heat for 8–10 minutes. Remove the perilla sprigs and discard.

Preheat the oven to 200°C/180°C Fan/Gas Mark 6.

While the liquid is reducing, dice the remaining 200g parsnips into pieces the same size as the mussels, scatter over a baking tray, drizzle with 1 tablespoon of the sunflower oil and bake in the oven for 10–12 minutes, or until tender.

For the mussels, warm the remaining 2 tablespoons of the oil in a medium heavy-based saucepan over a medium heat, add the shallots and garlic and sweat for 3–4 minutes until translucent. Turn up the heat and add the mussels, wine and perilla. Cover and cook for 3–4 minutes, or until the shells have opened. Remove the pan from the heat and remove the meat from the shells. Discard any shells that have not opened.

Wrap the mussels and diced parsnips in the blanched kalibos leaves to make eight parcels and warm them through in the reserved 100ml of blanching liquid. When warm, remove from the liquid and brush with the kalibos syrup.

Divide the cabbage parcels among plates and finish with the parsnip sauce and micro perilla shoots.

SERVES 4, AS A STARTER

Parsnip sauce and diced parsnip
1.4kg parsnips
1 litre whole milk
50g unsalted butter

Red cabbage
1 red cabbage, such as Kalibos
1 litre fresh apple juice
250ml red wine vinegar
1 red cabbage, juiced in a juicer
handful of perilla sprigs

Mussels
3 tbsp sunflower oil
2 shallots, thinly sliced
2 garlic cloves, thinly sliced
24 live mussels, washed thoroughly under
    cold running water, beards and grit
    removed
200ml white wine
2 sprigs of perilla

salt, for seasoning
micro perilla shoots, to serve

Make sure your oysters are really fresh – the oyster season begins in September and lasts for as long as there is an R in the month. They should smell of the sea, be firm in texture and surrounded by natural juice, and the heel of the oyster should be a creamy white colour. Hyssop is a strongly aromatic herb, similar to Mediterranean herbs such as lavender and rosemary, and its potent, hot and bitter flavours add a real kick to the salty, briney oysters. The pork adds a crunchy contrast to the chewy oysters, but it needs at least 12 hours in the oven to dry out properly. Put it in overnight and it will be ready by morning.

DUNCAN CABBAGE WITH OYSTERS, PUFFED PORK AND HYSSOP SAUCE

Put the pork skin in a large heavy-based saucepan and cover with water. Bring to the boil, then reduce the heat to a simmer. Simmer uncovered for 3 hours, or until soft and tender. Drain and remove any excess fat or meat from the skin. Cut the skin into 1cm squares, transfer to a baking tray and dry in the oven on its lowest temperature for at least 12 hours, or until completely dry.

To make the hyssop sauce, warm 2 tablespoons of the oil in a large, heavy-based saucepan over a medium heat and sweat the sliced shallots and fennel with the pinch of salt for 3–5 minutes, or until the shallots have become translucent. Deglaze the pan with the vinegar and white wine and reduce for about 3 minutes to a slightly thicker syrup consistency. Add the cream and 30ml water and bring to the boil, then reduce the heat and simmer for 5 minutes. Whisk in the butter gradually, a small piece at a time, to thicken the sauce. Remove from the heat and add the hyssop. Cover and leave to infuse for 30 minutes. Strain through a fine sieve and leave to one side.

Preheat the oven to 200°C/180°C Fan/Gas Mark 6. Remove any loose outer leaves from the cabbage to expose the heart, then cut the cabbage heart into quarters through the root. Warm the remaining 2 tablespoons of the oil in a large, ovenproof non-stick frying pan over a medium heat and colour both cut sides of the cabbage quarters until deeply golden, then finish the cooking in the oven for 10–12 minutes.

Shuck the oysters, keeping the juice and the meat separate. Pass the juice through a fine sieve into a small saucepan. Over a high heat, bring the oyster juice to the boil then immediately remove from the heat. Add the oysters and let them poach lightly for 30 seconds–1 minute in their own juices off the heat.

Deep-fry the pork skin in batches in a saucepan of oil heated to 180°C for about 1 minute until puffed and crisp like pork scratchings. Remove from the hot oil with a slotted spoon, leave to drain on kitchen paper and season them with salt.

Meanwhile, gently heat the hyssop sauce over a low heat to warm it through.

Fan the cabbage out on each plate, scatter the poached oysters and crispy pork on top, finish with the warm sauce and scatter over the hyssop flowers.

SERVES 4, AS A STARTER

1kg pork skin
1 tight-headed cabbage, such as Duncan
12 large fresh oysters
vegetable oil, for deep-frying

Hyssop sauce
4 tbsp sunflower oil
2 shallots, thinly sliced
½ fennel bulb, thinly sliced
15ml chardonnay vinegar
200ml white wine
150ml double cream
250g unsalted butter
20g anise hyssop
a pinch of salt

hyssop flowers, to serve

Blowtorching is a simple but effective way of cooking fish; the flame comes into direct contact with the mackerel, giving it a smoky, charred flavour. Mackerel works really well with strong, slightly acidic flavours, so the bitter chicory and orange marmalade balanced with a touch of sugar is is the perfect partner. Barley is often limited to soups and risottos, but toasting the grains gives them a wonderful depth of flavour and nuttiness. In the past I have given rosemary a supporting role because I've felt there are other, more interesting herbs, but I've come to really appreciate its qualities and here its warm, peppery notes allow the flavours of the pine and nutmeg to develop.

TORCHED MACKEREL WITH CHICORY MARMALADE AND TOASTED BARLEY SAUCE

Preheat the oven to 200°C/180°C Fan/Gas Mark 6.

For the sauce, toast the 80g pearl barley on a baking tray in the oven for 35–40 minutes until golden brown. Remove from the oven and leave to one side to cool. In a medium, heavy-based saucepan over a high heat, bring the chicken stock to the boil with the rosemary sprigs, then remove from the heat, add the toasted barley and allow to infuse for 1 hour.

Strain the barley from the stock and discard. Blitz the infused stock in a blender with the milk, egg and cooked barley until smooth, then pass through a fine sieve and season with lemon juice and salt.

For the mackerel, toast the coriander and fennel seeds in a dry non-stick frying pan over a medium heat for 4–5 minutes, then blitz them to a powder in a blender or grind them in a pestle and mortar. Combine the ground seeds in a bowl with the salt, sugar and lemon zest and mix well. Dust the mackerel fillets evenly on both sides with the salt mixture. Transfer to a plate and leave to cure in the fridge for 10 minutes. Rinse the fillets under cold running water and pat them dry with kitchen paper.

While the mackerel is curing, start the chicory marmalade. Preheat a medium heavy-based saucepan over a medium heat. Put the oil and butter in the saucepan with a pinch of salt, then add the chicory and sauté for 8–10 minutes until all the liquid has evaporated and the chicory is soft. Add the sugar and cook for a further 5 minutes to caramelise it, then add the orange juice, reduce the heat and reduce the liquid to a glaze.

Using a blowtorch, torch the skin side of the cured mackerel until lightly charred and smoky.

Spoon the warmed chicory marmalade on to the centre of each plate. Put the torched mackerel fillets on top and spoon the warmed sauce around. Finish with land seaweed and Maldon sea salt.

SERVES 4, AS A STARTER

Toasted barley sauce
80g pearl barley, plus 25g cooked
375ml White Chicken Stock (see page 286)
4 sprigs of rosemary
125ml whole milk
1 soft-boiled egg (cooked for 4 minutes)
lemon juice, for seasoning

Torched mackerel
25g coriander seeds
25g fennel seeds
500g rock salt
250g caster sugar
zest of 1 lemon
4 fresh mackerel fillets, skin on

Chicory marmalade
1 tbsp sunflower oil
30g unsalted butter
600g chicory, thinly sliced
20g caster sugar
350ml orange juice

Maldon sea salt, for seasoning
land seaweed, to serve

In early spring, all around Cartmel ramsons fill the air with their distinctive garlicky aroma. The season is brief, so we like to make as much use of it as we can, such as in this vibrant and delicious green sauce. This recipe makes a good quantity of sauce, but any left over can be kept in the fridge, covered, for 3–5 days and used with any simple dishes, such as grilled lamb chops. You need to plan ahead with this dish – the fish needs curing for 1 hour and the mousse needs to set in the fridge for a minimum of 3 hours for perfect flavouring and consistency.

SALT COD MOUSSE, BLACK RADISH AND RAMSON SAUCE

Dust the cod fillets with the salt and place on a plate in the fridge to cure for 1 hour. Rinse off the salt under cold running water and pat the fillets dry with kitchen paper. Blitz the parsley and oil together in a blender until smooth, strain through muslin into a bowl and put to one side.

Preheat the oven to 170°C/150°C Fan/Gas Mark 3.

Soak the gelatine in cold water for a few minutes until softened. Drain, squeeze out the excess water and leave the gelatine to one side.

Cook the potatoes in a saucepan of water over a high heat until tender. Bake the cod fillets on a baking tray for 6–8 minutes until flaky.

Drain the potatoes and flake the cod, and blitz them together in a blender with the softened gelatine leaves until smooth. Press through a fine sieve and fold in the parsley oil and crème fraîche. Transfer to an airtight container and leave in the fridge for 3 hours to set.

To make the sauce, bring a large saucepan of water to the boil and blanch the ramsons for 2 minutes. Remove from the water with a slotted spoon and transfer to a bowl of iced water to stop it cooking. Drain and squeeze out the excess water. In a medium, heavy-based saucepan, heat the oil over a medium heat and sweat the sliced shallots for 3–5 minutes, or until translucent. Add the milk and cream and bring to the boil, reduce the heat and simmer until reduced by two-thirds. Pour into a blender, add the blanched ramson leaves and blitz until smooth, then strain through a fine sieve into a bowl, cover and chill.

Just before serving, peel and slice the radish lengthways on a mandoline to create thin rectangles and season with salt just before serving.

Spoon the mousse into the centre of each bowl, shape the radish slices into curls and place alongside. Spoon the salmon roe on top of the mousse and finish with the green sauce and tagetes leaves and flowers.

SERVES 6, AS A STARTER

Salt cod mousse
125g fresh cod fillet, skinned
15g fine salt
40g flat-leaf parsley leaves
50ml sunflower oil
2½ gelatine leaves
130g potatoes (preferably Maris Piper),
    peeled and cut into even-sized chunks
300g crème fraîche

Ramson sauce
250g ramson leaves
2 tbsp sunflower oil
2 medium shallots, thinly sliced
200ml whole milk
200ml double cream

Black radish
1 large black radish, or any other radish

4 tsp salmon roe
salt, for seasoning
tagetes leaves and flowers, to serve

This is a real showstopper. The fish and prawn infusions need to be prepped two hours ahead, so you can prepare this in stages. This dish uses just the shells of the prawns, so either peel them off and freeze the prawns for another day, or use shells from another recipe. Arctic char is an underused fish similar in texture to salmon and trout but paler in colour; here it gets a lift from the lemon thyme gel, which adds spicy notes of clove, mint and camphor. We use pastry cutters to create a perfect flat mound of fish in the middle of the plate, but if you prefer a rougher look, pile it up and gently flatten it to support the radish discs.

ACCORD RADISH, CURED ARCTIC CHAR AND LEMON THYME

In a dry, non-stick frying pan over a medium heat, toast the coriander and fennel seeds for 4–5 minutes. When toasted, grind to a powder in a blender or pestle and mortar. In a bowl combine the ground seeds with the salt, sugar and lemon zest and mix well. Dust the Arctic char fillets evenly on both sides with the salt mixture. Put on a large plate and leave to cure in the fridge for 1½ hours.

While the fish is curing, preheat the oven to 200°C/180°C Fan/Gas Mark 6 and roast the prawn shells for 12–15 minutes, or until they turn a deep red colour. Blitz the roasted shells with the oil in a blender. Add the oil to a medium, heavy-based saucepan and warm through over a very low heat. Be careful not to get the oil too hot. Remove from the heat and leave to infuse for 2 hours.

Meanwhile, make the lemon thyme gel. Pour 200ml water into a small saucepan and bring to the boil. Remove from the heat, add the lemon thyme, cover and leave to infuse for 30 minutes. Strain the infused water into a small, heavy-based saucepan and discard the lemon thyme. Add the agar agar and salt and cook for 1 minute. Take off the heat and strain through a fine sieve into a heatproof bowl, then put in the fridge to set until firm, about 5–10 minutes. Once set, blitz until smooth with the yoghurt in a blender.

When you are ready to assemble the dish, rinse the cured Arctic char fillets under cold running water and pat them dry with kitchen paper, then cut the Arctic char into 1cm dice. Strain the cooled infused oil through a fine sieve and season with a little salt. Slice the radish thinly on a mandoline – if you want a uniform finish, cut each slice into equal-sized rounds using a 3cm pastry cutter. Lightly season the slices with salt.

Divide the cured fish evenly among plates. For a smart look, press each portion of diced char into a 6–7cm pastry cutter to shape, or just mound the fish in the centre of the plate and gently flatten the top. Cover the fish with a circle of radish slices or discs. Drizzle the prawn oil and the gel around the plate and finish with a few lemon thyme leaves and flowers.

SERVES 4, AS A STARTER

Arctic char
25g coriander seeds
25g fennel seeds
500g rock salt
250g caster sugar
zest of 1 lemon
250g fresh Arctic char fillets

Prawn oil
heads and shells from 250g fresh prawns
   (freeze the peeled prawns to use
   another day)
150ml sunflower oil

Lemon thyme gel
20g lemon thyme sprigs
1 level tsp agar agar
a pinch of salt
140g low-fat natural yoghurt

Radish
2 long radishes, such as Accord (about
   250g)

salt, for seasoning
lemon thyme leaves and flowers, to serve

3.5cm and 6–7cm pastry cutters (optional)

Sweet Cicely

(Myrrhis odorata)

From April right until October, the roadsides and fields around Cartmel are abundant with mounds of sweet cicely's fern-like leaves and tiny white flowers (much beloved of bees, and so important, as they are the first nectar plants in spring), growing in any bare patch of soil they can find. It's a prolific herb in Cumbria, where it is known as sweet brackens, which is how it appears on our menu. It has an incredibly long season, which is great for us as it has multiple uses in the kitchen, and this versatility is why this herb features so frequently in many of our dishes and why I also make sure that we preserve as much of it as we can for our larder. I'm a huge fan of the anise flavour, and this herb has it in spades – you can often smell a clump of sweet cicely before you see it.

Although sweet cicely grows on the roadside near the restaurant, I prefer to get a dawn start and forage for it on Bigland Hill, about 20 minutes away from Cartmel. I love going here before I start work; it is a high point in the landscape and on a clear summer morning the views are spectacular – and as an added bonus there's no phone signal, so I can pick in peace!

We use every part of the plant: the light-green lacy leaves, the delicate white flowers, the long, pointed seeds, and even the roots ¬ which make a great wine. Every bit is infused with the aroma of sweet aniseed when crushed. The leaves have more flavour when young and before the plant puts its

energies into its flowers, or you can wait for the seed pods in late summer, which have a sweet flavour and nutty texture. Once picked, the scent and flavours fade quickly, so they need to be used fresh, or if they are being preserved for another day, do it immediately. Be careful when picking this herb in the wild, though, as it looks similar to poison hemlock.

Sweet cicely complements a real array of ingredients. It is a natural sweetener, so the leaves and green seeds will reduce the tartness of rhubarb and gooseberries and add an anise note when used raw in fruit salads (it is especially good with peaches, apricots and strawberries), it also lends a spicy tang to cakes and makes beautiful ice cream. In savoury dishes it marries particularly well with fish and seafood, chicken and root vegetables, and it really lifts a green or cucumber salad. I like to use the fresh, barely opened flowers scattered over salads or as a garnish. Although sweet cicely already has a really long season, we like to extend it further by pickling the buds, using the leaves to make oils, salts and sugars, and dry the leaves for use over the winter. Its flavour does dissipate on cooking, though, so you need to add it to a hot dish at the end to get the best from it – it's fantastic in soups, stews and sauces.

Sweet cicely is a real gift from nature; there is no end to the uses for this beautiful, hard-working herb, so do keep an eye out for it, or grow a clump yourself.

Rhubarb is a versatile ingredient that shouldn't be kept only for desserts, as its sharp tang works so well with meats and strong-flavoured fish. In order to really absorb the full flavour of the rhubarb, cicely and spices, the herring needs to be marinated in the pickling mixture for 24 hours. Here sweet cicely is in its element, not only lending its aromatic flavour to the dish but also cutting through the oiliness of the herring and adding a natural sweetness to the pickle.

SWEET CICELY AND RHUBARB PICKLED HERRING

To make the pickle liquid, bring the rhubarb juice to the boil in a medium saucepan, then remove from the heat and add the sweet cicely stalks, sugar, vinegar, cloves, allspice berries and 2 pinches of salt. Return to the heat and bring to the boil again, then reduce the heat and simmer for 4–5 minutes. Remove from the heat and leave to infuse until it has cooled to room temperature. Strain through a fine sieve and chill. When the pickle liquid is cold, add the herring fillets, cover and leave to marinate in the fridge for 24 hours.

To make the gel, put the apple juice, lemon juice and agar agar in a small saucepan over a high heat and bring to the boil. Once the mixture has come to the boil, pour it into a heatproof container and leave to cool. Once cold, chill in the fridge until set firm – this will only take a few minutes.

Transfer the firm gel to a blender and blitz with the raw sweet cicely leaves until smooth. Pass through a fine sieve and chill until ready to serve.

Bring a large saucepan of water to the boil and blanch the frisée leaves for 1 minute 30 seconds. Remove and refresh in a bowl of iced water. Drain and squeeze out the excess water. Blitz the lettuce with the soft-boiled eggs in a clean blender until smooth, then gradually add the oil until the emulsion has a mayonnaise consistency. Pass through a fine sieve for a smoother texture and season with salt.

Divide the pickled herring among plates, add the sweet cicely gel and frisée lettuce emulsion and sprinkle each serving with the leaves, flowers and shoots.

SERVES 4, AS A STARTER

Sweet cicely stalk and rhubarb pickled herring
8 rhubarb stalks, juiced in a juicer (should yield about 500ml)
100g sweet cicely stalks (leaves reserved to use below)
20g caster sugar
50ml white wine vinegar
3 cloves
3 allspice berries
4 fresh herrings, cleaned and filleted

Sweet cicely gel
350ml fresh apple juice (shop-bought is fine)
juice of ½ lemon
1½ tsp agar agar
30g sweet cicely leaves

Frisée lettuce emulsion
230g green frisée leaves from the outer lettuce
2 soft-boiled eggs (cooked for 4 minutes)
300ml grapeseed oil

salt, for seasoning
young, yellow frisée from the lettuce centre, chervil leaves, garlic flowers, pak choi shoots, to serve

This is one for lovers of aniseed flavours – like me. The combination of fennel, sweet cicely and star anise packs an aniseed flavour punch against the sweet, delicate flavours of the langoustines and cream sauce. The whitecurrants are a lovely addition when in season as they add little bursts of sweetness and freshness. The recipe makes more oil than you will need, but it keeps in the freezer or for 3–5 days in the fridge – it might discolour over time but it's still fine to use.

LEEK AND LANGOUSTINES WITH SWEET CICELY AND FENNEL SAUCE

Preheat the oven to 180°C/160°C Fan/Gas Mark 4. Bring a large saucepan of water to the boil and blanch the langoustines for 20 seconds. Remove and refresh in a bowl of iced water. When cold, remove the tails from the heads with a short twist and pull. Peel the tails carefully and set the meat to one side. Roast the heads and shells in a roasting tin in the oven for 15–20 minutes.

Warm 2 tablespoons of the sunflower oil in a large, heavy-based saucepan over a medium heat, add all the vegetables and sweat them for 5–6 minutes. Add the tomato purée and cook for a further 2 minutes, stirring continuously. Add the star anise, bay leaf and roasted langoustine shells and heads, deglaze with the alcohol and reduce until almost all the liquid has evaporated. Cover with the chicken stock and bring to the boil, then reduce the heat and simmer for 30 minutes. Remove from the heat and leave to infuse for 2 hours. Strain through a fine sieve into a heavy-based saucepan over a low–medium heat and reduce by half. Add the cream and lemon juice and simmer for a further 5 minutes. Pass through a fine sieve and leave to one side.

While the sauce is infusing, make the sweet cicely oil. Toast the fennel seeds and star anise in a small dry frying pan over a medium heat for 3–4 minutes. Warm the oil in a small, heavy-based saucepan until it reaches roughly 80°C (check with a thermometer) then add the toasted spices. Remove from the heat and allow to infuse for 1 hour. Bring a heavy-based saucepan of water to the boil over a high heat and blanch the spinach for 30 seconds. Remove with a slotted spoon, refresh in a bowl of iced water, drain and squeeze out the excess water. Blitz the cicely, blanched spinach, spices and oil in a blender until smooth. Strain the herb oil through a muslin-lined sieve and chill immediately.

To make the fennel and sweet cicely purée, stir together 250ml water and the lemon juice. Add the finely sliced fennel to the acidulated water and allow to soak for a couple of minutes, then drain and transfer the fennel to a plastic container. Cover with microwave-safe cling film and microwave on full power for 5–6 minutes. After this time check the fennel is soft; if it still has a firm texture, cook it in

SERVES 4, AS A STARTER
_____

Langoustine and cream sauce
12 whole large fresh langoustines
4 tbsp sunflower oil
2 shallots, sliced
1 carrot, sliced
1 celery stick, sliced
1 garlic clove, sliced
1 small leek, sliced
2 tsp tomato purée
1 star anise
1 bay leaf
200ml white wine
25ml Cognac
400ml White Chicken Stock (see page 286)
100ml double cream
juice of ½ lemon

Sweet cicely oil
1 tsp fennel seeds
1 star anise
200ml grapeseed oil
50g spinach
50g sweet cicely leaves and young stalks

1-minute blasts until the fennel is soft and tender. When cooked, squeeze off the excess liquid. Transfer the fennel to a blender along with the reduced cream and sweet cicely leaves. Blitz until smooth and pass through a fine sieve for a smoother texture. Chill to maintain the vibrant green colour. Warm slightly before serving.

Fry the leeks in a non-stick pan over a high heat in 1 tablespoon of the remaining sunflower oil for 2–3 minutes until slightly charred and crispy and season with a pinch of salt. Remove from the pan, add the remaining tablespoon of oil to the same pan and cook the langoustines over a medium heat for 30 seconds on each side.

Drizzle each plate with the sauce and green oil, then divide the leeks and langoustines among the plates with the purée. Finish with whitecurrants that have been slightly warmed in the langoustine roasting tin.

Fennel and sweet cicely purée
1 tbsp lemon juice
325g fennel, thinly sliced
75ml double cream, reduced by half over a low heat
40g sweet cicely leaves

Wispy leeks
16 small baby leeks
a pinch of salt

whitecurrants, to serve

Sweet cicely might seem an unusual ingredient for a cake, but this herb is a natural sweetener, so you don't need sugar, and pairing it with star anise highlights its aniseed flavour. The leaves also add a wonderful colour to baking, so slice this cake in front of friends to show off the vibrant green in each piece and serve with a dollop of the creamy aniseed buttercream.

SWEET CICELY CAKE

Preheat the oven to 190°C/170°C Fan/Gas Mark 5 and line a 900g (2lb) loaf tin with baking parchment.

To make the cake, blitz the milk, eggs, honey and sweet cicely leaves in a blender until the mixture is bright green and smooth. Sift the flour, baking powder and ground star anise into a bowl. Fold the wet ingredients into the dry, transfer to the loaf tin and bake for 45 minutes, or until a skewer inserted into the centre comes out clean. Remove from the oven, leave to cool in the tin, then turn out on to a wire rack to cool completely.

To make the buttercream icing, cream the butter and the cream cheese together in a stand mixer until stiff, light and fluffy. Add three-quarters of the ground star anise and mix well to combine. Turn the speed down to low and gradually add the icing sugar, a tablespoon at a time, until fully incorporated. Remove from the machine and fold the lemon juice into the mixture. Transfer to the fridge for a couple of hours to set.

Put slices of the cake on plates with star anise buttercream, sprinkled with some of the remaining ground star anise.

SERVES 10

Sweet cicely cake
200ml whole milk
2 medium eggs
400g runny honey
80g sweet cicely leaves
440g plain flour
2 tsp baking powder
1 tsp ground star anise or 5–6 whole star
    anise, ground

Star anise buttercream
80g unsalted butter, softened
135g cream cheese
2 star anise, ground
150g icing sugar, sifted
juice of ¼ lemon

Sweet cicely adds an aromatic natural sweetness to the syrup here, which is the perfect complement to the tart yoghurt and ripe strawberries, finished off with the tangy citrusy leaves of sheep's sorrel. If you think you are not familiar with sheep's sorrel, think again: it is probably best known to most people as an irritating perennial weed that appears in summer on acidic grasslands, along roadsides and even in domestic gardens. It is widespread, so the leaves can be easily foraged or even cultivated.

STRAWBERRIES WITH SWEET CICELY SYRUP AND SHEEP'S YOGHURT

Slice the strawberries in half lengthways and put them in a bowl. Add the lemon juice and zest, sugar and split vanilla pod and stir gently to coat the strawberries in the mixture. Leave to macerate for 1 hour at room temperature, stirring at 10-minute intervals.

To make the sweet cicely syrup, boil the sugar, lemon juice and 150ml water in a medium, heavy-based saucepan over a high heat until the sugar has dissolved. Remove from the heat and chill (you can do this in a freezer for quick results). Once chilled, add to a blender with the sweet cicely leaves and blitz on high speed until smooth. Pass through a fine sieve. Pour back into a clean blender, add the xanthan gum, blitz to thicken then chill again.

Put a large spoon of sheep's yoghurt in each bowl, create a well in the top with the back of a spoon and fill with the sweet cicely syrup. Drain the macerated strawberries and arrange them around the outside. Finish with sheep's sorrel.

SERVES 4

Macerated strawberries
20 strawberries, hulled
juice and zest of ½ lemon
50g caster sugar
½ vanilla pod, split lengthways

Sweet cicely syrup
75g caster sugar
juice of ½ lemon
35g sweet cicely leaves
a pinch of xanthan gum

Sheep's yoghurt
750g natural sheep's yoghurt, hung in
    muslin over a bowl overnight to strain
    the whey from the curd

sheep's sorrel, to serve

This is a gently fragrant ice cream, infused simply with sweet cicely. The best way to retain the flavour of this herb is to keep cooking to a minimum, so here it is briefly blanched to preserve its colour, then added to the ice cream mixture at the last minute.

SWEET CICELY ICE CREAM

Bring a large saucepan of water to the boil and blanch the sweet cicely leaves for 30 seconds. Remove with a slotted spoon and refresh in a bowl of iced water. Drain and squeeze out the excess water.

In a medium, heavy-based saucepan, bring the milk, 175ml of the cream and 25g of the sugar to the boil. Once the mixture is boiling, remove it from the heat and gradually pour it on to the egg yolks in a large heatproof bowl, whisking constantly to prevent the eggs from scrambling. Return to a clean saucepan and cook over a low–medium heat, stirring constantly, until the temperature of the mixture reaches 80°C (check with a thermometer). Strain the mixture through a fine sieve into a clean bowl, cover and leave to one side.

Put the remaining 25g of sugar in a small, heavy-based saucepan with the remaining 50ml of cream and warm over a low heat. Once the sugar has dissolved, add the mixture to a blender with the blanched sweet cicely and blitz to a purée, then cool it down as quickly as possible by transferring it to a bowl set over ice to maintain the green colour.

Once cool, combine the two mixtures, then add the lemon juice and churn in an ice-cream maker until frozen. Serve at once or transfer to a freezerproof container and store in the freezer until required.

SERVES 4
_____

60g sweet cicely leaves
150ml whole milk
225ml double cream
50g caster sugar
4 egg yolks
juice of ½ lemon

Lemon verbena is an intense herb that has a floral, citrusy scent that is released when you crush the plant's leaves. Its flavour is slightly softer than its aroma, but you still get a good lemony tang, without the bitterness of a real lemon. It works beautifully with cream and juicy blueberries. The anise flavour of sweet cicely is the perfect partner to the citrus notes, making this a real celebration of fresh, summery ingredients.

SWEET CICELY POT WITH LEMON VERBENA AND BLUEBERRIES

Bring a large saucepan of water to the boil and blanch the sweet cicely leaves for 30 seconds. Remove with a slotted spoon and refresh in a bowl of iced water. Drain and squeeze out the excess water. Put to one side.

Put 300ml of the milk in a medium, heavy-based saucepan with the star anise and salt. Warm over a medium heat to 80°C (check with a thermometer), remove from the heat and leave to infuse for 30 minutes. Discard the star anise. Put the milk and blanched sweet cicely in a blender and blitz until very smooth. Strain the mixture through a fine sieve into a clean bowl, cover and leave to one side.

Put the remaining 150ml of milk in another medium, heavy-based saucepan with the double cream and pectin. Warm over a medium heat until it reaches 90°C (check with a thermometer). Remove from the heat and pour this liquid on to the egg yolks in a heatproof bowl, whisking constantly to prevent the eggs from scrambling. When fully incorporated, mix the two liquids together and skim any excess foam produced by the whisking from the top using a dessertspoon. Divide into four serving bowls and chill for about 6 hours until set.

Next, prepare the crème fraîche. Put the cream and the lemon verbena in a medium, heavy-based saucepan over a low–medium heat and simmer until reduced by half. Strain through a fine sieve into a heatproof bowl and discard the lemon verbena. Slowly fold the crème fraîche into the cream, cover and chill until needed.

To poach the blueberries, combine the sugar, lemon juice and dried lemon verbena with 100ml water in a small saucepan. Bring to the boil and remove from the heat. Strain the liquid and discard the lemon verbena. Return the liquid to a clean saucepan and bring to the boil again. Add the blueberries, then remove from the heat and allow to cool to room temperature. Strain the blueberries from the liquid before serving.

Spoon dots of the crème fraîche on to the set sweet cicely. Scatter the poached blueberries in and around the dots so you can see all the colours. Top with the young sweet cicely leaves.

SERVES 4

___

Sweet cicely pot
50g sweet cicely leaves
450ml whole milk
2 star anise
1 tsp salt
150ml double cream
1 heaped tsp pectin
5 egg yolks

Lemon verbena crème fraîche
500ml double cream
25g fresh lemon verbena
250g crème fraîche

Lemon verbena poached blueberries
100g caster sugar
juice of ½ lemon
10g dried lemon verbena
200g blueberries

young sweet cicely leaves, to serve

VEGETABLES

There are a few elements to this dish, but the radishes take centre stage. We use many different varieties; each offer something unique, but all are nutritional powerhouses. Use a few varieties if you can – we use Cherry Belle, bright red with crisp, mild, sweet white flesh; Albena, a white-skinned and white-fleshed mild variety; and Viola, with its bright violet skin and crisp white flesh. The truffle granola is one of my favourite recipes; it's really moreish and if it's around I can't help but pick at it. You can make a big batch and store it in an airtight container – but I promise you it won't hang around for long!

RADISH STEW

Preheat the oven to 200°C/180°C Fan/Gas Mark 6.

First, make the aubergine purée. Wrap the aubergine in foil and bake it in the oven for 35–40 minutes until completely soft, then halve it lengthways and scoop out the flesh. Put the flesh in a blender with the tahini, yoghurt and garlic and blitz until smooth. Pass through a fine sieve and season with a pinch of salt.

While the aubergine is cooking, make the radish sauce. Warm the oil in a medium, heavy-based saucepan over a medium heat, add the shallot and sweat for 5–6 minutes, or until translucent, stirring regularly. Add the mushrooms and sweat for a further 3 minutes, or until soft and tender. Stir in the tomato purée and cook for 3–4 minutes. Add the radishes and vegetable stock and bring to the boil. Reduce the heat and simmer for 8 minutes. Remove from the heat and blitz with a hand-held blender until smooth, then strain through a fine sieve. Finish the sauce by seasoning with sherry vinegar and salt and whisking in the butter.

Reduce the oven temperature to 160°C/140°C Fan/Gas Mark 2.

To make the granola, warm the honey, oils and 1 teaspoon of salt in a small saucepan over a low heat until the honey has melted and the salt dissolved. Mix in the oats. Transfer to a baking tray, spread it out in an even layer and bake for 15 minutes, or until golden. Remove from the oven and leave to cool, then break into small pieces. Leave the oven at the same temperature.

Put the radishes on a baking tray, chopping any larger ones in half, season with a pinch of salt, drizzle over half the oil and roast for 10–12 minutes.

Heat the remaining oil in a medium, non-stick saucepan and add the rhubarb chard leaves along with a splash of water. Cook gently until the leaves have wilted and season with a little salt.

Warm the radish sauce. Put a spoon of the purée in the centre of four plates and place the roasted radishes on top. Add the chard, purslane leaves and flowers. Spoon the sauce around the outside and sprinkle with truffle granola. Drizzle with rapeseed oil.

SERVES 4, AS A STARTER

Aubergine purée
1 large aubergine (about 450g)
½ tbsp tahini paste
1 tbsp natural yoghurt
½ tsp roasted chopped garlic

Radish sauce
1 tbsp sunflower oil
1 shallot, sliced
40g button mushrooms, sliced
1½ tsp tomato purée
250g red radishes, thinly sliced
500ml Vegetable Stock (see page 286)
sherry vinegar, for seasoning
5g unsalted butter

Truffle granola
135g honey
35g black truffle oil
35g chilli oil
150g porridge oats

Radishes
12 mixed radishes, such as Cherry Belle, Albena and Viola
2 tbsp rapeseed oil
8 stalks of rhubarb chard (or Swiss chard), stalks removed and cut in half

salt, for seasoning
rapeseed oil, for drizzling
assorted radish flowers and sea purslane, to serve

Once Britain's staple vegetable (until potatoes came along and took its crown), turnip has lost popularity in modern times, but it deserves a resurgence for its versatility and because it is a great source of vitamin C. Baby turnips have a sweet, delicate taste, while larger ones are stronger and more peppery, but even the more mature roots can burst with flavour when cooked in salt dough. This recipe makes a lot of lardo, but it can be frozen once cured. It needs almost 2 weeks to cure, so make it well ahead ready to use or store it in the freezer until you need it.

SALT-BAKED TURNIP WITH EGG YOLK AND PORK LARDO

For the pork lardo, finely grind the spices in a blender or pestle and mortar. Add the salt and sugar and pulse or grind to combine. Rub the spice mix over the pork fat. Wrap the pork fat tightly in cling film and chill for 11 days. Remove the fat from the cling film and brush off the spices. Place it on a wire rack set over a tray and chill, uncovered, for a further 2 days until dry to the touch.

When you are ready to cook the whole recipe, preheat the oven to 140°C/120°C Fan/Gas Mark 1. In a Pyrex dish or high-sided oven tray, cover the eggs with water and bake for 2 hours. Chill in a bowl of iced water to stop them cooking further. Once cool enough to handle, crack the eggs, remove the yolks and leave to one side. Discard the white.

For the salt-baked turnip, increase the oven temperature to 200°C/180°C Fan/Gas Mark 6. In a large mixing bowl, combine the salt, flour and enough cold water to form a dense dough (about 300ml). Dust a work surface with flour and roll out the dough to a thickness of 1cm. Wrap the turnips in the salt dough, covering them completely. Place on a baking sheet lined with baking parchment and bake for 25–30 minutes. Allow to cool to room temperature in the dough, then break open. Peel and grate the turnips into a bowl and leave to one side.

Put the turnip juice in a medium saucepan over a medium–high heat and bring to the boil. Remove from the heat, strain through a fine sieve to remove the scum that rises to the top and return the juice to a clean pan, on the heat. Stir in the cream and butter, add the xanthan gum and blitz using a hand-held blender. Season with salt and lemon juice. Remove from the heat and warm through before serving.

Cut 12 thin slices of lardo straight from the fridge. Warm the grated turnip and divide it among bowls. Sit an egg yolk on the turnip and top each with 3 slices of lardo. Finish with turnip tops and cornflowers and serve the broth hot on the side.

SERVES 4, AS A STARTER

Pork lardo
1 tsp black peppercorns
1 tsp fennel seeds
1 tsp ground allspice
1 tsp juniper berries
55g coarse sea salt
30g sugar
1kg pork back fat

Slow-cooked egg yolk
4 eggs

Salt-baked turnip
300g coarse salt
500g plain flour, plus extra for dusting
4 large white turnips

Turnip broth
2kg large white turnips, juiced
200ml double cream
50g unsalted butter
2 tsp xanthan gum
juice of 1 lemon
salt, for seasoning

turnip tops and cornflowers, to serve

This light and fresh dish is perfect for the hot days of summer, using a selection of ingredients that are at their best in the height of this season. Fennel packs my favourite aniseedy flavour, and it works so well with this chilled mousse, which is made from vegetable purée folded with cream and set with gelatine. The pickled red peppers make the most of summer surplus, as does the smoked tomato stock – leftovers can be sipped as a chilled soup or consommé with pearls of cooked courgette, carrot and torn basil leaves.

PICKLED RED PEPPERS AND FENNEL WITH SMOKED TOMATO STOCK

Mix all the tomato stock ingredients together in a bowl then transfer to the bowl of a food processor. Pulse gently in batches to break up and lightly purée the mixture then transfer back to the bowl. Cover with cling film and allow to infuse at room temperature for 6–7 hours. Line a bowl with muslin, pour the infused tomato mixture into the bowl, gather up the edges of the cloth into a bag and tie it with string, then leave it hanging over the bowl overnight to collect the juices. Do not be tempted to squeeze the bag to speed up the process.

For the fennel mousse, soak the gelatine in cold water for a few minutes until softened. Drain, squeeze out the excess water and leave the gelatine to one side. Warm the oil in a medium, heavy-based saucepan over a medium heat, add the shallots and fennel and sweat for 5–6 minutes, or until translucent. Add the fish stock and reduce by half. Add the cream on the heat and warm through with the rest of the ingredients, then transfer to a blender and blitz until smooth. Dissolve the softened gelatine in the hot liquid then pass the liquid through a fine sieve. Pour into a plastic container and leave in the fridge to set for 5–6 hours.

For the pickled peppers, put the vinegar, wine, herbs, salt and sugar into a small saucepan and bring to the boil over a medium heat. Reduce the heat and simmer for 3 minutes. Remove from the heat. Add the peppers and allow to cool in the pickle, then chill until needed. They will keep, submerged in the pickling juices, in an airtight container in the fridge for up to 1 month.

Put the smoking chips in a nice even layer in a large baking tray lined with foil. Sit a wire rack on top, that is a similar size to the tray, making sure the wire isn't touching the chips. Put the bowl of clear tomato juice on the wire rack. Cover the entire bowl, rack and tray with a tent of foil, so no smoke escapes. Sit the tray on the hob over a low–medium heat for 10 minutes. Remove the covered tray from the heat and let the tomato juice smoke in the foil tent for 30 minutes.

Put a spoon of the set fennel mousse in the centre of each bowl. Top each serving with 3 pickled peppers, followed by the corn salad leaves. Pour the smoked tomato stock around.

SERVES 4, AS A STARTER

Smoked tomato stock
2kg cherry tomatoes
1 garlic clove, chopped
1 celery stick, sliced
1 shallot, sliced
1 sprig of thyme
1 head of chive flowers
6 drops of Tabasco
1 tbsp Worcestershire sauce

Fennel mousse
2 gelatine leaves
2 tbsp sunflower oil
3 shallots, sliced
3 fennel bulbs, sliced
300ml Fish Stock (see page 287)
300ml double cream

Pickled red peppers
250ml white wine vinegar
125ml dry white wine
1 bay leaf
1 sprig of rosemary
1 tbsp salt
1 tbsp caster sugar
12 baby red peppers

enough wood smoking chips to create an
    even layer in a baking tray
corn salad leaves, to serve

THREE WAYS WITH KUZU DUMPLINGS

Kuzu root has long been used for its health benefits, but the starch that is made from the root is also excellent as a thickener to produce really smooth soups and sauces; it's also great in dumplings because it allows them to withstand high temperatures to produce meltingly soft, hot bites.
Here are a few flavour combinations to suit every palate – we serve three of each together, but if you prefer you can just make one batch.

Goat's cheese and beetroot is a classic combination, but we've added a twist by using the rich, caramelly-sweet flavours of one of my favourite British Cheddars, Westcombe, which is a slow-aged, traditionally handcrafted cheese.

EACH RECIPE SERVES 4–6,
AS A STARTER
_____

CHEDDAR CHEESE DUMPLINGS
WITH BEETROOT BROTH

In a small, heavy-based saucepan over a very low heat, warm the cheese in 300ml water for about 30 minutes, being careful not to let it boil. Remove from the heat, allow the 'cheese water' to cool to room temperature then put the whole pan in the fridge for about 4 hours, to allow the liquid to set.

Skim the fat which rises to the top from the liquid and discard. Strain the rest of the water through a fine sieve, discarding the solids. Weigh the 'cheese water', then weigh out the kuzu at 13 per cent of that figure. Combine in a medium, heavy-based saucepan and blitz together using a hand-held blender for about 8–10 minutes until it becomes thick and gloopy. Spoon or pipe into eighteen 15ml silicone moulds. Allow to cool before transferring to the fridge to chill until needed – they can stay in the fridge for up to 3 days before serving.

For the broth, combine the beetroot juice with the vegetable infusion and warm gently. Warm the dumplings through in a little water, then serve 3 in each bowl with the hot broth poured over. Finish with shaved beetroot and mibuna.

300g strong Cheddar cheese, such as
   Westcombe, grated
kuzu starch (13% weight to 'cheese water':
   see left)

Beetroot broth
50ml beetroot juice
½ quantity Aynesome Vegetable Infusion
   (see page 25)

shaved raw beetroot and mibuna, to serve

The Jerusalem artichoke dumpling is a little homage to the cheery sunflower that pops up in fields and gardens all over the country in summer. These funny knobbly roots are in fact a variety of this familiar plant, so here we've combined them with toasted, tasty sunflower seeds.

JERUSALEM ARTICHOKE DUMPLINGS WITH TOASTED SUNFLOWER SEED BROTH

Preheat the oven to 180°C/160°C Fan/Gas Mark 4. Put 600g of the Jerusalem artichokes in a deep-sided oven tray with 260ml water, cover with foil and bake for 2 hours. Remove and peel when cool enough to do so. Blitz the artichoke flesh with the vegetable stock in a blender until smooth and pass through a fine sieve.

Peel and juice the remaining raw artichokes in a juicer and add the lemon juice. Measure out 125ml of juice and 250g of purée and combine. Season with salt. Blitz the combined artichokes and kuzu together in a blender then put the mixture in a medium saucepan and set over a low–medium heat. Stir the mixture continuously for about 8–10 minutes until it becomes thick and gloopy. Spoon or pipe the mixture into the desired eighteen 15ml silicone moulds. Allow to cool before putting in the fridge to chill.

To make the broth, warm a medium saucepan over a medium heat and toast the sunflower seeds with a pinch of salt for about 5 minutes, stirring regularly to ensure even browning. Add the vinegar and Madeira and deglaze the pan. Reduce by half, then add the chicken stock, bring to the boil and immediately remove from the heat. Cover the saucepan with a lid and leave to infuse for 30 minutes.

Pulse the seeds and liquid in a blender. You do not want to blitz fully, just enough to break up the seeds. Strain. Season with salt if required and serve warm with the dumplings, warmed through in a little water.

900g Jerusalem artichokes
50ml Vegetable Stock (see page 286)
juice of ½ lemon
40g kuzu starch

Toasted sunflower seed broth
130g sunflower seeds
10ml chardonnay vinegar
20ml medium-dry Madeira
330ml White Chicken Stock (see page 286)

salt, for seasoning

Hyssop is one of my favourite flavours, so it just had to make an appearance in these dumplings. It has a delicate floral aroma that marries beautifully with this meaty, rich broth.

ANISE HYSSOP DUMPLINGS WITH CHESTNUT AND BACON BROTH

Warm the oil in a large, heavy-based saucepan over a medium heat, add the courgette and sweat for 5-6 minutes, or until soft, stirring regularly. Add the hyssop, chicken stock, sugar, vinegar and dashi granules and bring to the boil. Reduce the heat and simmer for a further 5 minutes. Remove from the heat and blitz in a blender until smooth. Pass through a fine sieve and leave to cool completely.

Weigh the mixture, then weigh out the kuzu at 13 per cent of the figure. Combine in a saucepan, blitz together using a hand-held blender and cook over a medium heat for about 8-10 minutes, stirring continuously, until it becomes thick and gloopy. Spoon or pipe into the desired eighteen 15ml silicone moulds. Allow to cool before putting in the fridge to chill.

For the crispy chestnuts, slice the chestnuts thinly with a mandolin then deep fry them at 170°C for 1 minute until crisp. Drain on kitchen paper, season and set aside until needed.

To make the broth, warm the oil in a medium, heavy-based saucepan over a medium heat, add the shallot, celery, garlic and bay leaf and sweat for 5-6 minutes, or until the shallot is translucent, stirring regularly. Add both stocks and the chestnuts and bring to the boil over a high heat. Reduce the heat and simmer for 10 minutes. Remove from the heat, blitz until smooth in a blender, thxen strain. Before serving, blitz the butter into the sauce bit by bit using a hand-held blender to enrich it.

Warm the dumplings through in a little water, then serve with the hot broth poured over. Finish with the crispy chestnuts.

2 tbsp sunflower oil
250g courgette, thinly sliced
100g anise hyssop
250ml White Chicken Stock (see page 286)
50g caster sugar
20ml white wine vinegar
1 tsp dashi granules
kuzu starch (13% weight to the broth: see left)

Chestnut and bacon broth
2 tbsp sunflower oil
1 shallot, sliced
1 celery stick, sliced
2 garlic cloves
1 bay leaf
250ml White Chicken Stock (see page 286)
250ml Ham Stock (see page 286)
250g peeled chestnuts (from a packet)
25g unsalted butter

Crispy chestnuts
100g fresh chestnuts, peeled
oil, for frying

In the restaurant this dish is a more vibrant affair, because we use Simane red onions and Red Epicure broad beans, for their deep flavour and fantastic crimson colour. You can use any good fresh baby onions and broad beans, you just won't get the colour. But if you've got some outside space, try planting a few seeds of this variety in a pot; they are easy to grow, and by picking them young you'll encourage more pods. Don't boil these beans if you want them to keep their colour, just steam or briefly blanch them. Again, we use all of the bean here, boiling the pods and skins into a flavourful broth.

BROAD BEANS WITH BABY ONIONS AND PANCETTA

Preheat the oven to 180°C/160°C Fan/Gas Mark 4.

Bring a large saucepan of salted water to the boil. Pod the broad beans and reserve the pods. Blanch the beans in the boiling water for 30 seconds. Remove with a slotted spoon and refresh in a bowl of iced water. Extract the bright green kernels from the outer skins, and leave both to one side.

Slice 200g of the pancetta into equal-sized lardons and cook in a dry, non-stick frying pan over a low heat for 15–20 minutes until golden and crispy. Remove and drain on kitchen paper. Bake the remaining 300g pancetta on a baking tray for 15–20 minutes until deeply golden and crisp. Pour off the fat. Keep warm.

To make the broth, warm the oil in a medium, heavy-based saucepan over a medium heat, add the shallots and garlic and sweat for 5–6 minutes, or until translucent, stirring occasionally. Add the thyme and the baked pancetta and cook for a further 2 minutes. Add 1.5 litres of water, the broad bean skins and 4 of the broad bean pods, bring to the boil, then reduce the heat and simmer until reduced by half. Strain through a fine sieve into a medium saucepan and boil the bacon and bean stock again. On the heat, add the cream and whisk in the butter little by little to thicken and emulsify the broth. Remove from the heat and warm through just before serving.

Peel the baby onions and halve them lengthways. Warm the oil in a non-stick frying pan over a medium heat and fry the onions cut side down for 5–6 minutes, or until charred. Season with salt. Remove from the pan and break the onion halves into petals.

Divide the broad beans and crispy lardons among bowls. Stand the onion shells up in the gaps. Warm the bacon broth through and give it a blitz with a hand-held blender until thickened and foamy, then pour the warm bacon broth around the veg. Scatter each serving with broad bean leaves and add a few drops of chive oil.

SERVES 4, AS A STARTER

400g broad beans in their pods
500g smoked pancetta

Broad bean shell and bacon broth
2 tbsp sunflower oil
2 shallots, sliced
1 garlic clove, sliced
2 sprigs of thyme
skins and pods from the broad beans
35ml double cream
100g unsalted butter

Simane onion shells
8 baby onions, such as Simane
1 tsp sunflower oil
salt, for seasoning

broad bean leaves, to serve
burnt chive oil (see page 225), to serve

A feast of autumn leaves cooked in the last embers of summer. This is a dish that we created for the Great British Menu in 2012, and it was so good that it still appears on our menu from time to time. Barbecuing the crunchy leaves gives them a wonderful smoky flavour which is complemented by the earthy truffle custard and delicate, yet full-flavoured cheese foam. If you can't get Isle of Mull Cheddar, any good mature Cheddar will do just as well.

GRILLED SALAD SMOKED OVER EMBERS

Preheat the oven to 140°C/120°C Fan/Gas Mark 1.

First, prepare the custard. In a medium, heavy-based saucepan over a high heat, bring the milk and cream to the boil, then remove from the heat. Add the truffle, season with salt and leave to infuse for 15 minutes. Put the egg and egg yolks in a bowl, gradually whisk in the truffle cream and set to one side until the air bubbles subside. Pour the custard mixture into a Pyrex dish, cover tightly with cling film and bake in a bain marie (see page 302) for about 30 minutes, or until just set. Chill in the fridge until fully set.

To make the garlic and herb oil, bring a large saucepan of water to the boil and blanch the parsley leaves for 30 seconds. Scoop them out with a slotted spoon and refresh in a bowl of iced water. Drain and squeeze out the excess water. In a medium, heavy-based saucepan over a low heat, warm together the garlic, chilli and grapeseed oil until the garlic is lightly golden. Strain through a fine sieve into a heatproof bowl and allow to cool. Blitz the flavoured oil, parsley and salt in a blender until smooth then pass through a muslin-lined sieve. Leave to one side.

To prepare the cheese foam, bring 450ml water to the boil in a medium saucepan over a high heat. Remove from the heat, add the grated cheese and stir until dissolved. Strain through a fine sieve into a heavy-based saucepan, whisk in the xanthan gum and season with salt. Leave to one side.

For the salad, preheat a barbecue or griddle pan. Break down the vegetables into their leaves and small florets and grill (in batches if necessary) until the florets are charred and tender and the leaves dry and crisp, turning regularly. Season with salt.

Spoon the truffle custard into each dish. Warm the cheese mixture slightly in the saucepan over a low heat and briefly blitz with a hand-held blender to create a foam. Spoon this over the dish, arrange the grilled vegetables and leaves on top and drizzle with garlic oil. Finish with mustard frills, black mustard flowers and freshly shaved black truffle.

SERVES 4, AS A STARTER

Truffle custard
200ml whole milk
200ml double cream
30g black truffle, finely chopped, plus extra to serve
1 egg, plus 3 egg yolks

Garlic and herb oil
40g flat-leaf parsley leaves
1 head of garlic, peeled and cloves finely sliced
1 small red chilli, sliced
200ml grapeseed oil
1 tsp salt

Isle of Mull cheese foam
500g Isle of Mull cheese, grated
1 tsp xanthan gum

Salad
1 baby Savoy cabbage
16 cavolo nero leaves
50g red curly kale, such as Scarlet
25g each 2 other red or green kales, such as Red Russian and Peacock
1 head of broccoli

salt, for seasoning
mustard frills, black mustard flowers, to serve

Cooking beetroot in a salt-dough crust is a simple way to steam it in its own juices, which intensifies its natural flavours to produce a succulent, juicy beet that contrasts well with the sharp, sour vinegar gel. The beetroot tapioca crisp looks really dramatic dressed with micro leaves and flowers, but it isn't as fiddly as it looks. You can make and dry the crisps well in advance, then keep them in an airtight container until you are ready to fry them for that special occasion. It makes an impressive snack for sharing with friends.

BEETROOT TAPIOCA CRISP

In a medium, heavy-based saucepan over a medium heat, stir together the tapioca pearls and beetroot juice, bring to the boil, then reduce the heat and simmer for 25–30 minutes, stirring continuously. Once the mixture begins to get thick and gloopy, gradually add 250ml water and continue cooking until the tapioca pearls have become translucent. Remove from the heat and spread in a thin layer on a parchment-lined baking sheet. Dry them in the oven overnight at 55°C or as low as the oven can go.

The next day, cook the beetroot. Preheat the oven to 200°C/180°C Fan/Gas Mark 6. In a large mixing bowl, combine the salt, flour and enough cold water to form a dense dough (about 300ml). Dust a work surface with flour and roll the dough out to a thickness of 1cm. Wrap the beetroots in the salt dough, covering them completely. Place on a baking sheet lined with baking parchment and bake for 45 minutes. Allow to cool to room temperature in the dough, then break open. Cut the beetroots into small dice and keep warm.

To make the vinegar gel, put all the ingredients in a medium saucepan with 130ml water, bring to the boil and boil rapidly for 1 minute. Remove from the heat and strain through a fine sieve into a small heatproof bowl, then chill for 5 minutes until set. When set, blitz until smooth in a blender.

Break the beetroot tapioca wafer into pieces about 3 x 5cm and deep-fry in batches in a pan of oil heated to 200°C until puffed up and crispy. Remove from the oil with a slotted spoon and drain on kitchen paper. Serve each wafer with diced beetroot and dots of vinegar and top with the leaves and flowers.

MAKES ABOUT 12, TO SERVE AS A STARTER

Beetroot tapioca
50g tapioca pearls
185ml shop-bought beetroot juice

Salt-baked beetroot
150g coarse salt
250g plain flour, plus extra for dusting
1 very large red beetroot

Apple vinegar gel
80ml apple cider vinegar
50g caster sugar
½ tsp agar agar

vegetable oil, for deep-frying
young beetroot leaves, red amaranth
   leaves and dianthus flowers, to serve

This is a wonderful dish for when the days grow shorter, full of autumnal, earthy flavours from the artichokes and truffles. Jerusalem artichokes are an odd, knobbly looking vegetable, but have a sweet, nutty flavour with a good crunch, and are fantastic roasted. In this recipe, we've made the most of the skins and the flesh, so nothing is wasted. Ragstone is one of my favourite British cheeses because it is so brilliantly versatile; it is a mature goat's cheese with a creamy, smooth texture and lemony flavour that lends itself to cooking, but any good goat's cheese log will do.

JERUSALEM ARTICHOKES AND GOAT'S CHEESE MOUSSE WITH TRUFFLE

First, prepare the Jerusalem artichokes. Preheat the oven to 180°C/160°C Fan/ Gas Mark 4. Place the artichokes in a single layer in a deep baking tray, add 500ml water and cover with foil. Bake for 35–40 minutes until tender.

While the artichokes are cooking, make the truffle vinaigrette. Put the stock in a small, heavy-based saucepan over a medium heat and reduce by half. Add the Madeira and vinegar and reduce by two-thirds. Remove from the heat. Slowly add the two oils, using a hand-held blender to emulsify the mixture into a thick vinaigrette.

Reduce the oven temperature to 60°C/40°C Fan or the lowest gas setting with the door slightly ajar. Slice the cooked artichokes in half lengthways. Using a spoon, remove the flesh from the skins. Put the skins back on the baking tray and into the oven for 1 hour to dry. Mash the flesh in a small bowl with a fork and season with salt.

To make the mousse, blitz the cheese in a blender until smooth, then transfer to a bowl, fold in the cream and season with a pinch of salt. Cover with cling film and leave to one side.

Deep-fry the artichoke skins in batches in a saucepan of oil heated to 180°C for 30 seconds–1 minute until lightly golden and crisp. Remove with a slotted spoon, drain on kitchen paper and season lightly with salt.

Dress the artichoke flesh with the truffle vinaigrette and fill half the shells with this mixture and the corresponding halves with the goat's cheese mousse. Add the herbs and flowers, then sandwich the two halves together.

SERVES 4, AS A STARTER

1kg Jerusalem artichokes, such as White Fuseau

Truffle vinaigrette
200ml Brown Chicken Stock (see page 286)
100ml medium-dry Madeira
40ml sherry vinegar
30ml truffle oil
30ml hazelnut oil

Ragstone mousse
1 goat's cheese log, such as Ragstone, about 250g, rind removed and at room temperature
120ml double cream

salt, for seasoning
vegetable oil, for deep-frying
micro green mustard leaf, viola, marigold and dianthus flowers, to serve

We use a variety of different carrots here for their individual colours and textures, so if you aren't growing carrots yourself, use a good selection of organic baby carrots for the sweetest and strongest flavours. Our favourite varieties are Sugar Snax, which is very sweet and orange, Purple Haze, sweet and purple in colour, both when raw and cooked, and Red Samurai, for its bright red skin and pink flesh. I love Iberico jamon, a rich, fat-marbled cured ham made from the meat of Iberian pigs, and this dish is a great way to use up the fat we trim off it. If you can't get Iberico jamon fat, a salted pork fat is fine.

ROASTED CARROTS WITH HAM FAT

First, make the carrot purée. Cook the sliced carrots and carrot juice in a medium saucepan over a medium heat, stirring regularly, until all the juice has evaporated and the carrots are tender. Blitz in a blender until smooth, strain through a fine sieve and season with salt. Leave to one side.

Chop the ham fat into small dice about 5 x 5mm and put in the blender. Bring the ham stock to the boil in a small saucepan over a high heat, then add to the blender. Blitz the two ingredients until smooth, adding the xanthan gum partway through. Strain through a fine sieve, then chill in the fridge.

Preheat the oven to 220°C/200°C Fan/Gas Mark 7.

Bring a large saucepan of water to the boil and blanch the tarragon leaves for 1 minute. Scoop them out with a slotted spoon and refresh in a bowl of iced water. Drain, squeeze out the excess water and blitz the tarragon with the oil in a blender until smooth. Pass the herb oil through a muslin-lined sieve.

Season and dress the baby carrots with the oil and a pinch of salt, put on a baking tray and cook in the oven for 10–12 minutes, or until tender and slightly shrivelled.

Smear the ham fat emulsion across four plates and put the roasted carrots on top. Spoon on the carrot purée and drizzle over the tarragon oil. Finish with nasturtium leaves and flowers.

SERVES 4, AS A STARTER

Carrot purée
250g carrots, thinly sliced
250ml carrot juice (shop-bought is fine)

Ham fat emulsion
200g cured ham fat or salted pork fat
275ml Ham Stock (see page 286)
1 tsp xanthan gum

Tarragon oil
150g tarragon leaves
100ml sunflower oil

Roasted carrots
36 baby carrots, such as 12 each of
    Sugar Snax F1, Purple Haze F1, Red
    Samurai F1
2 tbsp sunflower oil

salt, for seasoning
nasturtium leaves and flowers, to serve

The name should hint that this is another dish with its roots (literally!) in Our Farm. There is nothing fancy about this salad, it simply came about because one very fruitful summer we had so much produce we didn't know what to do with it all! Wastage not being an option, we made it our mission to create a dish to use up the glut but also reflect what our food is all about. The result was this celebration of vegetables, flowers and herbs, picked fresh and served straight to the table. The varieties used here are ones we grow, but if you can't get these, just use organic baby veg – a really fresh, clean flavour is key.

AYNSOME OFFERINGS

Preheat the oven to 160°C/140°C Fan/Gas Mark 2.

Slice the wedge of fennel lengthways into two slender pieces. Cut the carrot into bite-size chunks. Cut the celeriac into 2cm cubes, dress with rapeseed oil, season with salt and bake all the vegetables together on one baking tray for 5–6 minutes.

Use an apple corer to cut two cylinders from the cooled salt-baked kohlrabi. Slice the French beans in half at an angle. Halve any larger radishes lengthways, keeping the smaller ones whole, with leaves intact. Use a mandoline to shave the radishes into thin slices. Thinly slice the cucumber into rounds.

Neatly spoon the warmed carrot and broccoli purée between two plates and arrange the prepared vegetables and baby spinach leaves evenly on to each plate. Drizzle with a little tarragon oil and finish with black radish cress, iron cross sorrel flowers, lovage salt, nasturtium leaves and violas.

SERVES 2, AS A STARTER

a wedge of baby fennel

1 small carrot, such as Atomic Red, Sugar
    Snax, Purple Haze

1 small piece of baked celeriac

rapeseed oil

4cm piece of Salt-baked Kohlrabi (see
    page 110)

2 French beans

6 radishes, such as Viola, Breakfast,
    Albina, Accord

¼ seedless cucumber, such as Diva

4 tbsp Carrot Purée, warmed (see
    page 85)

4 tbsp Broccoli Purée, warmed (see
    page 204)

1 heritage cherry tomato, peeled (see page
    34) and halved

a few of leaves of baby spinach, such
    as Fuji

Tarragon Oil (see page 85), for drizzling

salt, for seasoning

black radish cress, iron cross sorrel flowers,
    lovage salt, nasturtium leaves, violas,
    to serve

This recipe is a sort of homage to another under-used ingredient – celeriac. Again, like so many overlooked vegetables, it's knobbly and not particularly appealing to look at, but it has a fantastic nutty, celery-like flavour which compensates for its lack of beauty. Here appearance isn't an issue, as we've juiced the celeriac and used it as a glaze to get its pure flavour, and also sliced it into a salad to showcase its wonderful crunchy texture alongside the acidic tang of Granny Smith apples.

CELERIAC AND MUSTARD-GLAZED CHICKEN WINGS WITH CELERIAC AND APPLE SALAD

Preheat the oven to 200°C/180°C Fan/Gas Mark 6.

For the glazed chicken wings, peel and juice the celeriac in a juicer. Put the juice in a small saucepan over a medium heat with a pinch of salt and reduce by half. Remove from the heat and add the mustard, honey and butter. Mix well. Toss the wings in the glaze and put in a single layer on a baking tray. Bake for 40 minutes until golden and sticky.

While the chicken is cooking, put all the ingredients for the emulsion, except the oil, in the blender along with 1½ teaspoons of water. Blend together slowly. Gradually add the oil until the emulsion has a mayonnaise consistency.

To make the salad, peel the celeriac then shave it using a peeler and cut the shavings into strips. Put the strips in a bowl. Peel the apples and grate them into the celeriac. Dress with the oil, lemon juice and a pinch of salt.

Divide the warm chicken wings among plates and add the salad, emulsion and leaves.

SERVES 4, AS A STARTER

Celeriac and mustard-glazed chicken wings
1 medium celeriac (about 450g)
45g whole grain mustard
100g honey
20g unsalted butter
12 chicken wings

Whole grain mustard emulsion
1 soft-boiled egg (cooked for 4 minutes)
25g whole grain mustard
5ml white wine vinegar
1½ tsp honey
a pinch of salt
150ml sunflower oil

Celeriac and apple salad
1 medium celeriac (about 450g)
2 Granny Smith apples
20ml rapeseed oil
juice of 1 lemon

salt, for seasoning
chickweed and golden streak mustard
    leaves, to serve

Black garlic is becoming more widely available to buy, but it's also really easy to make by slow-roasting the bulbs in stout until caramelised. Unlike ordinary garlic, black garlic has a sweet yet savoury flavour, a little smoky with a hint of aged balsamic. These three recipes are some of our favourite ways to showcase this versatile and mouth-watering ingredient.

THREE WAYS WITH BLACK GARLIC

This has a soft, slightly thick and oozy texture, almost like a paste, which makes it perfect as a flavouring to add to creams, butter and many sauces.

BLACK GARLIC BASE

Preheat the oven to 110°C/90°C Fan/Gas Mark ¼. Place the garlic in a small, deep-sided tray. Pour over the stout, cover with foil and bake in the oven for 12 hours. When baked, remove the garlic from the oven and reduce the oven temperature to 95°C/75°C Fan/lowest Gas Mark.

Transfer the garlic to a clean tray and dry in the oven for a further 12 hours. Store in an airtight container in the fridge until required.

MAKES 6 BULBS
_____

6 heads of garlic
500ml stout beer

This is great as a dressing for all sorts of dishes, but particularly fish – it's excellent as a dip for crispy fried goujons.

BLACK GARLIC YOGURT

Blitz all the ingredients in a blender until smooth. Put in an airtight container and transfer to the fridge to chill.

MAKES 500G

350g natural yoghurt
150g black garlic, skins removed (shop-bought or see page 90)
1 tsp salt

You can make this up and freeze it, so it's ready to be sliced straight from the freezer. Drop it cold on to resting meats so that it melts and oozes over them.

BLACK GARLIC BUTTER

Put the ingredients in the bowl of a stand mixer fitted with the paddle attachment and beat together on medium speed for 3 minutes. Roll the black garlic butter into logs, wrap in cling film and store in the freezer until required.

MAKES 1 STICK

250g unsalted butter, softened
80g black garlic, skins removed (shop-bought or see page 90)
1 tsp salt

The first stems of summer purple broccoli are a real treat, and we like to pick them as fresh as possible for their deliciously sweet flavour, which is intensified when roasted. They are perfectly complemented here with buttery sweetbreads which curb the richness of the goat's butter and the acidic ramsons. I love ramsons, and pickling the seeds is a fantastic way to preserve them and extend their availability. Pick the little green seed buds as soon as they appear, before they dry, and after just one week you will have delicious garlicky capers which will keep in a cool dark place for several months – great also for serving with cured meats and firm-textured fish.

SUMMER PURPLE BROCCOLI AND SWEETBREADS WITH RAMSON CAPERS

First, make the pickled ramson capers. Put the vinegar, sugar and 150ml water in a medium, heavy-based saucepan, bring to the boil and boil for 3 minutes. Remove from the heat and allow to cool, then add the ramson caper buds. Transfer to a sterilised 350ml Kilner jar and place a circle cut out of baking parchment on top. Seal the jar and leave in a cool, dark place to pickle for 1 week.

To make the sauce, warm the oil in a large, heavy-based saucepan over a medium heat, add the shallots and fennel and sweat for 5–6 minutes until soft and translucent, stirring regularly. Add the sprig of thyme and the wine and bring to the boil, then turn down the heat and simmer to reduce by half. Add the vinegar and simmer for a further 3 minutes. Strain through a fine sieve into a clean saucepan and return to the boil over a medium heat. Using a hand-held blender, add the goat's butter little by little until the sauce has a creamy consistency. Season with a pinch of salt and leave to one side in a warm place.

Bring a large saucepan of water to the boil and blanch the sweetbreads for 30 seconds. Remove with a slotted spoon and refresh in a bowl of iced water. Peel the outer membrane away and leave the sweetbreads to dry on kitchen paper. Heat a non-stick frying pan over a medium heat, add the butter and, when it foams, add the sweetbreads and move them around the pan to give them an even colour, cooking them for 3–4 minutes on each side until they are deep golden. Remove from the pan and season with salt.

While the sweetbreads are cooking, warm the oil for the broccoli in another non-stick frying pan over a medium heat, add the broccoli, season with salt, turn the heat to high and cook for 3–5 minutes until slightly charred and tender but still with a little bite. Remove from the pan.

Put 1 tablespoon of pickled ramson capers in the sauce and warm through. Put 6 or 7 pieces of broccoli on each plate, add 3 or 4 sweetbreads to each and spoon over the sauce. Finish with herbs and flowers.

SERVES 4, AS A STARTER

Pickled ramson capers
50ml white wine vinegar
100g caster sugar
100g ramson caper buds

Goat's butter sauce
2 tbsp sunflower oil
2 shallots, sliced
1 fennel bulb, sliced
1 sprig of thyme
400ml white wine
1 tsp chardonnay vinegar
200g goat's butter

Sweetbreads
12–16 small lamb sweetbreads
200g unsalted butter

Purple sprouting broccoli
1 tbsp sunflower oil
24–28 purple sprouting broccoli stalks

salt, for seasoning
buckshorn plantain, brassica flowers, to serve

The thick, firm leaves of Cos make these brilliant lettuces for roasting or grilling. If you are having a barbecue, cook a few extra and set them aside to make this dish, or just char them on a hot griddle pan. Here we've taken the lovely charred flavours of this slightly sweet lettuce and juiced them to make a herby sauce. If you've got leftover verbena oil, store it in the fridge for 3–5 days or freeze it, and drizzle it over fish or poultry dishes.

CONFIT SARDINES WITH GRILLED COS LETTUCE SAUCE

Preheat a griddle pan or a barbecue. Brush the outside of the lettuce with the oil. Cook on the griddle or barbecue grill, turning it continuously, until a deep golden colour all over. Remove from the heat and let it cool, then put it through a juicer. Blitz the juice with the mayonnaise and herbs in a blender until smooth, then pass through a fine sieve.

To make the verbena oil, blitz the leaves and the oil in a blender until smooth. Strain through a muslin-lined sieve and reserve in the fridge.

Bring a large pan of water to the boil and blanch each of the tomatoes for 10 seconds. Remove with a slotted spoon and refresh in a bowl of iced water, then when cool enough to handle, remove the skins. Season with salt and drizzle lightly with the verbena oil.

For the sardines, dissolve 100g of the salt in 1 litre of cold water. Soak the sardine fillets in the resulting brine for 15 minutes, then dry them on kitchen paper. Heat the olive oil with the remaining salt, the garlic and bay leaf in a small, heavy-based saucepan over a low heat until it reaches 50°C (check using a thermometer). Add the fillets to the pan, turn off the heat and allow the fish to cook in the residual heat for 6–8 minutes, then drain on kitchen paper and serve warm with the Cos lettuce sauce, tomatoes and arrowgrass and red lace mustard leaves.

SERVES 4, AS A STARTER

Grilled Cos lettuce sauce
1 Cos lettuce
2 tbsp rapeseed oil
2 tbsp mayonnaise
5g dill fronds
5g chervil
5g flat-leaf parsley leaves

Verbena oil
100g lemon verbena leaves
200ml sunflower oil

Miele tomatoes
12 yellow baby plum tomatoes, such as
    Miele F1
salt, for seasoning

Confit sardines
105g table salt
8 fresh medium sardines, filleted
400ml olive oil
2 garlic cloves
1 bay leaf

arrowgrass and red lace mustard leaves,
    to serve

With Morecambe Bay and Flookborough on our doorstep up at Cartmel, we have a fantastic array of shellfish available to us. We are constantly thinking up new ways to serve this local produce, and asparagus is a really great pairing. The British asparagus season runs from May to July, and our spears are said to be the best in the world – they have an intense flavour that doesn't need a lot of dressing up, so in this dish we've kept the flavours quite simple. The shrimp butter sauce is really moreish, but also very rich, so don't overload the asparagus with it!

ASPARAGUS WITH BROWN SHRIMP BUTTER SAUCE

First, make the pickle for the asparagus spears. Put the vinegar and sugar in a small saucepan with 100ml water, bring to the boil then remove from the heat and leave to one side to cool completely.

To make the sauce, warm the oil in a large saucepan over a medium heat, add the onion and sweat for 5–7 minutes until translucent, stirring regularly. Add the mace and sweat for 1 minute. Deglaze the saucepan with the white wine vinegar and white wine and reduce to a syrup. Pass through a fine sieve. Put the reduced syrup in a medium saucepan over a medium heat and add the cream. Stir well, bring to the boil, then reduce the heat and simmer. Gradually add the butter in small pieces, whisking constantly and adding the next only when the previous piece has fully melted and become incorporated into the sauce. Do not add the butter too quickly or in large amounts, as this may cause the sauce to split. Remove from the heat, season with salt and add the parsley. Stir the shrimps into the warm sauce.

Using a vegetable peeler, peel 4 of the asparagus spears into long strands and put these in the cooled pickling liquid. Leave them in the pickling liquid for 6 minutes.

Bring a large saucepan of salted water to the boil and blanch the 12 remaining asparagus spears for 1 minute. Remove with a slotted spoon and refresh in a bowl of iced water. Drain on kitchen paper and preheat the grill to high. Season the blanched asparagus with a pinch of salt and cook under a preheated grill for 1–2 minutes until slightly browned.

Place 3 asparagus spears in the centre of each plate. Spoon over the warm shrimp sauce and put the pickled ribbons of asparagus over the top. Thinly slice the raw mushrooms on a mandoline and add them to each serving, then scatter over the chrysanthemum shoots.

SERVES 4, AS A STARTER

50ml white wine vinegar
25g caster sugar
16 spears of green asparagus

Brown shrimp butter sauce
2 tbsp sunflower oil
140g white onion, diced
5g mace
50ml white wine vinegar
150ml white wine
160ml double cream
300g unsalted butter
1 tbsp finely chopped flat-leaf parsley
100g brown shrimps, peeled

salt, for seasoning
100g brown chestnut mushrooms and
  chrysanthemum shoots, to serve

You can use any baby potatoes here but Pink Fir have a particularly nice nutty flavour which works well with the strong flavours of Tabasco and horseradish. It's a great late-season potato, going well into the autumn, and is becoming more widely available in markets now, so keep an eye out for it. Although potatoes are the star of the show, the dish is lifted by adding crab flavours and piquant horseradish, and who doesn't like crispy roasted chicken skin?

POTATOES AND CRAB WITH CHICKEN SKIN AND HORSERADISH

To confit the potatoes in poultry fat, put all the ingredients in a medium, heavy-based saucepan over a low heat and cook slowly for about 2 hours until the potatoes are tender.

In a heavy-based saucepan over a medium heat, bring the fresh horseradish, creamed horseradish and cream to the boil and boil for 3 minutes. Remove from the heat and leave to infuse for 20 minutes.

Preheat the oven to 200°C/180°C Fan/Gas Mark 6.

For the crab mix, blitz together the brown crab meat, soft-boiled egg, lemon juice and Tabasco in a blender. Slowly add the oil until the mixture has a mayonnaise consistency. Pass through a fine sieve and season with salt. Fold 6 tablespoons of the brown crab emulsion through the white crab meat in a bowl and put the rest in the fridge to use another time.

Scrape away any excess fat from the chicken skin and discard. Lay the skin flat on baking sheet lined with baking parchment, season with a pinch of salt and bake in the oven for 15–20 minutes until lightly golden. Remove from the oven and drain on kitchen paper. Leave to one side.

Reduce the brown chicken stock over a medium heat in a heavy-based saucepan until it reaches a sauce consistency (see page 286). Keep warm.

Strain the horseradish-infused cream through a fine sieve into a clean saucepan, bring back to the boil and add the lemon juice and a pinch of salt.

Divide the crab mix among four plates and put halved warm potatoes on top. Break the chicken skin into shards and add them to the plates. Drizzle around the warm horseradish sauce and the chicken jus. Finish with baby red choi leaves.

SERVES 4, AS A STARTER

Potatoes in poultry fat
300g poultry fat (duck or goose)
500g baby potatoes, such as Pink Fir
10g salt
2 bay leaves
1 tsp white peppercorns
4 garlic cloves, crushed

Horseradish sauce
20g freshly grated horseradish
40g creamed horseradish
250ml double cream
1 tbsp lemon juice

Crab mix
100g brown crab meat
1 soft-boiled egg (cooked for 4 minutes)
2 tsp lemon juice
4 drops of Tabasco
250ml grapeseed oil
200g white crab meat

Chicken skin
200g chicken skin

Chicken jus
250ml reduced Brown Chicken Stock,
    (see page 286)

salt, for seasoning
baby red choi leaves, to serve

There is a little Italian influence here with the base obviously being a type of pasta, but it is teamed with the very British chestnut – so great for using up the glut of chestnuts that grow on the perimeter of the farm. This is warming and indulgent for those darkening chilly evenings. The unmistakeable taste of autumn is created by the natural pairing of smoky chestnut flour and shavings, earthy mushrooms and the mighty truffle. Chestnut flour (*farina di castagna*) does not contain gluten, so we add a little gluten powder to give the pasta the characteristics that we all know and love.

CHESTNUT PASTA WITH TRUFFLE SAUCE AND CHANTERELLES

First, make the pasta dough. Mix the dry ingredients together on the work surface and form a well in the centre. Lightly beat the eggs and oil together in a bowl and pour into the well. Mix the wet ingredients into the dry to form a dough, bringing the flour from the outside in. Knead the dough on a lightly floured work surface for 4–5 minutes, then wrap it in cling film and leave it to rest in the fridge for 30 minutes.

While the dough is resting, soak the mushrooms for the sauce. Bring 100ml water to the boil in a small saucepan, remove from the heat, add the dried ceps and leave to soak for 30 minutes.

Roll the rested pasta dough through a pasta machine, starting at the thickest setting and gradually working your way down to the second thinnest setting. Cut the pasta sheet into strips about 5mm wide and 25cm long. Dust them with flour and leave to dry for 30 minutes.

While the pasta is drying, continue with the sauce. Melt the butter in a medium, heavy-based saucepan over a medium heat, add the shallots and garlic and sweat for 4–5 minutes until soft and translucent. Strain the ceps through a fine sieve (set the ceps aside for another recipe or discard) and add the strained soaking water. Bring to the boil, reduce the heat and simmer for 5 minutes. Add the cream and reduce to a thick sauce consistency. Remove from the heat, add the chopped truffle and season with salt. Keep warm.

Bring a large saucepan of salted water to the boil. Cook the pasta for 3–4 minutes, or until it still has a slight bite. Add to the warm sauce and mix well to coat.

Meanwhile, heat a non-stick frying pan over a high heat and sauté the chanterelles in the oil for 3–4 minutes, tossing frequently. Drain on kitchen paper.

Serve the pasta and sauce in bowls with the chanterelles on top and grate over some fresh black truffle and chestnut.

SERVES 4

Chestnut pasta
180g plain flour, plus extra for dusting
140g chestnut flour
2 tsp gluten powder
3 eggs
1 tbsp rapeseed oil

Sauce
60g dried ceps or porcini
3 tbsp unsalted butter
12 shallots, finely diced
6 garlic cloves, finely chopped
300ml double cream
3 tbsp finely chopped black truffle
salt, for seasoning

Chanterelle mushrooms
200g chanterelle mushrooms
2 tbsp sunflower oil

black truffle, to serve
peeled fresh chestnut, to serve

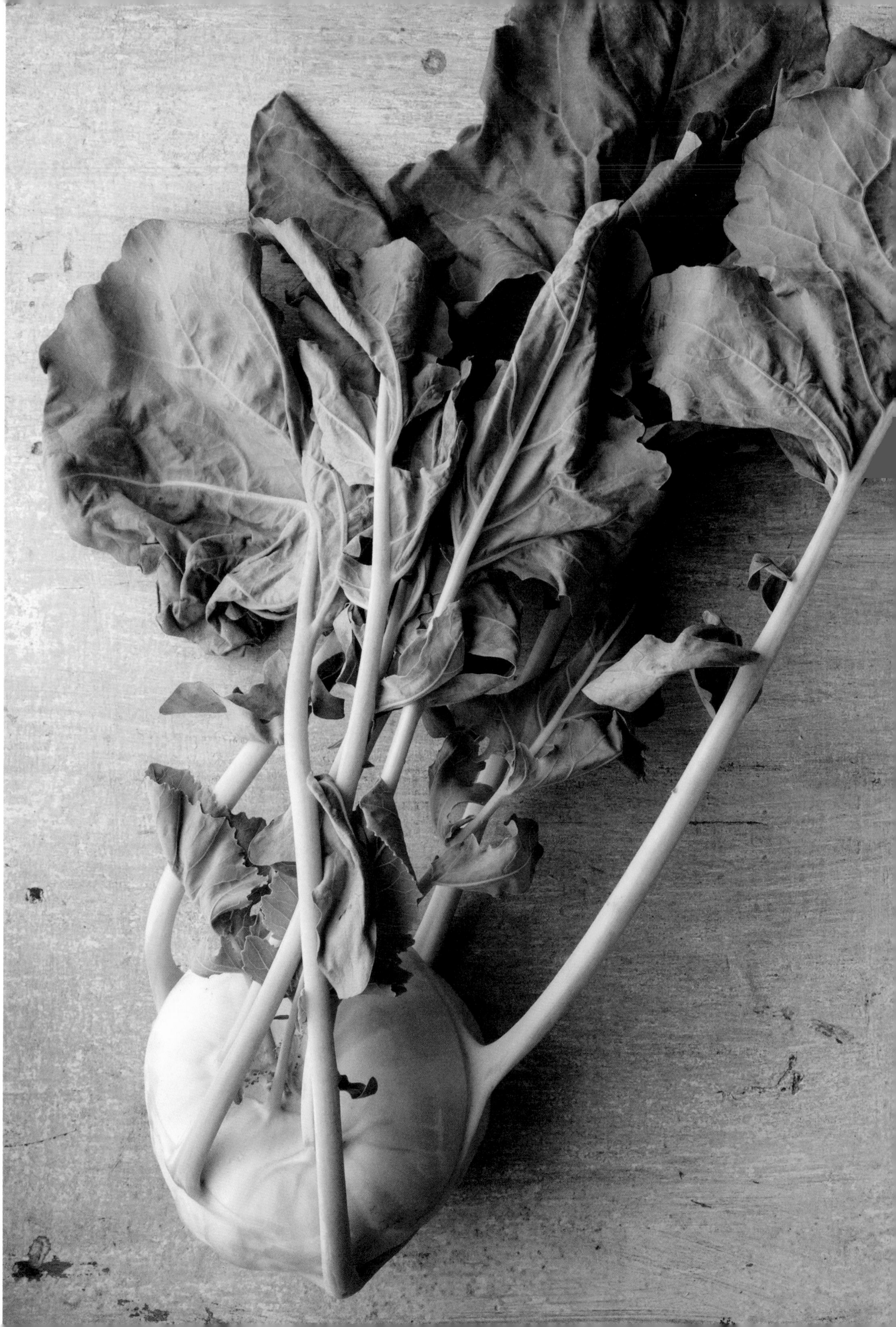

Kohlrabi

(Brassica oleracea)

True, kohlrabi isn't the prettiest-looking plant; it's a bit like a Sputnik in vegetable form, with a squat bulb and antennae-like shoots, but it is a secret weapon on the farm because it is such a quick grower over a long season and we can get a lot of produce for use in the restaurants. We like to use the swollen stem at about tennis-ball size, because they provide the most intense flavour; any larger it starts to get woody, so we sow seeds in March in the tunnels and by May the kohlrabi are at the perfect size for pulling. We then repeat sow throughout the summer right up until September to keep a crop going until November.

There are many different varieties of kohlrabi available, in shades of pale green to dusky purple, and each is unique, not just in how they look, but their depth of flavour and also speed of maturity. Kohlrabi (from the German *kohl* for cabbage and the Latin *rapa* for turnip), has a mild, sweet, slightly nutty flavour that is somewhere between cauliflower and broccoli when raw, closer to turnip when cooked, and a crisp, crunchy and refreshing texture and peppery kick. It's also a two-in-one vegetable, in that the leaves, when gently steamed or sautéed, taste almost as good as the root.

We use kohlrabi raw or cooked, preparing it in lots of different ways. Raw is one of best ways to eat it – grated in salads, served thinly sliced with hard cheeses, which bring out its potency and nuttiness. When roasted, though, the outside of the root caramelises, mellowing and sweetening its flavour, but one of my favourite ways to bake it is wrapped in salt dough – the casing enables the root to steam in its own juices, intensifying its natural flavours and keeping it succulent and juicy, ready to eat with cheese sauce and grated truffle or even to be encased in kale leaves and fried for a crunchy exterior. I also like pickling the roots so that they keep their lovely crunch and mild spicy notes. These pickled kohlrabi are great for slicing into wafer-thin discs that we use as wonton wrappers to encase ingredients such as raw meat and fish. Being low in calories and high in fibre, and containing more carbs than most veg, kohlrabi is great with proteins, such as stir-fried with beef and anchovies or cooked with bacon for a delicious bittersweet salty combination.

For this recipe we tend to use one of the two varieties of kohlrabi that we grow, Kref F1, because it is wonderfully tender and has a light green colour and smooth shape. Salt-baking the stems really intensifies the flavour and makes them beautifully soft and tender, so for contrast, nutty, toasted butter is scattered over for bite and a crisp texture. To really push up the flavours, the egg yolks are blended with earthy, smoked oil to make a wonderfully rich purée. Altogether this is a simple yet impressive and deeply flavoursome dish.

SALT-BAKED KOHLRABI WITH SMOKED EGG YOLK

To make the toasted butter, melt the butter in a medium, heavy-based saucepan over a medium heat, then then leave to one side until cooled. Add the kuzu, mix well, return to a medium heat and cook for 10 minutes, whisking regularly to break down the solid pieces to a crumb. Cook for a further 5–6 minutes without stirring, let the foam rise and then disappear, and let the crumb brown slightly. Strain through a fine sieve (discard the liquid) and transfer the crumb to kitchen paper to dry, changing the paper if necessary until the crumb is free from oil and crispy. Transfer the crumb to an airtight container until needed, or store at room temperature for up to 1 week.

Now, bake the kohlrabi. Preheat the oven to 200°C/180°C Fan/Gas Mark 6. In a large mixing bowl, combine the salt, flour and enough cold water to form a dense dough (about 300ml). Dust a work surface with flour and roll the dough out to a thickness of 1cm. Wrap the kohlrabi in the salt dough, covering them completely. Place on a baking sheet lined with baking parchment and bake for 25–30 minutes. Allow the salt-baked kohlrabi to cool to room temperature in the dough, then break open. Peel the cooked kohlrabi and break them into large chunks.

To make the smoked egg yolk purée, peel away the shells and put the soft yolks in a bowl. Discard the whites. Slowly add the smoked oil to the yolks, whisking constantly with a hand-held blender, until the mixture has a mayonnaise consistency. Season with salt.

Melt the butter in a frying pan over a medium heat, add the the warm chunks of salt-baked kohlrabi and fry for 5–6 minutes until golden on all sides.

Divide the fried kohlrabi chunks among plates, dot with egg yolk purée and dust with the crispy kuzu butter. Finish with watercress.

SERVES 4, AS A STARTER

Salt-baked kohlrabi
300g coarse salt
500g plain flour, plus extra for dusting
4 large kohlrabi

Toasted butter
200g unsalted butter
80g kuzu starch, blitzed to a powder

Smoked egg yolk purée
2 soft-boiled eggs (cooked for 4 minutes)
200ml smoked oil (you can buy this online)
salt, for seasoning

125g unsalted butter, for frying
red watercress, to serve

We all know the issues with raising veal, so make sure the meat you use is humanely reared and of the highest quality. This is important not only for the flavours but also for the animals and the environment. Veal and oysters is a popular pairing, and this is a modern interpretation of the British classic, steak and oyster pie. Often oysters are dressed with lemon juice, but I use apple marigold for its natural acidity and burst of freshness. It's a herb you don't see used often but I love its minty taste with an intense apple flavour. It's a member of the marigold family and great for growing in your garden as it has a reputation for fending off invasive weeds such as ground elder!

VEAL AND POACHED OYSTER KOHLRABI PARCELS

To poach the oysters, bring the kombu, dashi granules, lemon juice and 500ml water to the boil in a small, heavy-based saucepan, then remove from the heat. Shuck the oysters from their shells and add the oyster meat to the warm dashi stock. Leave for 2 minutes, or until firm, then remove from the stock, put in a bowl and chill until cold, then chop into 7mm dice.

Chop the veal fillet into dice the same size as the oysters and season with salt and a small amount of Tabasco.

Blitz the apple marigold leaves with the sunflower oil in a blender until smooth and leave to stand for 1 hour to infuse. Pass the herb oil through a muslin-lined sieve and chill.

Blitz the apple juice, lemon juice, spinach and a pinch of salt in a clean blender until smooth. Transfer to an airtight container and chill until needed, to maintain the green colour.

Peel and slice the raw kohlrabi thinly on a mandoline into 24 discs about 6–7cm in diameter. Into the centre of each put about 15g of veal, a dice of oyster and a small amount of oyster emulsion. Squeeze the sides of discs together to create little parcels.

Put 6 parcels into each bowl and top with apple marigold leaves. Pour the juice into each bowl and split with droplets of apple marigold oil.

SERVES 4, AS A STARTER

Poached oysters
15g dried kombu
1 tsp dashi granules
juice of ½ lemon
12 fresh oysters

Raw veal
300g veal fillet
Tabasco, for seasoning

Apple marigold oil
10g apple marigold leaves
100ml sunflower oil

Apple and spinach juice
300ml fresh apple juice
    (shop-bought is fine)
2 tsp lemon juice
50g baby spinach leaves

Kohlrabi discs
2 large kohlrabi

Oyster emulsion
see page 181

salt, for seasoning
apple marigold leaves, to serve

We grow a variety of kales, but Red Russian is a favourite for its deep green leaves and red/purple midribs and veins. It has a sweeter flavour than most kales, which makes it the perfect partner for kohlrabi. Here, the kohlrabi is gently roasted and then fried wrapped in crispy kale leaves ready for dipping into a rich dill emulsion. Abandon the cutlery for this one, fingers are the way forward. It makes a fabulous snack to eat with friends, or to serve as one of an array of sharing dishes.

BUTTER-ROASTED KOHLRABI AND KALE ROLLS

Preheat the oven to 200°C/180°C Fan/Gas Mark 6. Melt the butter for the kohlrabi parcels in a large, deep, heavy-based saucepan over a medium heat and add the whole, unpeeled kohlrabi. Transfer to a baking dish, uncovered, and bake in the oven for 35–40 minutes. Carefully open the oven door and quickly baste the kohlrabi with the hot foaming butter every 5 minutes. After 40 minutes, remove the dish from the oven and allow to cool to room temperature. Discard the butter and place the kohlrabi in the fridge for a couple of hours to chill.

While the kohlrabi chills, bring a large saucepan of water to the boil and blanch the dill fronds for 1 minute. Scoop them out with a slotted spoon and refresh in a bowl of iced water. Drain, squeeze out the excess water and blitz the dill with the oil in a blender until smooth. Pass the dill oil through a muslin-lined sieve.

Blitz the eggs in a clean blender on medium speed, adding the dill oil slowly until the emulsion has a mayonnaise consistency. Pass it through a fine sieve and season with salt. Leave to one side.

Cut the top and bottom off each of the kohlrabi. Using an apple corer, punch out 24 barrels from the centres. Wrap the barrels of kohlrabi in the kale leaves and secure using a toothpick.

Heat a non-stick frying pan over a low heat. Place the kohlrabi rolls in the dry pan and toast for 2–3 minutes until the kale leaves are crisp, turning the rolls halfway through the cooking time.

Remove the toothpicks and serve the wrapped kohlrabi on a plate to share, with the dill emulsion on the side as a dip and scattered with a few micro leaves of Red Russian kale, if you have them.

SERVES 4, AS A STARTER

Butter-roasted kohlrabi rolls
500g unsalted butter
4 large kohlrabi
24 red kale leaves, such as Red Russian

Dill emulsion
75g dill fronds
200ml sunflower oil
2 soft-boiled eggs (cooked for 4 minutes)
salt, for seasoning

When cooked, kohlrabi becomes sweeter, making this a delicious warming and comforting dish. Thinly sliced and baked with rich cream and cheese, this twist on the traditional potato gratin makes the best of the more mature kohlrabi that are last to leave the ground in November. We like to use a purple variety called Azur here, for its beautiful blue colouring and tender stems. The fruity and nutty flavours of the Berkswell are the perfect foil for the richness of this gratin. If you can't get Berkswell, make sure you use a really good-quality hard sheep's cheese, such as Manchego.

KOHLRABI GRATIN

Preheat the oven to 220°C/200°C Fan/Gas Mark 7. Butter a 25cm square ovenproof dish.

In a medium, heavy-based saucepan over a medium heat, slowly bring the milk, cream and thyme to the boil. Season with salt. Remove from the heat and allow to cool slightly. Strain through a fine sieve and pour the liquid over the sliced kohlrabi in a bowl. Toss through, making sure all the slices are covered.

Layer the kohlrabi evenly in the buttered dish and pour the liquid left in the bowl over the final layer. Sprinkle the cheese on top and cover with foil. Bake for 20 minutes, then remove the foil and bake for a further 20 minutes until golden brown. Serve hot.

SERVES 6–8, AS A SIDE

Kohlrabi gratin
butter, for greasing
130ml whole milk
200ml double cream
2 sprigs of thyme
1.5kg kohlrabi, peeled and thinly sliced
100g hard cheese, such as Berkswell, grated

salt, for seasoning

Kohlrabi is at its best in the summer months when it is tennis-ball size, although it will linger on in the soil into autumn and winter. Pickling our beautiful raw kohlrabi keeps them at their crunchy best once they are pulled fresh from the ground, and this pickle is the perfect accompaniment to the terrine. Rabbit is a subtle meat that easily takes on the flavours of its braising ingredients, and together adds a punch to the terrine. The terrine isn't too fiddly but it does need overnight refrigeration to get the flavours working and to set, so it's a good one to make ahead when feeding a crowd. It's a real showstopper and well worth the effort.

RABBIT TERRINE WITH PICKLED KOHLRABI

Preheat the oven to 180°C/160°C Fan/Gas Mark 4. Dust each rabbit leg lightly in flour. Heat a non-stick frying pan over a medium heat, add 2 tablespoons of oil and fry the legs in batches for 2–3 minutes on each side until lightly golden. Transfer to a deep-sided baking tray. Sauté the roughly chopped carrots, onion, celery and garlic in the frying pan (you don't need to add more oil) for 4–5 minutes until lightly browned, then add to the tray. Deglaze the frying pan with the wine and reduce by half. Add to tray along with the chicken stock and whole tarragon sprigs. Cover the tray with foil and braise in the oven for 2 hours.

Once the rabbit is cooked, remove from the oven and allow to cool slightly. Strain the cooking juices through a fine sieve into a medium saucepan and cook over a low heat to reduce the liquid to a slightly thicker sauce consistency.

Pick the meat from the rabbit legs and put in a mixing bowl, being sure not to add any bone. Discard the vegetables.

Melt the butter in a small saucepan over a low heat, add the diced carrots and shallots and sweat for 3–5 minutes until translucent. Add them to the rabbit meat with the reduced cooking liquid and chopped tarragon. Mix well.

Line a 1-litre terrine mould or loaf tin with a triple layer of cling film which is twice the size of the tin, so that the cling film hangs over the sides. Place a slice of Parma ham widthways in the tin and repeat with the rest of the ham, each new slice slightly overlapping the previous one and overhanging the edge of the tin, until the tin is lined. Spoon the rabbit mixture into the lined terrine, pressing down into the edges. Bring the overlapping Parma ham over the top to cover. Cover with the overhanging cling film to seal, then place a heavy weight on top – such as another loaf tin with two tins inside – and put in the fridge for 12 hours.

The next day, make the pickle. Put the vinegar and sugar in a medium, heavy-based saucepan with 600ml water, bring to the boil then remove from the heat and allow to cool. Peel the kohlrabi, shave them thinly on a mandoline and add to the cool pickling liquor. Leave for 1 hour.

Turn the terrine out on to a chopping board and cut it into thick slices. Serve with the pickled kohlrabi, some fresh watercress and walnuts.

SERVES 8–10, AS A STARTER

Rabbit terrine
6 rabbit legs
plain flour, for dusting
sunflower oil, for shallow-frying
6 carrots, 2 roughly chopped, 4 finely
    diced
1 onion, roughly chopped
1 celery stick, roughly chopped
2 garlic cloves
300ml white wine
500ml White Chicken Stock (see
    page 286)
2 whole sprigs of tarragon, plus 3 tbsp
    finely chopped tarragon leaves
10–12 slices of Parma ham
20g unsalted butter
4 shallots, finely diced

Pickled kohlrabi
300ml white wine vinegar
150g caster sugar
4 kohlrabi

watercress leaves and walnut halves,
    to serve

Fermenting food is a great way to preserve ingredients and flavours by natural processes, and it also offers fantastic health benefits, in particular enhancing the natural good bacteria in the gut to help with digestion. When fermented, kohlrabi has a wonderful earthiness that makes it a beautiful accompaniment to oysters. Make a good-sized batch of the fermented kohlrabi and you can add it to salads or use it as a side dish for oriental foods, a bit like a kimchi. This is a real 'get stuck in' dish for sharing amongst friends – just put all the elements into separate serving bowls in the middle of the table and let your guests help themselves.

BUTTERMILK FRIED OYSTERS WITH FERMENTED KOHLRABI AND FENNEL

Peel and coarsely grate the kohlrabi. Weigh the kohlrabi and measure out the salt at 3g per every 100g of kohlrabi. Combine the kohlrabi, salt, chilli, garlic, horseradish juice and yeast flakes and transfer to a sterilised 1-litre Kilner jar and seal. Store in a cool, dry place away from direct sunlight for 2 weeks. After 2 weeks, open the jar and transfer the contents to an airtight plastic container. Chill until required.

Shuck the oysters, discard their juice and dry the oyster meat on kitchen paper. Combine the buttermilk and Tabasco in a bowl, add the oysters and leave to marinate for 10 minutes at room temperature. In a medium bowl, mix together the flours, ground fennel and 1 teaspoon of salt. Drain the oysters and coat them in the flour, one at a time, then deep-fry in batches in a pan of oil heated to 200°C for 3–4 minutes, or until lightly golden. Remove with a slotted spoon, drain on kitchen paper and season with salt.

Shave the fennel thinly on a mandoline and toss in a bowl with the remaining ingredients and a pinch of salt.

Serve the deep-fried oysters alongside the fermented kohlrabi and fennel salad.

SERVES 4, AS A STARTER

Fermented kohlrabi
1 kohlrabi
Maldon sea salt, for fermenting (see method)
½ red chilli, finely chopped
1 garlic clove, crushed
50ml fresh horseradish juice
1 tsp yeast flakes

Buttermilk fried oysters
24 fresh oysters
150ml buttermilk
5 drops of Tabasco
60g plain flour
60g tapioca flour
10g fennel seeds, ground

Shaved fennel
2 fennel bulbs
2 tbsp rapeseed oil
juice of 1 lemon
1 tbsp finely chopped chives

salt, for seasoning
vegetable oil, for deep-frying

Kombucha is made from a culture known as scoby, which is an acronym for symbiotic culture of bacteria and yeast. As it is a living colony of bacteria and yeast, kombucha makes a probiotic tea that contains significant amounts of B vitamins, and has many health benefits such as improved digestion and mood stability, and it also fights yeast infections. It's a drink of goodness, but here we've rung the changes with a few flavour options, adding fruit, herbs and vegetables to perk up the slightly sour, fizzy tea.

THREE WAYS WITH KOMBUCHA

We have an abundance of rosehips near us, and hibiscus thrives in the tunnels on Our Farm, so we use these flavours together as a perfect, tangy infusion and an excellent source of vitamin C.

ROSEHIP AND HIBISCUS KOMBUCHA

Put the maple syrup, rhubarb, hibiscus, rosehips and 1 litre of water into a large, heavy-based saucepan over a high heat. Bring to the boil, then turn down the heat and simmer for 5 minutes. Remove from the heat, add the tea leaves and leave to steep for 5 minutes, stirring regularly, then strain the liquid, discarding the tea leaves and all the other flavourings. Leave the liquid to cool to 20°C (check with a thermometer), transfer to a 1.5-litre sterilised container or jar (see page 302) and add the scoby. Cover the jar with muslin secured with an elastic band, leaving the lid off. Store in a cool, dry place away from direct sunlight for 4 days.

Strain through a fine sieve into a clean, sterilised plastic container. Keep the scoby to use again, seal the container and store the strained liquid in a cool, dark place for 2 days to carbonate. Once carbonated, store in the fridge for up to 2 weeks and serve chilled.

MAKES 1 LITRE

150g maple syrup
50g rhubarb stalks, chopped
1 tbsp dried hibiscus
130g dried rosehips, chopped
1 tsp black tea leaves
1 kombucha scoby

This kombucha came about because I love cabbage. When we make this we add the cabbage juice to a rotary evaporator which reduces it in a vacuum at a very low temperature so that we don't lose the leaves' fresh flavours. At home, reducing the leaves in a pan results in a sweeter taste as its pepperiness is lost through heating, but both methods still produce a fantastic flavour.

RED CABBAGE KOMBUCHA

In a large, heavy-based saucepan set over a medium heat, reduce the cabbage juice by half. Remove from the heat. Add the sugar and mix well to dissolve, then add the apple juice. When the liquid has cooled to 20°C (check with a thermometer), transfer to a 1.5-litre sterilised container or jar (see page 302) and add the scoby. Cover the jar with muslin secured with an elastic band. Store in a cool, dry place away from direct sunlight for 1 week.

Strain through a fine sieve into a clean, sterilised plastic container. Keep the scoby to use again, seal the container and store the strained liquid in a cool, dark place for 2 days to carbonate. Once carbonated, store in the fridge for up to 2 weeks and serve chilled.

MAKES ABOUT 2.5 LITRES

5kg red cabbage, juiced in a juicer to make 2 litres juice
100g caster sugar
500ml fresh apple juice
1 kombucha scoby

Pumpkin is another ingredient that is prolific on the farm, and this is a wonderful way to preserve the dramatic-looking jewels of our veg patch and to capture this vegetable's sweet, nutty flavour characteristics in a refreshing fizzy drink.

PUMPKIN KOMBUCHA

In a large, heavy-based saucepan set over a medium heat, reduce the pumpkin juice by half. Add the sugar and filtered water, bring to the boil and remove from the heat. Add the oolong tea and leave to steep for 10 minutes, stirring regularly, then strain the liquid, discarding the tea leaves. Leave the liquid to cool to 20°C (check with a thermometer), transfer to a 3-litre sterilised container or jar (see page 302) and add the scoby. Cover the jar with muslin secured with an elastic band, leaving the lid off. Store in a cool, dry place away from direct sunlight for 1 week.

Strain through a fine sieve into a clean, sterilised plastic container. Keep the scoby to use again, seal the container and store the strained liquid in a cool, dark place for 2 days to carbonate. Once carbonated, store in the fridge for up to 2 weeks and serve chilled.

MAKES ABOUT 2 LITRES

2kg pumpkin, juiced in a juicer to make 600ml pumpkin juice
100g cane sugar
1.7 litres filtered water
20g oolong tea leaves
1 kombucha scoby

MEAT

Hen of the wood is one of my favourite mushrooms, which can be foraged for from late August, but you can also get hold of it under its Japanese name, maitake. The crisp-fried mushrooms enhance the crunchy textures from the fried skin and yeast-flake crumb and are beautiful against the tender chicken and soft mushroom purée. Make sure you use an organic, free-range and corn-fed chicken here for maximum flavour, not to mention animal welfare.

CHICKEN WITH MUSHROOMS AND CREAMED KALE

Preheat the oven to 200°C/180°C Fan/Gas Mark 6. Scrape any excess fat from the chicken skin and discard. Lay the skin flat on a baking sheet lined with baking parchment, season with a pinch of salt and bake for 15–20 minutes until lightly golden. Remove and drain on kitchen paper. When cool, chop to a fine crumb.

Lower the oven to 160°C/140°C Fan/Gas Mark 2. Melt the butter in a small, heavy-based saucepan over a low–medium heat. Add the yeast flakes and toast, stirring, for 1–2 minutes until golden, then fold through the chicken-skin crumb.

Season the chicken breasts with salt on both sides. Warm the oil in a non-stick ovenproof frying pan over a medium heat and fry the chicken breasts for 3–4 minutes until lightly coloured, then turn them over and finish in the oven (still in the pan) for 12–15 minutes. Remove from the oven and put to one side to rest. Meanwhile, reduce the brown chicken stock to a sauce consistency in a large, heavy-based saucepan (see page 286).

To make the mushroom purée, melt the butter in a large, heavy-based saucepan over a medium heat, add the mushrooms with a pinch of salt and cook, stirring regularly, for 8–10 minutes until soft and slightly caramelised. Add the milk, bring to the boil and boil for 2 minutes. Remove from the heat and blitz until smooth in a food processor. Pass the purée through a fine sieve into a bowl.

For the creamed kale, warm the oil in a medium, heavy-based saucepan. Sweat the shallot and bay leaf for 3–4 minutes until the shallot is soft and translucent. Add the stock and reduce to a thick, syrup-like consistency. Pour in the cream, add the savory and reduce by half, then strain through a fine sieve and allow to cool.

Sauté the kale in a little oil in a saucepan over a high heat for 30 seconds, adding 2–3 tablespoons of water to help it steam. Once the kale has wilted, add the reduced cream to glaze the kale. Remove the pan from the heat.

Heat a large non-stick frying pan over a medium heat. Add the oil followed by the mushrooms and sauté for 3–5 minutes. Add the butter and cook for 4 minutes until lightly golden and crispy. Remove from the heat and season with a pinch of salt.

Put a spoon of warm mushroom purée on each plate, brush the chicken with a little jus, top with crispy crumb and add to the plates. Serve the creamed kale alongside with a bowl of crispy hen of the woods and the remaining jus.

SERVES 4

Chicken breast and yeast-flake crumb
100g chicken skin (from the 4 large breasts)
50g unsalted butter
40g yeast flakes
2 tbsp sunflower oil
4 large chicken breasts, skin on, such as Goosnargh

Chicken jus
1 litre Brown Chicken Stock (see page 286)

Mushroom purée
80g unsalted butter
500g chestnut mushrooms, sliced
120ml whole milk

Creamed kale
1 tbsp sunflower oil, plus extra for the kale
1 shallot, sliced
1 bay leaf
200ml Ham Stock (see page 286)
500ml double cream
10g summer savory
150g kale leaves, such as Pentland Brigg, Red Russian, Peacock

Hen of the wood
3 tbsp sunflower oil
200g hen of the wood or maitake mushrooms
50g unsalted butter

salt, for seasoning

Nose-to-tail eating is not widely embraced in Britain today, although previous generations would have happily made use of every part of an animal, and we like to follow their example. There's a fair bit of prep for this dish, but it's necessary for a really good flavour and texture – soaking the offal in milk overnight helps remove impurities, and long, slow cooking tenderises every part until it melts in the mouth. This recipe will give you more dough than you need because the quantities allow for enough volume to create a well-worked dough, but you can cook the excess and freeze it for another day.

POULTRY OFFAL DUMPLINGS

Make the ferment the night before by mixing the flour, caster sugar and milk powder together in a bowl. Dissolve the yeast in 50ml tepid water and mix it into the dry ingredients until smooth. Chill overnight.

For the ragout, soak the hearts, gizzards and livers separately in milk in the fridge overnight.

The next day, make the dough. In a stand mixer fitted with a dough hook, mix the flour, sugar, salt, prepared ferment and egg yolks together until smooth. Add the butter, dice by dice, until it's fully incorporated. Remove the dough from the mixer, wrap in cling film and allow to rest in the fridge for 20 minutes. Weigh the dough into 7g balls and roll into smooth dumplings. Place the dumplings on a baking tray lined with baking parchment and leave to prove at room temperature, covered with a clean cloth, for 1 hour.

Preheat the oven to 155°C/135°C Fan/Gas Mark 2. Bake the dumplings in the oven for 8 minutes, then turn off the heat and leave the door halfway open with the dumplings inside for 3 minutes. Remove and put to one side to cool.

Increase the oven temperature to 200°C/180°C Fan/Gas Mark 6. Drain and thoroughly rinse the livers, place on a baking tray and bake in the oven for 5 minutes. Remove from the oven and leave to one side. Put the gizzards and hearts separately in two small, heavy-based saucepans over the lowest heat possible and cover in melted duck fat. Cook the hearts for 2 hours and the gizzards for 6 hours, or until tender. When all the hearts and gizzards are cooked, remove from the duck fat with a slotted spoon and mince together with the livers using a mincer or pulse in a food processor until coarsely chopped and put in a medium saucepan with the reduced chicken stock, butter and salt to season. Heat gently over a low heat to warm through.

Dust the sliced shallots with tapioca flour and deep-fry them in oil heated to 180°C for 2–3 minutes until lightly golden. Remove with a slotted spoon and drain on kitchen paper. Once cool, chop them finely to make a crumb.

Using a melon baller, scoop out a small amount of the cooked dumpling from the bottom of each and fill the holes with the offal. Cook the buns in a steamer for 15 minutes. Remove and divide among plates, lightly brush with a little melted butter and sprinkle with the shallot crumb.

SERVES 6, AS A STARTER

Ferment
65g strong bread flour
1 tsp caster sugar
1 tsp milk powder
8–10g fresh yeast

Offal ragout
250g duck hearts
250g duck gizzards
125g chicken livers
milk, for soaking
1kg duck fat, melted
1 litre Brown Chicken Stock, reduced to a
    sauce consistency (see page 286)
25g unsalted butter, plus extra, melted,
    for serving
salt, for seasoning

Dough
190g strong bread flour
1 tsp caster sugar
½ tsp salt
2½ egg yolks
75g unsalted butter, at room temperature,
    diced

Shallot crumb
6 shallots, thinly sliced
tapioca flour, for dusting
vegetable oil, for deep-frying

Cumberland sauce is a popular and traditional English condiment, made with sweet ruby red port and redcurrant jelly to give it extra depth. It is fantastic with rich meats such as goose or game, and it works really well with the intense flavour of chicken livers. Here the Cumberland sauce is reduced and spooned over the finished parfait; it needs a little time to set, which makes this a really impressive get-ahead dish.

CUMBERLAND CREAMED CHICKEN LIVERS

To make the parfait, put the shallots, thyme, garlic and all the alcohol in a medium, heavy-based saucepan over a medium heat and cook for about 7–10 minutes until the liquid has reduced to a glaze. Strain through a fine sieve and leave to cool.

Put the livers, eggs and pink salt in a blender, add the shallot reduction and blitz until smooth. Strain through a fine sieve into a bowl. Using a hand-held blender, gradually add the melted butter, blitzing all the time. Pour the parfait into six individual 500ml Kilner jars or ramekins and cover with cling film. Put the jars or ramekins in a tiered steaming pan and steam the parfaits over simmering water for 20–25 minutes, or until just set with a little wobble. Remove from the steamer and allow to cool to room temperature before covering and putting in the fridge to chill until ready to serve.

To make the sauce, warm the oil in a medium, heavy-based saucepan over a medium heat, add the shallots and sweat for 3–5 minutes, or until translucent. Deglaze the pan with the red wine vinegar and reduce to a syrup consistency. Add the rest of the ingredients, increase the heat and bring to the boil, then turn down the heat and reduce until the liquid coats the back of a spoon. Remove from the heat and allow to cool a little. Strain through a fine sieve while it's still warm then spoon on to the parfaits and return them to the fridge to chill until set.

Serve the creamed chicken livers with toasted sourdough.

SERVES 6, AS A STARTER

Chicken liver parfait
3 shallots, sliced
2 sprigs of thyme
1 garlic clove, smashed
150ml medium-dry Madeira
150ml port
75ml white port
50ml brandy
400g chicken livers
4 eggs
15g Himalayan pink salt
400g unsalted butter, melted

Cumberland sauce
2 tbsp sunflower oil
5 shallots, finely diced
100ml red wine vinegar
5g sage leaves
1 tsp white peppercorns
250ml White Chicken Stock (see page 286)
250ml port
150g redcurrant jelly
50ml Worcestershire sauce
35ml fresh orange juice (shop-bought is fine)
zest of 2 lemons

toasted sourdough bread, to serve

Grouse is considered to be the king of game, and the The Glorious Twelfth – the start of grouse shooting season on 12 August – is eagerly anticipated. Grouse has a distinctive gamey flavour and is very rich, so you don't need much of it, which makes it perfect for these faggots. If you want to make the most of the grouse season, make lots of these and freeze them. Elder trees begin to be covered with juicy purple berries from late summer, perfectly matching the grouse season. Their deep, intense flavour means they stand up well to the richness of game.

GROUSE FAGGOTS WITH ELDERBERRY SAUCE

Combine all the ingredients for the faggots in a large bowl, including the truffles if using, (it really improves the flavour) and mix well. Roll between your hands into golf ball-size faggots, place on a plate, cover and leave to firm up in the fridge for 1–2 hours.

To make the sauce, warm the oil in a casserole dish over a medium heat and fry the carcasses for 12–15 minutes, or until deeply caramelised, stirring regularly. Add 200g of the elderberries and all the chicken stock, increase the heat and bring to a rapid boil. Regularly skim the surface and cook until reduced by half. Pass the stock through a fine sieve into a clean saucepan and season with salt. Add the remaining elderberries and cook over a low heat for 8–10 minutes.

Preheat the oven to 180°C/160°C Fan/Gas Mark 4. Warm the oil for the grouse faggots in a large, non-stick ovenproof frying pan over a medium heat and fry the faggots for 3–4 minutes, turning them so that they are evenly browned, then transfer to the oven to cook for 5 minutes.

Divide the faggots into bowls and serve with the hot sauce.

SERVES 6, AS A LIGHT MAIN

Grouse faggots
2 grouse: remove 400g breast meat and
    cut it into strips, and mince the leg
    meat
180g minced pork
25g button mushrooms, finely chopped
1 tbsp brandy
4 slices of stale white bread, blitzed to
    crumbs
100ml whole milk
2 egg whites
15g salt
50g chicken livers, chopped
20g black truffle, chopped (optional)
sunflower oil, for frying

Elderberry sauce
2 tbsp sunflower oil
2 grouse carcasses from above, chopped
500g elderberries
1 litre White Chicken Stock (see page 286)
salt, for seasoning

Rich and intensely flavoured, duck is classically paired with quite a few different fruits, but here we have gone for the traditional combination with tart cherries and brought it into the twenty-first century by adding the earthy flavours of sweet baby beetroots. For this recipe, buy two duck crowns and remove the breasts yourself, or ask a butcher to do it for you, and keep the carcasses to make the stock. If you have a duck carcass already, you can make the stock ahead of time and store it in the freezer.

DUCK BREAST WITH CHERRIES AND SMOKED BEETROOT

For the duck stock, warm the oil in a large, heavy-based saucepan over a low heat, add the vegetables and cook for 2–3 hours, stirring regularly, until completely soft and darker in colour, and no moisture is left in the pan.

Preheat the oven to 200°C/180°C Fan/Gas Mark 6. Roast the duck carcasses on a baking tray for 40 minutes, or until deeply golden. Add the carcasses to the stock pan. Deglaze the baking tray with 200ml water and add it to the pan. Cover with the chicken stock and bring to the boil over a high heat. Reduce the heat and simmer for 2 hours, skimming it regularly. Strain through a fine sieve into another heavy-based saucepan then reduce by two-thirds over a medium heat.

Put the baby beetroots, oil, thyme and garlic in a small, heavy-based saucepan on the lowest heat and cook for 1 hour, or until tender. Remove from the heat and allow to cool slightly, then scoop out the beetroots, rub off the skins and leave to one side. Discard the cooking liquid.

Meanwhile, make the beetroot sauce. Reduce the red beetroot juice by half in a small, heavy-based saucepan over a medium heat. Pour into a small heatproof bowl and allow to cool. Put the smoking chips in a baking tray lined with foil. Sit a wire rack on top, one of similar size to the tray, making sure the wire isn't touching the chips. Put the bowl on the wire rack. Cover the entire bowl, rack and tray with a tent of foil, so no smoke escapes. Sit the tray on the hob over a low–medium heat for 5 minutes. Turn the heat off and leave the bowl covered in the foil tent for 15 minutes to cool to room temperature.

Combine the smoked beetroot juice and reduced duck stock in a small, heavy-based saucepan over a low heat and reduce to a sauce consistency. Keep warm while you prepare the rest of the dish.

To make the cherry gel, put all ingredients with 50ml water in a small saucepan, bring to the boil and boil for 1 minute. Strain the mixture through a fine sieve into a heatproof bowl and allow to cool, then leave in the fridge for a few minutes to set. Once set, blitz in a blender until smooth.

SERVES 4

4 duck breasts, taken from 2 crowns

Duck stock
2 tbsp sunflower oil
2 carrots, roughly chopped
2 onions, roughly chopped
2 celery sticks, roughly chopped
1 leek, roughly chopped
2 garlic cloves
duck carcasses, from the crowns above
3 litres White Chicken Stock (see page 286)

Confit beetroots
16 baby beetroots, such as Pablo F1
400ml rapeseed oil
3 sprigs of thyme
4 garlic cloves, smashed

Smoked beetroot sauce
1kg red beetroot, juiced in a juicer
6 tbsp wood smoking chips
300g reduced Duck Stock, from above

Preheat the oven to 160°C/140°C Fan/Gas Mark 2. Put the duck breasts skin side down in a dry, non-stick, ovenproof frying pan over a medium heat and cook for 4–5 minutes, or until the skin is lightly golden. Turn them over and transfer them to the oven for 6 minutes. Remove from the pan and allow to rest for 10 minutes.

Drizzle the smoked beetroot sauce around each plate. Carve the duck breasts and divide the slices among the plates along with the confit beetroots. Add dots of cherry gel to each serving. Finish with red orache and burgundy oxalis.

Cherry gel

250g frozen cherry purée (shop-bought or just blitz together frozen cherries in a blender)

1 tbsp caster sugar

2 tbsp kirsch

1 tsp agar agar

red orache and burgundy oxalis, to serve

Guinea fowl are delicious, slightly gamey birds, but because they are smaller than most chickens, they need careful cooking, as they can become quite dry when overcooked. The offal ragout is extremely rich, but it is complemented by the acidic hit from the elderflower vinegar in the sauce. This vinegar is a great way to preserve the abundant supply of elderflowers that smother the bushes and trees around Cartmel in early summer. The vinegar can be kept for up to 4 months in a cool dry place, unopened, and in the fridge once opened.

GUINEA FOWL AND OFFAL RAGOUT WITH BROAD BEANS AND ELDERFLOWER

Preheat the oven to 180°C/160°C Fan/Gas Mark 4.

Warm the oil in a large, non-stick ovenproof frying pan over a low–medium heat, add the guinea fowl crowns and cook for 5–7 minutes, turning them until the breasts and skin are lightly and evenly golden. Stand the crowns in the pan, transfer to the oven and roast for 15–20 minutes. Remove from the oven and leave to one side to rest.

Put the elderflowers and vinegar in a small saucepan over a low heat and bring to the boil. Remove from the heat and allow to infuse for 20 minutes. Strain through a fine sieve into a bowl and allow to cool.

Pod the broad beans. Bring a large saucepan of water to the boil and blanch the beans for 1 minute. Remove with a slotted spoon and refresh in a bowl of iced water. Discard the outer skins and set the bright green kernels to one side.

Remove the guinea fowl breasts from the crowns. Warm through the offal ragout.

Spoon a portion of ragout on to each plate and arrange the guinea fowl breasts alongside the ragout. Warm the broad bean kernels in a saucepan with a small amount of water and a knob of butter, drain and add to the plate. Warm the reduced stock and split it with a small amount of the elderflower vinegar, then spoon it around the plate. Finish with fresh elderflower flowers and broad bean leaves.

SERVES 4

Guinea fowl
2 tbsp sunflower oil
2 guinea fowl crowns

Elderflower vinegar
100g fresh elderflowers
200ml chardonnay vinegar

Broad beans
330g broad beans, such as Aquadulce, in
    their pods
knob of butter

Offal ragout
120g Offal Ragout (see page 130)

Sauce
200ml reduced Duck or White Chicken
    Stock (see page 134 or 286)
elderflower vinegar (above), to taste

fresh elderflowers and broad bean leaves,
    to serve

Pork and smoked eel is a combination I have been using for years, both in the restaurant and at home, because the flavours and textures work so well together. Pork jowl is an under-used cheek cut ideal for curing and smoking. The meat is cured with aromatic seeds and herbs, then slow-roasted to absorb the flavours and become deliciously tender. We grow lots of varieties of onion for their varying colours and degrees of sweetness – such as red Kamal F1 and Simane and yellow Reks F1 – so get a good selection to brighten up the plate. Wood-firing the onions gives them a smoky edge, so it's worth the effort.

PORK JOWL WITH WOOD-FIRED ONIONS AND SMOKED EEL

For the pork jowls, toast the fennel and coriander seeds in a dry frying pan over a medium heat for 2–3 minutes. Remove from the heat and allow to cool, then combine with the parsley and a small handful of salt and grind to a coarse powder with a pestle and mortar. Transfer the mixture to a plastic container or bowl, add the remaining salt and sugar and pack in the pork jowls. Put in the fridge for 2 hours.

Meanwhile, preheat the oven to 200°C/180°C Fan/Gas Mark 6 and prepare the onion tapioca sauce. Peel the onions, cut them in half and lay them cut side down on a baking tray. Bake for 45–50 minutes until deeply golden. Transfer the onions to a large, heavy-based saucepan and add 4 litres of water, using some of the water to deglaze the baking tray and pouring the liquid from the tray into the pan, too. Bring to the boil over a high heat, then turn the heat down as low as possible, cover the pan with a lid and cook for 1 hour.

Meanwhile, reduce the oven temperature to 170°C/150°C Fan/Gas Mark 3. Wash the cure off the jowls with cold running water and put them on a baking tray. Cover with foil and roast for 3 hours, turning up the oven temperature to 200°C/180°C Fan/Gas Mark 6 for the last 30 minutes.

Strain the onion stock through a fine sieve and divide equally between two saucepans. Reduce one pan of stock by half, then remove from the heat. Put the other pan over a low heat, add the tapioca pearls and cook for 20–25 minutes, or until the tapioca is tender, stirring regularly. Strain out the pearls, transfer to a tray and chill until cold.

To make the purée, melt the butter in a medium, heavy-based saucepan over a low heat, add the onions and sweat them without letting them brown for 15–20 minutes, or until soft, stirring regularly. Add the cream and reduce to a thick sauce. Blend until smooth, pass through a fine sieve and season with salt.

Put the onions in a baking tray, coat in oil and season with salt. Roast in the wood-fired oven or on a hot barbecue grill for 4–5 minutes until tender and charred.

Return the pearls to the reduced warm stock, add the smoked diced eel and serve in small jugs alongside the pork jowl, white onion purée, wood-fired onions and buckler sorrel.

SERVES 4, AS A STARTER

Pork jowl
25g fennel seeds
25g coriander seeds
25g flat-leaf parsley leaves
375g salt
125g caster sugar
2 pork jowls

Onion tapioca sauce
4 large white onions
50g tapioca pearls
100g smoked eel, diced

White onion purée
70g unsalted butter
4 large white onions, sliced
500ml double cream

Wood-fired onions
12 onions, such as baby browns, silverskins and baby red, peeled
4 tbsp rapeseed oil

salt, for seasoning
buckler sorrel, to serve

This is a real favourite of mine. Fatty pork belly is a fantastic partner to smoked eel wrapped in a spicy crumb. Dipping it into the fermented sweetcorn sauce makes this a really comforting dish. The two weeks' fermentation for the sweetcorn might seem a long time but is well worth the wait, as it adds a slight sourness to the sauce which really cuts through the fatty elements. Lovage has a surprisingly strong celery-like flavour, so use this oil sparingly and keep the leftovers to liven up salads, root vegetables or poultry dishes.

PORK AND EEL CROQUETTES WITH FERMENTED SWEETCORN SAUCE

Drain the sweetcorn and tip the corn kernels into a sterilised 1-litre Kilner jar (see page 302) with the salt. Mix well, seal the jar with the lid and allow to ferment for 2 weeks in a cool, dry place away from direct sunlight.

On the day of cooking, cover the pork belly with the coarse sea salt, transfer to a container, cover and chill for 2 hours.

While the pork is curing, make the lovage oil. Bring a large saucepan of water to the boil and blanch the parsley and lovage leaves separately for 1 minute each. Remove with a slotted spoon and refresh in a bowl of iced water. Drain, squeeze out the excess water and blitz the herbs with the oil in a blender until smooth. Pass the herb oil through a muslin-lined sieve, then chill in the fridge.

Preheat the oven to 140°C/120°C Fan/Gas Mark 1. Rinse the salt off the pork under cold running water and pat it dry with kitchen paper. Put the pork belly in a small baking tray, cover with foil and cook in the oven for 2 hours, or until tender. Remove and allow to cool, then dice into 5mm pieces. Dice the smoked eel into pieces the same size and add to the pork. Melt the reduced brown chicken stock in a small saucepan, add to the pork and eel, season with salt and mix well. Roll the pork and eel mixture into golf ball-size balls and chill on a plate in the fridge for 30 minutes until firm.

For the crumb, season the flour with salt and put in a shallow dish. Put the beaten eggs in a second shallow dish and the breadcrumbs in a third. Coat the pork and eel in the flour, then egg, and finish with a generous coating of the breadcrumbs. Return to the fridge to set for 10 minutes.

Blitz the fermented corn with the cream in a blender until smooth, then pass through a fine sieve into a small saucepan and warm through.

Deep-fry the pork and eel balls in batches in a pan of oil heated to 180°C for 2 minutes, or until golden. Remove with a slotted spoon, drain on kitchen paper and season with salt.

Serve the warm sauce in small jugs on plates, split with droplets of the green oil, and place the pork and eel croquettes on the plates, scattered with salad leaves and dianthus flowers.

SERVES 4, AS A STARTER

Fermented sweetcorn sauce
200g cooked sweetcorn
6g sea salt
200ml double cream

Pork and eel croquette
150g skinned and boned pork belly
200g coarse sea salt
85g smoked eel
100ml reduced Brown Chicken Stock (see page 286)

Croquette crumb
75g plain flour
2 eggs, beaten
100g panko breadcrumbs

Lovage oil
50g flat-leaf parsley leaves
50g lovage leaves
150ml sunflower oil

salt, for seasoning
vegetable oil, for deep-frying
mixed salad leaves and dianthus flowers, to serve

A whole shoulder might seem extravagant, but it's not an expensive cut of meat, and every part of the joint is used, including the bones to make a rich, flavourful stock. Mead or honey wine is our favourite drink at Cartmel, made with the honey collected from own hives, and creates a boozy, slightly fermented sauce. It is not sweet, but the fresh honey taste is the perfect partner to the rich garlicky flavours of the pig. This is a real showstopper and great for sharing with a group of friends – just put the meat, sauce and vegetables on the table and let everyone serve themselves.

SUCKLING PIG WITH MEAD SAUCE

For the suckling pig, mix the salt, thyme and garlic together and rub it into and all over the shoulder. Chill in the fridge for 12 hours.

Preheat the oven to 190°C/170°C Fan/Gas Mark 5. Combine the pork ribs and the minced pork in a baking tray and place in the oven for 1 hour.

Once the ribs and mince are cooked remove from the oven and set aside. Reduce the oven temperature to 160°C/140°C Fan/Gas Mark 2. Wash the salt off the shoulder under cold running water and pat dry with kitchen paper. Put the shoulder and the stock in a large roasting tin, cover with foil and cook for 3 hours before removing the foil and cooking for a further 30 minutes.

While the pork is cooking, warm the sunflower oil in a large, heavy-based saucepan over a medium heat, add the chopped vegetables and sweat for 6–8 minutes, or until soft. Stir in the tomato paste and cook for 2 minutes. Add the cooked ribs and mince and deglaze with the mead, then reduce by half. Cover with 2 litres of water, increase the heat and bring to the boil, then reduce the heat and simmer for 3 hours, skimming it regularly.

Strain the mead sauce through a fine sieve into a clean, medium saucepan, discarding all the solids. Skim the fat from the top. Reduce the stock to a sauce consistency over a low heat, and spike with extra mead to add freshness.

Add the baby beetroots, turnip and new potaoes to another baking tray, drizzle with rapeseed oil and roast alongside the pork shoulder for the last 35 minutes. With 15 minutes to go, add the carrots to the other baby vegetables and return to the oven – they should all be just cooked through.

Remove and reserve the bones from the shoulder and cut the meat into 4–6 portions. Serve the meat in the centre of the table for everyone to help themselves. Cut the pork into chunky portions and serve on a plate alongside a bowl of roasted vegetables and a jug of the sauce.

SERVES 4-6

Suckling pig
250g coarse sea salt
1 tbsp thyme leaves
6 garlic cloves, sliced
1 shoulder of suckling pig
500ml White Chicken Stock (see page 286)

Mead sauce
2 tbsp sunflower oil
2 carrots, finely chopped
2 onions, finely chopped
2 celery sticks, finely chopped
2 tbsp tomato paste
500ml mead, plus extra for seasoning
2kg pork ribs
2kg minced pork

For the roasted vegetables
8 each of baby beetroots, baby turnips new potatoes and baby carrots
rapeseed oil, for drizzling

For me, this dish sums up the change from summer to autumn, as a feast of the deep flavours of seasonal game and the rich jewel-like colours of elderberries, along with crisp lettuces fresh from the soil. If you can get it, use wild venison for an unrivalled flavour – available from mid October to mid February. This rich, dark, lean meat has an earthiness that works really well with root vegetables. Don't miss the elderberry season in late summer, as these wonderful capers can be bottled up and used as a sharp acidity to cut the richness of meat, helped here by sweet yet slightly bitter red gem lettuce.

ROAST VENISON WITH GRILLED GEM LETTUCE AND ELDERBERRY CAPER SAUCE

To make the sauce, warm the oil in a large casserole dish over a medium heat, add the venison bones and brown them for 8–10 minutes. Strain through a colander, return the oil to the dish, add the sliced vegetables and bay leaf and sweat for 5–6 minutes, stirring regularly. Return the browned bones to the dish, deglaze with the vinegar and wine and reduce by three-quarters. Add the stock, bring to the boil, reduce the heat and simmer for 20 minutes, skimming it regularly. Strain through a fine sieve into a clean saucepan, skim the surface and reduce by half. Finish the sauce with the cream and capers, bring to the boil one final time and remove from the heat. Put to one side until needed.

Preheat the oven to 240°C/220°C Fan/Gas Mark 8.

Season the venison meat with a generous amount of salt. Heat the duck fat in a baking tray over a medium heat. When hot, add the haunch of venison and caramelise and brown it all over, for 3–4 minutes on each side. Transfer the meat to a rack in another baking tray and cook for 20 minutes in the oven. Reduce the heat to 150°C/130°C Fan/Gas Mark 2 and cook for a further 20 minutes. Remove from the oven, wrap in foil and allow to rest in a warm place for 15 minutes.

Peel and thinly slice the parsley root. Melt the butter in a large, heavy-based saucepan over a low–medium heat, add the parsley root and sweat it without browning for 8–10 minutes, stirring regularly. Add the milk, cream and salt and cook for 15–18 minutes until the parsley is soft and most of the liquid has evaporated. Remove from the heat and blitz in a blender until smooth. Pass through a fine sieve into a heatproof bowl.

Slice the gem lettuces in half lengthways. Warm the oil in a non-stick frying pan over a medium heat, add the lettuce cut side down and cook for 1–2 minutes until lightly browned. Add the chicken stock and butter and turn the lettuce over. Reduce the stock and butter to a glaze while basting the lettuce.

Spoon the purée into the centre of each plate, spreading it in circular motion, and carve the venison into 5mm-thick slices. Arrange the venison slices on top of the purée in a curve, fan the grilled gem lettuce in the open part of purée. Spoon over the sauce, dividing the capers evenly among the plates.

SERVES 4

Elderberry caper sauce
2 tbsp sunflower oil
venison bone pieces from the haunch (see below)
2 carrots, sliced
1 onion, sliced
1 bay leaf
2 tbsp red wine vinegar
100ml red wine
1 litre White Chicken Stock (see page 286)
125ml double cream
20g Elderberry Capers

Venison leg
1 haunch of venison (about 750g), bones removed and cut into 2.5cm pieces (ask the butcher to do this for you)
salt, for rubbing in
200g duck fat

Parsley root purée
350g parsley root
25g unsalted butter
150ml whole milk
150ml double cream
1 tsp salt

Grilled red gem lettuce
2 red gem lettuce
1 tbsp sunflower oil
250ml White Chicken Stock (see page 286)
30g unsalted butter

Sweetbreads are another part of the animal that have fallen out of favour, but I use them a lot. Sweetbreads are glands taken from calves and lambs, which admittedly doesn't make them sound very appealing, but they are delicate and creamy. You can order them from your butcher, but do make sure they come from rose veal, which have been humanely produced. Cooking the sweetbreads until deeply caramelised makes a wonderful contrast to the softer elements here; yellow beans add a vibrant colour and pair beautifully with the earthy sweetness of corn. The dash of savory oil uses one of my favourite herbs to add a piquant note reminiscent of thyme, mint and marjoram.

SWEETBREADS WITH SWEETCORN PURÉE

Bring a large saucepan of water to the boil. Blanch the French beans for 1 minute then remove them with a slotted spoon and refresh in a bowl of iced water. Scoop out and drain on kitchen paper. Blanch the sweetbreads in the same pan for 1 minute. Scoop them out, peel away the outer membrane of the sweetbreads and leave the sweetbreads to dry on kitchen paper. Cut into 4 equal-sized pieces.

Put the fresh sweetcorn kernels in a medium, heavy-based saucepan with the milk and cream and a pinch of salt and cook over a medium heat for 6–8 minutes, or until most of the liquid has evaporated. Remove from the heat, transfer to a blender and blitz until smooth. Pass through a fine sieve into a bowl and leave to one side.

Preheat the oven to 180°C/160°C Fan/Gas Mark 4.

Blitz the savory leaves and oil in a blender until smooth, then pass the oil through a muslin-lined sieve into a bowl. Put the oil in the fridge to chill.

Lightly dust the sweetbread pieces with flour and heat the sunflower oil in a non-stick ovenproof frying pan over a medium heat. Add the sweetbreads to the hot pan. Cook on one side for 5–6 minutes for veal sweetbreads, slightly less for other kinds, until lightly golden and crispy. Add the butter, turn the sweetbreads over and repeat on the other side. Transfer to the oven to finish cooking for 5–6 minutes.

Divide the sweetcorn purée among plates with a spoon, add the sweetbreads and finish with the blanched yellow beans. Drizzle the savory oil around the dish and finish with savory flowers.

SERVES 4

Yellow beans
300g yellow French beans, such as Minidor

Sweetbreads
750g sweetbreads, such as veal
plain flour, for dusting
2 tbsp sunflower oil
100g unsalted butter

Sweetcorn purée
200g fresh sweetcorn, removed from the cob (from 2 cobs)
200ml whole milk
100ml double cream

Savory oil
100g savory leaves
150ml sunflower oil

salt, for seasoning
savory flowers, to serve

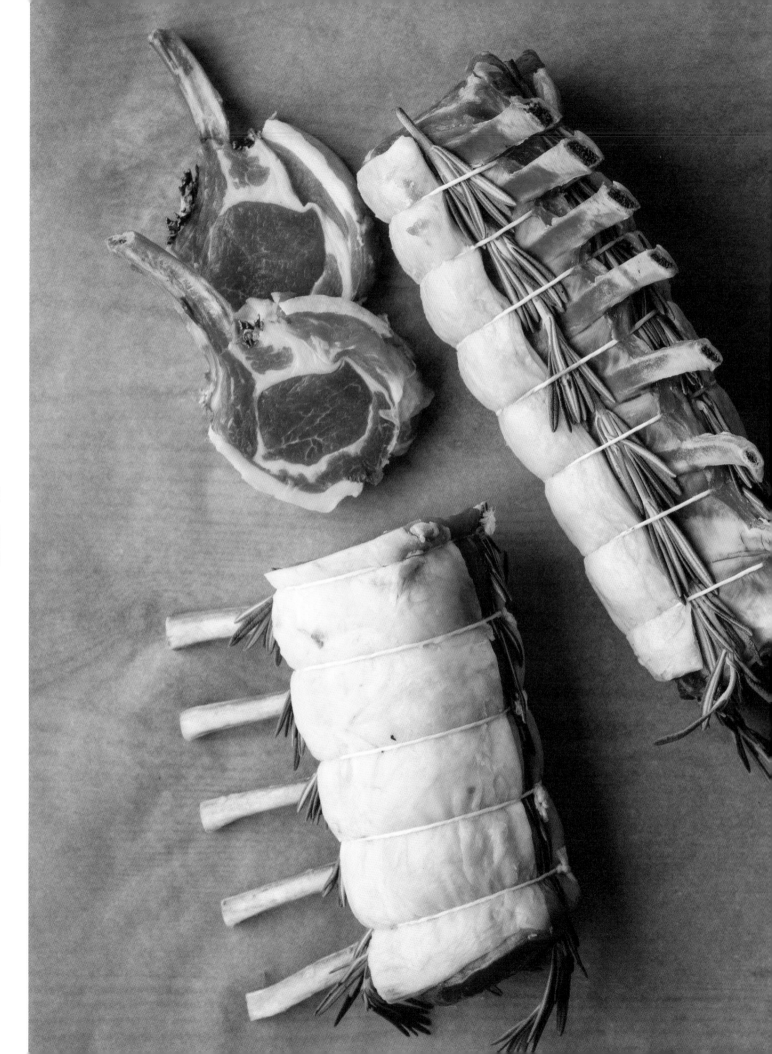

Herdwick lamb

In an area where there are more sheep than people, it's no surprise to hear that my favourite meat ingredient is Herdwick lamb. This traditional, hardy local breed has a superior flavour to other varieties, in part because these animals are slow-reared, foraging on heather and grasses over the rough but lush terrain to produce a darker, juicier and firmer meat with a slightly gamey flavour.

The traceability of our all ingredients is really important to me: knowing that the lamb I buy comes from an animal that has been humanely treated while alive, had the shortest possible journey to the slaughterhouse and has been expertly handled once slaughtered. Not only are these things important in respecting the animals we produce, but they also have an impact on the meat's flavour and tenderness.

Choosing really good-quality local lamb is now helped by the fact that the Herdwick has recently been awarded a PDO (Protected Designation of Origin) – which means that for a supplier to sell Herdwick as 'Lakeland', it must have been born, reared and slaughtered in Cumbria. We have great suppliers around us at Cartmel, but recently we have also begun to rear a few sheep ourselves, as part of our approach to widen the remit of our farm.

As fits our ethos, we use every part of the animal – the prime cuts and those that need long, slow braising or roasting on the bone to keep all their delicious flavour. We slow cook or braise the shank, shoulder, neck and cheek, while the leg, loin and chump cuts are good for grilling or roasting. Cuts such as loin and fillets are great roasted or fried, and we love to marinate the breast meat then roast it or coat in herby in crumbs and pan-fry until golden and crispy. As ever, one of my favourite flavours is anise, which is perfectly suited to roasted or grilled lamb. Don't chuck out the bones, either, as bold and fatty lamb stocks are a wonderful and rich accompaniment to freshly cooked cabbage leaves.

The belly of spring lamb is one of my favourite cuts because the meat is rich and flavoursome and lends itself perfectly to slow-roasting until meltingly tender. This is a good recipe for a relaxed weekend, as you can do much of the prep the day before and leave the fritter to set in the fridge overnight. The ramson emulsion adds a delicious seasonal flavour and wonderful garlicky punch to this springtime dish.

SPRING LAMB BELLY FRITTERS WITH RAMSON EMULSION

Preheat the oven to 160°C/140°C Fan/Gas Mark 2.

Put the lamb belly in a deep-sided roasting tin and pour in the white chicken stock to cover. Cover in foil and braise in the oven for 2–3 hours until very tender. Remove from the oven and allow to cool slightly before picking the meat away from the bones. Shred the meat with your fingers and add it to a bowl along with the reduced brown chicken stock, capers and shallot. Season with salt and mix well.

Press the mixture into a 450g (1lb) loaf tin lined with two layers of cling film, to a thickness of about 2cm. Cover the mixture with cling film and place a heavy weight on top, such as the same size container with two tins inside, and put in the fridge for 4 hours to set. Remove from the tin and cut into about 18 fingers roughly 6cm long.

For the crumb, season the flour with salt and put in a shallow dish. Put the beaten eggs in a second shallow dish and the breadcrumbs in a third. Coat the lamb belly fingers in the flour, then egg and finish with a generous coating of the breadcrumbs. Return to the fridge to set for 10 minutes.

Deep-fry the fritters in batches in a saucepan of oil heated to 180°C for 4 minutes, or until golden. Remove with a slotted spoon, drain on kitchen paper and season with salt.

Serve the fritters with a generous amount of ramson emulsion and scatter over the pickled ramson capers and brassica flowers, if using.

SERVES 4–6, AS A STARTER

Spring lamb belly fritter
1 spring lamb belly (about 1.2–1.5kg)
300ml White Chicken Stock (see page 286)
100ml reduced Brown Chicken Stock (see page 286)
1 tbsp chopped capers
1 shallot, finely diced

Crumb
75g plain flour
2 eggs, beaten
100g panko breadcrumbs

salt, for seasoning
vegetable oil, for deep-frying
Ramson Emulsion (see page 32), to serve
pickled ramson capers and brassica flowers, to serve (optional)

Making your own bresaola is a bit of a project, but it produces a beautifully salted and air-dried meat that lasts for months. We don't feature proteins on our menu when they are out of season, so drying meat is an ideal way to preserve spring lamb while at its best and get proteins on the plate when we can't get them fresh. Other than a cool, slightly moist environment in which to hang your meat, and a fair amount of patience, you don't need any special equipment for this. The process can't be rushed; the meat must cure for 16 days before it is dried and wrapped, then hung for a further 10 days, after which you can tuck in.

LAMB BRESAOLA

To make the cure, combine the salt, cloves, garlic, pepper, herbs and citrus zests. Rub the mixture into the lamb, place in a container and leave to cure in the fridge for 4 days, turning the lamb after 2 days.

Rinse the lamb under cold running water and pat it dry with kitchen paper. Place in a large dish, cover the meat with red wine, cover and return to the fridge to cure for 10 days, turning the lamb every day.

Pat the lamb dry with kitchen paper. Wrap it in muslin completely with no meat showing through, and hang it from the ceiling for 10 days in a cool, dry place away from direct sunlight where air can circulate around it.

This makes a large quantity that will keep in the fridge, well wrapped, after the hanging time, for several weeks. Thinly slice the meat as needed and serve with a drizzle of good-quality rapeseed oil, crusty bread and homemade pickles.

SERVES 6, AS A STARTER

500g silverside or topside of hogget

The cure
20g coarse sea salt
3 cloves
1 garlic clove, crushed
2 tsp black peppercorns, crushed
1 tsp chopped rosemary needles
2 bay leaves, chopped
zest of ½ lemon
zest of ½ orange
red wine (enough to cover, approx 75cl)

rapeseed oil, pickled onions, cornichons, halved radishes, capers, caper berries and sliced fresh bread, such as sourdough, to serve

This showstopper of a lamb dish is really straightforward. The meat needs to be left in brine for 24 hours before the delicious, fragrant and warmly spiced rub is massaged into the meat and finally it is smoked and slow-cooked. The long, slow preparation is well worth it, though, for the intense, sweet smoky flavour it produces. Home smoking is much easier than you might think; just make sure the meat is raised above the wood chips and both the smoking tray and the joint are tightly encased in tin foil. And open a window ...

SMOKED LAMB SHOULDER

Dissolve 300g of the salt in 1.5 litres of water in a large bowl. Submerge the lamb shoulder in the brine and put it in the fridge for 24 hours. The next day, rinse the shoulder under cold running water and pat it dry with kitchen paper. Mix the remaining ingredients together in a bowl, including the 100g salt, and rub into the shoulder.

Put the smoking chips in a nice even layer in a large roasting tin lined with foil. Sit a wire rack on top, one that is a similar size to the roasting tin, making sure the wire isn't touching the chips. Put the shoulder on the rack and cover the entire rack and tin with a tent of foil, so no smoke escapes. Sit the tin on the hob over a low-medium heat for 10 minutes. Remove the covered tin from the heat and allow the shoulder to smoke in the foil tent for 30 minutes.

Preheat the oven to 150°C/130°C Fan/Gas Mark 2. Transfer the smoked lamb shoulder to a clean baking tray, place in the oven and cook for 4 hours until tender.

Top and tail the runner beans and remove the stringy sides. Bring a large saucepan of salted water to the boil, add the butter and cook the beans for 3 minutes. Drain.

Serve the lamb in the middle of the table with a jug of sauce for guests to help themselves and with the runner beans and confit potatoes in a large bowl alongside.

SERVES 6-8

Lamb shoulder
400g coarse sea salt
1 lamb shoulder (about 2.8–3kg)
100g soft light brown sugar
200g granulated sugar
20g garlic powder
50g smoked paprika
50g sweet paprika
6 star anise
1 tbsp yellow mustard seeds
1 tbsp juniper berries
1 tbsp cayenne pepper
1 tbsp ground cumin
1 tbsp ground black pepper
1 tbsp coriander seeds

Runner beans
500g young, tender runner beans, such as
    Tenderstar
40g unsalted butter
salt, for seasoning

enough wood smoking chips to create an
    even layer in the baking tray
Lamb Jus (see page 158), to serve
Confit Potatoes (see page 29), to serve

The loin is a prime cut of lamb, so it is best served simply, with subtle ingredients that complement but don't overwhelm the flavours of the tender meat. Separating curds and whey might sound like something from days gone by, but it is so easy to do and gives you two ingredients from one (see page 302). Leave the yoghurt to hang overnight and you will be left with the curds but also an acidic whey, which, when combined with the butter and cream, balances out to create a rich sauce. You won't need all the curd here, but don't chuck it out – use just as you would any thick plain yoghurt, or eat it with fresh fruit or some truffle granola (see page 64).

BAKED LAMB LOIN WITH SPINACH, CURDS AND WHEY

Put the whey in a large, heavy-based saucepan over a medium heat and reduce it by three-quarters, until you have 80–100ml of liquid. Add the cream and simmer for a further 5 minutes, reducing by half. Once you have a thicker, sauce-like consistency, remove from the heat and whisk in the butter and salt to taste and the xanthan gum, then blitz with a hand-held blender to incorporate. Leave to one side.

Preheat the oven to 180°C/160°C Fan/Gas Mark 4.

Heat a large non-stick ovenproof frying pan over a medium heat. Season the lamb loin with salt and fry in the oil for 4 minutes, moving it around until it is browned on all sides. Add the butter and transfer to the oven to cook for 6–8 minutes, or until the core temperature reaches 50°C on a probe thermometer. Remove the lamb from the pan and allow to rest.

For the spinach, melt the butter in a medium frying pan over a medium–high heat, add the spinach with a pinch of salt and cook for 2 minutes until wilted.

Drain the spinach and divide it among plates. Spoon the sauce on to the plates. Carve the lamb loin and put the meat on top of the sauce and finish with a dollop of curd and young spinach leaves.

SERVES 4

Whey sauce
320ml whey, from 1kg natural yoghurt
    (see page 302)
40ml double cream
40g unsalted butter
a pinch of xanthan gum

Lamb loin
600g lamb loin
1 tbsp sunflower oil
20g unsalted butter

Spinach
20g unsalted butter
250g baby spinach

Curds
60g yoghurt curd (from above)

salt, for seasoning
young spinach leaves, such as Fuji spinach,
    to serve

Mutton has an unfair reputation for being the tough, chewy meat of mature or ageing sheep. However, this is not the case, and in fact mutton is very well-flavoured, and although firmer than lamb, it is certainly not tough. Buy it through a trusted butcher to make sure it has been properly hung and is the best quality. Cooking mutton in hay gives an earthy, slightly smoky flavour, and it is a great technique that can be used for other meats, too, such as beef or chicken. The potato terrine and bitter endive cooked in sweet orange add rich, caramelly flavours that perfectly complement the mutton.

HAY-BAKED MUTTON WITH POTATO TERRINE AND BRAISED ENDIVES

To make the lamb jus, warm the oil in a large, heavy-based saucepan over a low heat, add the vegetables and cook for 2–3 hours, stirring regularly, until completely soft and no moisture is left in the pan.

Preheat the oven to 220°C/200°C Fan/Gas Mark 7. Put the lamb bones in a roasting tin and roast for 40 minutes, or until deeply golden. Add the bones to the pan with the vegetables, reserving the fat for the potatoes. Deglaze the roasting tin with 200ml water and add it to the pan. Cover with the chicken stock and bring to the boil over a high heat. Reduce the heat and simmer for 2 hours over a low heat, skimming it regularly. Strain through a fine sieve into another heavy-based saucepan then reduce the stock over a medium heat to a sauce consistency.

Preheat the oven to 180°C/160°C Fan/Gas Mark 4. Grease a 450g (1lb) terrine mould or loaf tin with butter and line it with baking parchment. Slice the potatoes thinly on a mandoline. Melt the butter in a saucepan over a low heat. Layer the sliced potatoes in the mould, brushing with butter and lamb fat between each layer and seasoning with salt. Cover with foil and bake in the oven for 1½ hours. Remove from the oven and allow to cool then cover with cling film and chill in the fridge for 3 hours with a heavy weight on top, such as the same size container with two tins inside.

Preheat the oven to 180°C/160°C Fan/Gas Mark 4. Place an ovenproof dish in the centre of a large casserole dish and surround it with hay to create a ring between the two dishes. Warm the oil for the mutton rumps in a non-stick frying pan over a medium heat and cook the mutton rumps, fat side down, for 4 minutes, turning them every minute until evenly browned. Transfer to the dish inside the casserole and set over a high heat until the hay starts to smoke. Cover the casserole dish with a lid and cook in the oven for 15 minutes. Remove from the oven and leave to rest for 5 minutes.

While the mutton is cooking, braise the endive. Melt the butter in a small heavy-based saucepan over a low heat, then cook for 15–20 minutes until the

SERVES 4

Lamb jus
2 tbsp sunflower oil
2 carrots, roughly chopped
2 onions, roughly chopped
2 celery sticks, roughly chopped
1 leek, roughly chopped
2 garlic cloves
1kg lamb bones
3 litres White Chicken Stock (see page 286)

Lamb-fat potato terrine
250g unsalted butter, plus extra for greasing
2kg potatoes (preferably Maris Piper)
lamb fat, for greasing

Hay-baked mutton rumps
1 tbsp sunflower oil
2 mutton rumps, trimmed and oven ready (ask your butcher to do this for you)

Braised endive
200g unsalted butter
4 endives
200ml fresh orange juice (shop-bought is fine)
zest of 2 oranges

salt, for seasoning
4 handfuls of hay, for cooking

aroma is nutty and you have a light golden colour. Remove from the heat. Slice the endives in half lengthways and add them to a non-stick frying pan, cut side down, with the rest of the ingredients (including the browned butter) and 2 teaspoons of salt. Bring to the boil over a high heat, reduce the heat and simmer for 20 minutes. Drain the endive on kitchen paper.

Turn out the chilled potato terrine on to a chopping board and thickly slice it. Warm the slices through in the oven or fry in a non-stick frying pan until crisp on both sides.

Carve each rump into 3 pieces. Lay them on top of the potato terrine, place 2 braised endive halves on the side and drizzle the jus over the whole plate.

One of my favourite dishes is moussaka, because I love the combination of juicy lamb mince and meltingly soft aubergine – and my first job was in a Greek restaurant! I think aubergine is underused and more versatile than it is given credit for, as its spongy flesh soaks up strong flavours beautifully, including the natural sweetness of maple syrup. A few foraged ingredients balance the dish, with earthy nettles and peppery, acidic nasturtium capers. You can get ahead on these elements, or save the leftovers for another day – nasturtium capers can be stored in a sterilised jar, while excess nettle butter can be wrapped and frozen.

LAMB CHOPS WITH AUBERGINE, NASTURTIUM CAPERS AND NETTLE BUTTER

Preheat the oven to 220°C/200°C Fan/Gas Mark 7.

Cut the aubergines in half lengthways and put them cut side up on a baking tray. Score diagonally across the flesh with a small knife without piercing the skin. Sprinkle salt over the flesh and leave for 20 minutes. Rinse off the salt thoroughly under cold running water and pat the aubergine halves dry with kitchen paper. Mix together the oil, maple syrup and vinegar, drizzle over the aubergines and roast in the oven for 15–20 minutes. Keep warm until ready to serve.

For the capers, bring the vinegar, sugar and 200ml water to the boil in a small saucepan, remove from the heat, add the capers and allow to cool.

Bring a large saucepan of water to the boil and blanch the nettles for 2 minutes. Remove with a slotted spoon and refresh in a bowl of iced water. Drain, squeeze out the excess water and chop the nettles finely. Blitz together with the softened butter and garlic in a blender. Transfer the garlic butter to a bowl and fold through the nettles. Lay out a sheet of cling film and top with the nettle butter, then wrap and roll into a log shape. Twist the ends and transfer to the fridge.

Lower the oven to 200°C/180°C Fan/Gas Mark 6. Heat a non-stick ovenproof frying pan over a medium heat. Coat the lamb chops with oil and season with a pinch of salt, then cook on all sides for a total of 2–3 minutes until caramelised. Transfer the lamb chops to the oven and cook for 3 minutes. Allow to rest before serving.

Warm the lamb jus, add a few nasturtium capers and add 1 teaspoon of the nettle butter to split the sauce.

Divide the chops among each plate, add the aubergines and spoon the sauce around it. Slice the butter log and serve a few slices on each plate (any leftover butter can be stored in the freezer for another time).

SERVES 4

Baby aubergines
8 baby aubergines
2 tsp rapeseed oil
2 tsp maple syrup
2 tbsp sherry vinegar

Nasturtium capers
100ml white wine vinegar
50g caster sugar
100g nasturtium capers

Nettle butter
175g nettles
125g unsalted butter, softened
1 garlic clove, sliced

Lamb chops
8 lamb loin chops
2 tbsp olive oil

salt, for seasoning and salting
Lamb Jus (see page 158), to serve

Brisket is a cheaper cut, so to get it really tender it needs long, slow cooking. The cut is quite thick, so the brine helps the flesh take on the seasoning and spices, and the soaking time ensures these penetrate to the centre of the meat and build layers of flavour. The accompaniments make this a well-balanced main, with a deeply umami sauce, the hot, horseradishy flavour of the dittander, which grows on the coast, earthy mushrooms and delicious fried crosnes. Some say crosnes, or Chinese artichokes, look like grubs, but I prefer to think of them more like pasta twists. Don't be put off by their appearance, these little root veg have a crunchy texture and a taste similar to Jerusalem artichoke.

SLOW-COOKED BEEF BRISKET WITH MUSHROOMS

Put all the ingredients for the brine along with 1 litre of water in a heavy-based saucepan over a medium heat and bring to the boil. Remove from the heat and allow to infuse and cool. Submerge the brisket in the cooled brine and chill in the fridge for 12 hours.

Preheat the oven to 140°C/120°C Fan/Gas Mark 1. Rinse the meat under cold running water and pat it dry with kitchen paper. Warm the oil in a non-stick frying pan over a medium heat, add the brisket and seal for 3–4 minutes on each side. Transfer to a roasting tin with the beef stock and cover with foil. Cook in the oven for 6–8 hours, or until extremely tender.

For the crosnes and mushrooms, melt the butter in a non-stick frying pan over a medium heat until it foams. Add the crosnes and cook for 5–6 minutes, turning them constantly, until lightly golden and tender. Add the trompettes and cook for 2 minutes. Strain through a fine sieve and season with salt.

Warm the marrow fat sauce and blend it with the black garlic until smooth, pass through a fine sieve and keep hot.

Blitz the dittander and oil in a blender until smooth, pass through a muslin-lined sieve into a bowl and keep in the fridge until needed.

Divide the mushrooms and crosnes among plates and put a generous portion of beef brisket on each plate. Spoon around some sauce and split it with the dittander oil.

SERVES 6

Brine
200g salt
2 bay leaves
1 tbsp coriander seeds
5 sprigs of thyme
2 star anise
1 tsp juniper berries
zest of 1 lemon
zest of 1 orange
1 head of garlic, halved

Beef brisket
1kg beef brisket
2 tbsp sunflower oil
200ml Beef Stock (see page 287)

Crosnes and mushrooms
125g unsalted butter
200g crosnes
200g fresh trompettes

Beef sauce
150ml Marrow Fat Sauce (see page 166)
125g Black Garlic (see page 90), skins
    removed

Dittander oil
100g dittander
200ml sunflower oil

This is a really meaty broth that is deliciously warming when you're feeling under the weather or on a chilly day. The slow-baked swede, creamy fresh cheese and sweet and crisp lettuce hearts add texture to the clear rich beef stock, which has added umami from the yeast flakes. Serve it with the pickled mustard seeds for a touch of acidity.

BEEF BROTH WITH SLOW-BAKED SWEDE

Preheat the oven to 200°C/180°C Fan/Gas Mark 6. Roast the beef bones in a roasting tin for 1 hour, or until golden brown. Remove and set aside.

Lower the oven temperature to 120°C/100°C Fan/Gas Mark ¼. Bake the swede on a baking tray at the reduced oven temperature for about 3 hours, or until tender. Remove, allow to cool, then peel and break into small pieces.

Meanwhile, warm the oil in a large, heavy-based saucepan over a medium heat, add 500g of the minced beef and cook for 15–20 minutes, or until dark brown, stirring regularly. Remove the beef and leave to one side. Add the shallots, garlic, 2 of the thyme sprigs and bay leaf to the pan and sweat for 5–6 minutes until translucent, then return the browned beef to the pan. Add the bones along with the peppercorns, star anise and stock. Bring to the boil, reduce the heat and simmer for 2 hours, skimming it regularly.

Strain the liquid through a fine sieve and allow to cool, then transfer to a medium, heavy-based saucepan. Mix the remaining 200g minced beef with the egg whites and remaining thyme. Whisk into the cooled liquid and cook over a low heat for 30 minutes. The solids and particles will rise to the top. Strain through a muslin-lined sieve into a small saucepan and reduce by half. Leave to one side.

For the pickled mustard seeds, put all the ingredients in a small saucepan with 100ml water and bring to the boil over a low heat. Remove from the heat and allow to cool to room temperature.

Slice the lettuces in half lengthways. Warm the oil in a non-stick frying pan over a medium heat and cook the lettuce halves cut side down for 4–5 minutes until deeply golden. Remove from the heat.

Sprinkle the yeast flakes over the lettuce halves and divide among bowls with the diced swede, pickled mustard seeds and a spoonful of the ricotta. Pour the broth around the ingredients and finish with the leaves and flowers.

SERVES 4

Beef broth
1.5kg beef bones
2 tbsp sunflower oil
700g minced beef
4 shallots, sliced
1 garlic clove, cut in half
3 sprigs of thyme
1 bay leaf
1 tsp black peppercorns
1 star anise
2 litres White Chicken Stock (see page 286)
2 egg whites

Slow-baked swede
1 large swede

Pickled mustard seeds
2 tbsp yellow mustard seeds
50ml white wine vinegar
25g caster sugar

Lettuce hearts
2 small lettuces, such as gem
1 tbsp sunflower oil
2 tbsp yeast flakes

Westcombe Somerset ricotta cheese, perilla leaves, wasabi leaves and chive flowers, to serve

Shorthorn beef is Britain's fastest-growing native breed, and one of the reasons I like this meat so much is not just for its outstanding quality but also for its traceability. The meat is rich and marbled with fat, which imparts flavour as well as moisture, leaving you with a really succulent bit of beef. As the number of animals being reared across the country increases, so too does the meat's availability, so seek it out if you can. Marrow fat is another underused ingredient, so do make use of it; not only does it mean less wastage, it also adds flavour and a richness to the finished dish.

SHORTHORN BEEF FILLET WITH HORSERADISH AND MARROW FAT SAUCE

Preheat the oven to 200°C/180°C Fan/Gas Mark 6. Roast the beef bones in a roasting tin for 35–40 minutes, or until deeply golden.

Warm the oil in a large, heavy-based saucepan over a high heat, add the minced beef and brown it, stirring continuously, for 6–8 minutes. Drain the meat through a colander over a bowl to catch the fat. Set the mince to one side, return the fat to the same pan, reduce the heat to low, add the herbs and vegetables and cook for 20 minutes, stirring occasionally. Drain the herbs and vegetables in the colander, this time discarding the fat, then return the mince, herbs and vegetables to the pan over a medium heat. Add the red wine and reduce by half, then add the bones to the pan and deglaze the roasting tin with 1 litre of water over a medium heat. Add the water to the pan along with the beef stock, increase the heat and bring to the boil, then reduce the heat and simmer for 2 hours, skimming it regularly. Strain through a fine sieve into a clean saucepan and reduce the liquid over a low–medium heat by about two-thirds to a sauce consistency.

Put the bone marrow in a small, heavy-based saucepan over a low heat, and cook for 6–8 minutes to release the fat. Strain through a fine sieve.

To make the horseradish gel, combine the vinegar and horseradish in a small, heavy-based saucepan over a high heat and bring to the boil. Remove from the heat and allow to infuse for 20 minutes. Strain through a fine sieve. Put the sugar and agar agar in a small, clean heavy-based saucepan over a high heat with 300ml water and the infused vinegar and bring to the boil for 1 minute, whisking constantly. Transfer to a heatproof bowl, allow to cool and chill in the fridge for 5 minutes to set. Once set, blend until smooth and leave to one side.

Warm the oil for the beef fillet in a large non-stick ovenproof frying pan over a high heat, add the fillet and season with a pinch of salt. Cook on all sides for a total of 4–5 minutes for even caramelisation. When sealed all the way around, transfer to the oven, still at 200°C/180°C Fan/Gas Mark 6, for a further 5–6 minutes. Remove from the oven and rest.

SERVES 4

Marrow fat sauce
2kg beef bones
2 tbsp sunflower oil
1kg minced beef
3 sprigs of thyme
1 bay leaf
2 carrots, roughly chopped
1 onion, roughly chopped
4 garlic cloves, roughly chopped
300ml red wine
1 litre Beef Stock (see page 287)
50g bone marrow

Horseradish gel
200ml chardonnay vinegar
30g fresh horseradish, grated
100g caster sugar
1 level tsp agar agar

Shorthorn beef
2 tbsp sunflower oil
800g shorthorn beef fillet

Leeks
12 baby leeks, such as Bulgarian
unsalted butter, for frying

salt, for seasoning

While the meat is resting, bring a large saucepan of salted water to the boil and blanch the leeks for 1 minute. Remove and refresh in a bowl of iced water, then drain on kitchen paper. Fry in a small amount of butter over a medium heat for 2–3 minutes.

Meanwhile, warm the sauce and whisk in the bone marrow fat.

Carve the fillet and divide among plates. Add small spoonfuls of the gel and finish with the sauce and fried leeks.

FISH

Mallow is a wild herb that is abundant in fields and roadsides, and when cooked, the mild-flavoured leaves create a fluid that is very similar to that produced by okra, which can be used as a thickener in soups and stews and is wonderful bound with cucumber. We get lovely crabs from just off the Cumbrian coast, and I love pairing them with tender, raw squid. Crab, squid and cucumber all have very delicate tastes, so the mallow soup is the perfect medium to bring together all these elements. This is a beautiful, fresh-looking soup with flavours to match.

CRAB, SQUID AND MALLOW SOUP

Insert your knife into the squid and cut down one side to open the squid out. Scrape the squid using the back of your knife to clean and remove the excess membrane. When clean, lay the squid flat and freeze until firm. When frozen, dice the squid into 5mm squares and leave to one side to defrost on kitchen paper.

To make the mallow soup, warm the oil in a small saucepan over a low–medium heat, add the sliced onion and sweat for 3–5 minutes until translucent but not coloured. Add the sliced cucumber and cook for a further 2 minutes. Add the cream and mallow and bring to the boil. Remove from the heat and blitz in a blender until smooth. Pass through a fine sieve and season with salt.

To make the pickled cucumber, peel the cucumber and scoop out and discard the seeds. Cut the cucumber into 5mm dice. Bring 200ml water, the vinegar and sugar to the boil in a small saucepan over a high heat. When boiled, remove from the heat and add the diced cucumber. Leave the cucumber to cool in the pickle.

Dress the white crab meat with the rapeseed oil, lemon juice and salt and add to the centre of each bowl. Add the raw cut squid and the pickled cucumber. Serve the soup poured around the crab, squid and pickle and finish with borage flowers and baby cucumbers.

SERVES 4, AS A STARTER

Raw squid
1 fresh squid, about 100g

Mallow soup
2 tbsp sunflower oil
½ onion, sliced
350g cucumber, thinly sliced
400ml double cream
250g mallow

Pickled cucumber
1 cucumber
100ml white wine vinegar
50g caster sugar

Crab
240g white crab meat
2 tbsp rapeseed oil
juice of ½ lemon
a pinch of salt

salt, for seasoning
borage flowers and baby cucumbers, to
    serve

To the west of Cartmel, Humphrey's Head is one of the peninsulas of Morecambe Bay, where there are a series of rock pools that have been created by five rivers that feed into the Irish Sea. It is a beautiful, peaceful spot, and a wonderful place to forage in the early hours of the morning, when the whole place is deserted. I created this dish as a sort of homage to Humphrey's Head – it is essentially a pool of broth which you can dive into with a spoon to fish out little chunks of seafood and shellfish.

HUMPHREY'S POOL

To make the dashi stock, put the dried shiitake and dried kombu in a large, heavy-based saucepan with 2 litres of water. Bring to the boil over a high heat, reduce the heat to a simmer and cook for 1 hour. Strain through a fine sieve into a clean saucepan and discard the solids. Bring the stock back to the boil, then remove from the heat, add the bonito flakes and stir for 2 minutes. Strain through fine sieve once more and add the white soy and lemon juice. Leave to one side.

Hydrate the wakame seaweed for the seaweed butter in 250ml warm water for 5 minutes. Drain and squeeze out the excess water. Chop the seaweed finely then mix it through the softened butter with the salt in a bowl. Chill in the fridge for 30 minutes. When firm, roll into small marble-size balls and chill again.

Bring a medium saucepan of boiling water to the boil over a medium–high heat, drop in the shellfish – except the scallops – and cook for 2–3 minutes until all the shells have opened. Remove the shellfish with a slotted spoon. Blanch the prawns in the liquid for 3 minutes, turning them halfway through.

Divide the shellfish meat between bowls, keeping a few shells for presentation, if you like. Add small balls of the seaweed butter in the gaps. Finish with the sea herbs and serve the hot dashi stock on the side to pour at the table.

SERVES 4, AS A STARTER

Dashi stock
30g dried shiitake
30g dried kombu
25g bonito flakes
40g white soy sauce
juice of ½ lemon

Seaweed butter
1 tsp dried wakame seaweed
70g unsalted butter, softened
½ tsp table salt

Shellfish
12 live mussels
12 live clams
12 fresh prawns, shelled and deveined
2 raw scallops, diced

sea lettuce, sea purslane and sea blite, to
    serve

This is something for a really special occasion when you want to impress with a tasty pre-dinner bite; it's not particularly difficult to make but has a few elements that need prepping ahead of time. The idea for this is based in the landscape around Cartmel, with the green-clad hills around our valley farm. The smoked cod roe is delicately sprinkled with the vibrant green parsley snow, then served with fennel biscuits, which can be used as wafers to scrape up the roe.

SMOKED COD ROE WITH FENNEL BISCUITS AND PARSLEY SNOW

Push the cod roe through a fine sieve into a bowl. Whisk the cheese in a stand mixer until smooth then add 2 tablespoons of water. Slowly add the oil to the cheese while still whisking, to emulsify the mixture. When all the oil has been added, whisk in the cod roe, lemon juice and salt. Check the seasoning and adjust accordingly. Transfer the mixture to an airtight container and chill in the fridge to firm up.

Soak the gelatine in cold water for a few minutes until softened. Drain, squeeze out the excess water and leave the gelatine to one side. Bring 100ml water to the boil in a small saucepan with the butter and oil. Remove from the heat and add the softened gelatine. Add the herbs to a blender along with the gelatine water and salt and blitz until smooth. Transfer the mixture to a bowl which is resting over an iced bath to cool. When cooled, use cling film to roll the mixture into a log about the diameter of a 50p piece, then freeze.

Preheat the oven to 190°C/170°C Fan/Gas Mark 5 and line a baking tray with baking parchment.

To make the fennel biscuits, mix together the flour, salt and fennel seeds in a stand mixer fitted with the paddle attachment. Dice the butter and add it to the dry ingredients with the mixer set at low speed until you have a breadcrumb consistency. Mix together the milk and 35ml cold water and add it to the mixture gradually until just combined (do not overwork the dough). Wrap it in cling film and transfer it to the fridge to rest for 30 minutes. Unwrap the chilled dough and roll it out as thinly as possible on a floured work surface. Transfer in one piece to the lined baking tray and bake for 15–18 minutes until crisp and lightly golden. Remove from the oven, leave to cool on the tray and snap into shards.

Spoon or pipe the cod roe on to each plate, remove the parsley snow from the freezer and, using a fine grater, grate it all over the cod roe – any left over can be stored in the freezer. Serve the fennel biscuits on the side.

SERVES 6, AS A STARTER

Smoked cod roe
50g smoked cod roe
200g cream cheese
200ml sunflower oil
juice of 1 lemon
a pinch of salt

Parsley snow
6 gelatine leaves
10g unsalted butter
10ml rapeseed oil
90g flat-leaf parsley
45g chervil
45g chives
a pinch of salt

Fennel biscuits
110g plain flour, plus extra for dusting
1 tsp salt
1 tsp fennel seeds
45g unsalted chilled butter, diced
30ml whole milk

This is a delicious snack that plays on the ever-popular combination of meat and fish, and it's a really fun one for friends and family to dive in and help themselves to. Squid ink is often used in pasta for its unique briny flavour as well as natural black dye, which gives it a dramatic quality. We've rung the changes using it for another Italian classic – breadsticks. The ham emulsion spread over the grissini and topped with shredded crispy pork makes a nice finish to the crunchy breadsticks.

SQUID INK GRISSINI

Preheat the oven to 160°C/140°C Fan/Gas Mark 2. Put the pork belly in a baking tray and cook for 2 hours. Remove the pork from the oven and shred the meat with two forks. Add the shredded meat to a medium, heavy-based saucepan with the butter and place over a medium heat. Cook the pork in the butter for 8–10 minutes until deeply golden and crispy. Remove the pork from the pan and drain on kitchen paper. Allow to cool and season with salt. Serve in a small dish next to the grissini and fat for dipping.

Preheat the oven to 220°C/200°C Fan/Gas Mark 7. Put the butter for the grissini in a small saucepan over a low heat. Once melted add the milk to the pan and remove from the heat.

Beat the egg and squid ink in a small bowl. In a large bowl mix together the flour and salt, then add the squid ink and egg mixture. Slowly add the butter and milk mixture to the dry ingredients to form a dough. Knead the dough for 5 minutes.

Wrap the dough in cling film and leave it to rest in the fridge for 1 hour. Once rested, unwrap the dough, dust a work surface with flour and roll out the dough to a thickness of 5mm. Cut the dough into long, thin 1 x 15cm strips. Bake on a baking tray lined with baking parchment for 15 minutes, then remove from the oven and allow to cool on the tray.

Spread the ham fat emulsion on to the cooled grissini and sprinkle with crispy pork. Alternatively, serve the ham fat in a small dish for dipping, and a separate dipping dish for the crispy pork.

SERVES 4, AS A STARTER

Grissini
15g unsalted butter
75ml whole milk
10g squid ink
1 egg
250g plain flour, plus extra for dusting
1 tsp table salt

Crispy pork
500g boneless pork belly, skin removed
125g unsalted butter
salt, for seasoning

Ham Fat Emulsion (see page 85), to serve

Don't let the presentation here fool you – these are undeniably showstoppers, but they are also much simpler to make than they look and worth every moment spent making them. Essentially, these little pebbles are mouth-watering meringues that are slowly dehydrated overnight in the oven, then hollowed out and filled with apple dice and oyster emulsion. These are a hugely popular snack at the restaurant, and served over pebbles and dressed with an oyster leaf, they have the wow factor, too!

OYSTER PEBBLE

Using a hand-held blender, blitz together the apple juice, xanthan gum, silver powder and squid ink until the mixture is an even grey colour without any black speckling. Transfer this to a stand mixer fitted with a whisk attachment. Add the egg white powder and whisk on high speed until thick and aerated. Gradually add the icing sugar little by little while whisking continuously. Stop the mixer when all the sugar has been incorporated and the meringue forms stiff peaks. Spoon the mixture into a piping bag and pipe on to baking parchment-lined trays in the shape of a small half pebble (do not make them too big as they need to be bite-size). Dehydrate in an oven set to 75°C, or the lowest setting on your oven, for 12 hours.

While the meringues are dehydrating, make the oyster emulsion. Shuck the oysters, separating the juice and the meat. Discard the juice and add the meat to a blender with the egg white, lemon juice and salt. Blitz on medium speed until smooth, then gradually add the oil while blending on slow speed, until the mixture has a mayonnaise consistency. Pass through a fine sieve and reserve in the fridge.

Peel and finely dice the apple as small as possible then add to the lemon and apple juice in a bowl. Leave to one side.

Using a teaspoon or melon baller make a small hole in the bottom of the dehydrated meringues. Fill the holes with the oyster emulsion and a small amount of diced apple. Put 2 halves together to form a pebble shape and serve in a bowl with oyster leaves.

MAKES 30 OYSTER PEBBLES, TO SERVE AS A STARTER

Oyster pebble
330ml fresh apple juice (shop-bought is fine)
¼ tsp xanthan gum
¼ tsp silver powder colouring
1 tsp squid ink
35g egg white powder
150g icing sugar

Oyster emulsion
3 live oysters
1 egg white
juice of ¼ lemon
a pinch of salt
250ml grapeseed oil

Apple dice
1 Granny Smith apple
100ml fresh apple juice (shop-bought is fine)
5 drops of lemon juice

oyster leaves, to serve

This is a variation on the classic 'surf and turf' combination, when often you see black pudding married with prawns. Here we've gone with a more widely appealing white sausage, made from chicken and pork. It's a bit fattier, but it complements the lean and sweet prawns perfectly. The puffed quinoa is scattered through for a crispy texture, while the squash is a simple yet satisfying addition.

PRAWNS WITH WHITE SAUSAGE

Start by making the white sausage. Warm 1 tablespoon of the oil in a small, heavy-based saucepan over a medium heat, add the chopped shallot and sweat for 4–5 minutes, or until translucent. Add the breadcrumbs and cream and mix well to form a firm paste. Transfer the mixture to a bowl and chill.

Combine the meats in the bowl of a stand mixer fitted with the beater attachment on slow speed. Add the egg and the breadcrumb mix and continue to mix until fully incorporated. Season with salt and pepper.

Lay three layers of cling film on a work surface, and use a towel to push all the air out between each layer. Add the sausage mix to the cling film and form it into a sausage shape with the circumference of a 50p piece. Fold over the cling film and roll it tight, twisting the ends until tightly closed.

Bring a medium saucepan of water to the boil then reduce the heat to a very gentle simmer. Place the cling film-wrapped sausage in the pan and poach for 12–15 minutes. When cooked, transfer the sausage to a bowl of ice-cold water to cool.

To puff the quinoa, bring a small saucepan of water to the boil, reduce the heat, add the quinoa and simmer for 10–15 minutes until the quinoa kernels start to break down. Drain the quinoa and spread it out on a baking tray. Set the oven to its lowest possible temperature, add the tray of quinoa and leave it for 2 hours, or until completely dry. When dried, deep-fry in a pan of oil heated to 200°C for 2–3 minutes until crisp and slightly puffed. Remove with a slotted spoon, drain on kitchen paper and season with salt.

Melt the butter with the rosemary in a medium, heavy-based saucepan over a medium heat. When the butter starts to foam, remove the rosemary and add the grated squash. Reduce the heat to low and cook for 5–8 minutes, stirring frequently, until the squash is just cooked. Season with a pinch of salt.

Meanwhile, slice the sausage into 2cm-thick rounds. Warm the remaining tablespoon of oil in a heavy-based frying pan over a low–medium heat and fry the

SERVES 4, AS A STARTER

White sausage
2 tbsp sunflower oil
1 shallot, finely chopped
20g breadcrumbs
25ml double cream
85g chicken breast, medium minced
85g pork fillet, medium minced
40g pork lardo (available from butchers)
1 egg
salt and pepper, for seasoning

Puffed quinoa
25g red quinoa
vegetable oil, for deep-frying

Grated squash
100g unsalted butter
1 sprig of rosemary
½ butternut squash, such as Summer
    Crookneck, peeled and coarsely grated
a pinch of salt

Prawns
16 raw tiger prawns
50g unsalted butter
a pinch of salt
Prawn Oil (see page 44)

Sunset sorrel, to serve
finely grated Berkswell cheese, or other
    hard sheep's cheese, to serve

sausage rounds for 3 minutes on each side until lightly golden. Remove from the pan, drain on kitchen paper and keep warm.

Bring a large saucepan of water to the boil and blanch the prawns for 30 seconds. Scoop them out and refresh in a bowl of iced water. Peel the prawns and discard the shells and heads. Melt the butter in a medium, non-stick frying pan over a low–medium heat, add the prawns and fry for 2 minutes on each side. Coat the prawns with a little prawn oil and remove from the pan. Season with salt. Divide the prawns and white sausage rounds between bowls, then sprinkle over the squash, quinoa and sorrel. Drizzle with prawn oil and finish with grated cheese.

Mylor prawns are a delicious treat. These tiny prawns are in season between September and February, caught in the harbour outside Falmouth, in Cornwall. Their miniature size is misleading, as they have a really strong prawn flavour and should be eaten raw to get the best from them. If you can't get Mylors, use any other raw, super-fresh prawn, but make sure they are chopped into very small pieces. The light and crispy pork cracker is the perfect way to eat these delicate little prawns. Just pop them in your mouth and enjoy!

PORK CRACKER WITH PRAWNS AND TARRAGON EMULSION

Put the pork skin in a large, heavy-based saucepan and cover with water. Bring to the boil, then reduce the heat to a simmer. Simmer for 3 hours, or until soft and tender. Drain and remove any excess fat or meat from the skin. Cut the skin into 1cm squares, transfer to a baking tray and dry in the oven on its lowest temperature for 12 hours, or until completely dry.

When dry, deep-fry the pork skin in a pan of oil heated to 180°C until puffed and crisp. Remove from the hot oil with a slotted spoon, drain on kitchen paper and season with salt.

To make the tarragon emulsion, bring a large saucepan of water to the boil and blanch the tarragon leaves for 2 minutes. Scoop them out with a slotted spoon and refresh in a bowl of iced water. Blitz the blanched tarragon with the sunflower oil in a blender until smooth. Pass the tarragon oil through muslin-lined sieve and put straight in the fridge to chill until cold.

In a clean blender blitz the soft-boiled eggs on medium speed. Add the green oil slowly until the emulsion has a mayonnaise consistency. Strain through a fine sieve and season with a pinch of salt.

Carefully peel the shells from the mylar prawns and remove and discard the heads. Season them lightly with salt and drizzle with a little rapeseed oil.

Place the dressed prawns on the pork crackers to cover, spoon on small dots of the tarragon emulsion and finish with a few tarragon leaves.

MAKES ABOUT 20 BITES

Pork cracker
1kg pork skin
vegetable oil, for deep-frying

Tarragon emulsion
150g tarragon leaves
200ml sunflower oil
2 soft-boiled eggs (cooked for 4 minutes)

Mylor prawns
200g raw Mylor prawns
rapeseed oil

salt, for seasoning
tarragon leaves, to serve

Combining seafood and meat is a popular pairing. In this dish, lobster sits alongside cubes of fried sweetbread and girolle mushrooms. Eucalyptus isn't to everyone's taste but do try it, as it adds a refreshing touch to the meaty lobster and rich sweetbreads and a floral note to the creamy hollandaise. Most of what we grow is indigenous, but eucalyptus is an example of a plant I've seen on my travels that I've then wanted to grow on the farm. It was so popular on the menu that it is something for which I will relax our rule about using non-native ingredients.

CUBES FROM LAND AND SEA WITH EUCALYPTUS HOLLANDAISE

To make the hollandaise, put 4 tablespoons of water in a small, heavy-based saucepan with the vinegar, peppercorns and eucalyptus leaves, place over a medium heat and reduce by a third. Strain through a fine sieve into a heatproof bowl. Place a pan of water (small enough for the bowl to fit on top without touching the water) on the hob and bring to the boil. Reduce to a simmer. Add the egg yolks to the reduction and whisk over the simmering water for 6–8 minutes until you reach a very thick ribbon stage.

    Meanwhile, clarify the butter. Put the butter in a heavy-based saucepan over a low heat and melt, skimming off any froth. Carefully pour the clear part of the butter into a bowl and discard the milky residue. Gradually add the warm clarified butter to the hollandaise, whisking continuously. Remove from the heat, finish with the eucalyptus oil, season with salt and whisk in the lemon juice. Leave in a warm place until ready to serve.

    Insert the tip of a large, sharp, heavy knife through the centre of the cross on the lobster's head with force. This will kill the lobster immediately. Twist and pull the tail away from the body to remove it, and pull back the claws to remove them. Bring a large saucepan of water to the boil. Quickly blanch the claws for 6 minutes, then after 2 minutes add the tail for the last 4 minutes. Remove and refresh in a bowl of iced water. Peel the shell away from the tail and discard. Using the back of a knife, tap the claw shell to crack it and remove the meat. Dice the lobster meat into 1cm cubes and leave to one side.

    Bring another large saucepan of water to the boil and blanch the sweetbreads for 30 seconds. Remove with a slotted spoon and refresh in a bowl of iced water. Peel the outer membrane away and leave the sweetbreads to dry on kitchen paper. Cut the sweetbreads into pieces of a similar size to the lobster meat and lightly dust them with flour. Warm the oil in a large, non-stick frying pan over a medium–high heat, add the sweetbreads and fry for 5–6 minutes, or until lightly golden. Add the butter, lobster meat and girolle mushrooms, turn over the sweetbreads and cook for a further 3–4 minutes until the sweetbreads are deeply golden and crispy. Season to taste, if you like.

    Remove the lobster, mushrooms and sweetbreads from the pan using a slotted spoon and divide among bowls. Cover with a generous spoonful of hollandaise.

SERVES 4, AS A STARTER

Lobster
2 fresh, live lobsters

Sweetbreads
300g sweetbreads
plain flour, for dusting
2 tbsp sunflower oil
150g unsalted butter

Girolles
200g girolle mushrooms, cleaned

Eucalyptus hollandaise
1 tbsp white wine vinegar
1 tsp black peppercorns, crushed
3 eucalyptus leaves
4 egg yolks
250g unsalted butter
2 drops of eucalyptus essential oil
juice of ½ lemon

salt, for seasoning

Sea bass is a popular fish that always looks beautiful on the plate, but it is at its best when it's not messed around with too much. Here we've added a little punch with a sauce made from roasting the fish bones that would normally make their way to the bin, but otherwise we've let the fresh ingredients do the talking. Delicately cooked sea bass with simply roasted carrots and young crisp spinach leaves make this a lovely light dish for a warm summer's evening.

PAN-FRIED SEA BASS WITH ROASTED FISH BONE SAUCE

First make the sauce. Preheat the oven to 200°C/180°C Fan/Gas Mark 6.

Roast the fish bones in a large baking tray for 25–30 minutes, or until lightly golden, stirring them regularly. Warm the oil in a large, heavy-based saucepan over a medium heat, add the fennel, shallots and garlic and sweat for 6–8 minutes until the shallots have become translucent, stirring regularly. Add the star anise and deglaze the pan with the wine, reducing to a syrup consistency. Add the roasted fish bones and chicken stock and bring to the boil over a high heat. Once boiled, reduce the heat to a simmer and cook for 2 hours, regularly skimming the impurities from the top of the stock. Pass through a fine sieve into a clean, medium, heavy-based saucepan. Bring back to the boil, reduce the heat to a simmer then reduce to a sauce consistency. Leave to one side.

While the sauce is reducing, poach the carrots. Put the carrots in a small, heavy-based saucepan with all the other ingredients and add water to just cover the carrots. Place over a high heat and bring to the boil, then reduce the heat to a simmer and poach gently for 2–3 minutes. By this time the water should have evaporated and the butter should be glazing the carrots. Remove the carrots from the pan and discard the tarragon.

Warm the oil for the sea bass in a large, heavy-based saucepan over a medium heat then carefully place the sea bass fillets in the pan skin side down. Cook for 5–6 minutes, or until the skin has become crispy, then turn the heat off, season the fish and turn the fillets over. Let the fillets continue cooking with the residual heat of the pan for 3 minutes, then serve.

Put the carrots on plates, followed by the fish and seaweed butter. Spoon around the sauce and finish with the raw spinach leaves .

SERVES 4

Sea bass
2 tbsp sunflower oil
4 fillets of sea bass, skin on, about
    80–100g each

Roasted fish bone sauce
1kg fish bones, heads removed
2 tbsp sunflower oil
1 fennel bulb, sliced
4 shallots, sliced
3 garlic cloves, sliced
1 star anise
250ml white wine
3 litres White Chicken Stock (see page
    286)

Atomic Red carrots
12 young, small, baby Atomic Red carrots
2 sprigs of tarragon
50g unsalted butter
a pinch of salt
2 pinches of sugar

salt, for seasoning
melted Seaweed Butter (see page 174),
    to serve
24 Koto F1 spinach leaves, to serve

Kelp is a really versatile seaweed that is packed with vitamins and minerals and has a deeply savoury taste. It is known as the 'King of Seaweed' for its unique property to be used as a base ingredient for stocks and sauces, and it works really well as an umami hit against the mild-flavoured cod. Cobra French beans are a particularly reliable and prolific variety that we grow on the farm, but any will do as long as they are really fresh. Lightly blanched, they add a vibrant colour and crunch along with the sweet lettuce chunks.

ROAST COD WITH KELP BUTTER SAUCE

To make the kelp butter sauce, warm the oil in a medium, heavy-based saucepan over a medium heat, add the shallots and kelp and sweat for 5–6 minutes, or until the shallots are translucent, stirring regularly. Add the vinegar and wine and reduce by two thirds, then add the cream and bring to the boil. When it has reached the boil, remove from the heat and strain through a fine sieve; discard the solids and transfer the liquid to a small saucepan. Using a hand-held blender gradually incorporate the butter until the liquid has a sauce consistency. Season with a pinch of salt and leave to one side.

Break the lettuce down into individual leaves and wash them in cold water. Cut into large dice and leave to one side.

Warm the oil for the fish in a large, non-stick pan over a medium heat. Lightly dust the fish skin with flour. Place skin side down in the pan and cook for 5–6 minutes. As the colour changes on the sides from opaque to white halfway up the fish, carefully turn it over and add the butter to the pan, basting the fish with the melted butter. Reduce the heat to low and cook for a further 4–5 minutes. Turn off the heat and allow the fish to rest.

Bring a large saucepan of salted water to the boil and blanch the French beans for 1 minute. Remove and refresh in a bowl of iced water. Warm through slowly in a small pan with the butter and a pinch of salt just before serving.

Wilt the squares of lettuce in the kelp butter sauce in a small saucepan over a low heat. Divide among plates with the warmed beans and cooked cod and spoon over the sauce.

SERVES 4

2 tbsp sunflower oil
4 portions of cod loin, skin on, about 80g each
plain flour, for dusting
20g unsalted butter

Kelp butter sauce
1 tbsp sunflower oil
3 shallots, sliced
30g dried kelp
30ml chardonnay vinegar
100ml white wine
50ml double cream
100g unsalted butter, diced

Butterhead lettuce
1 butterhead lettuce

Cobra French beans
200g French beans
25g unsalted butter

salt, for seasoning

The firm white flesh of brill has a sweet taste which marries perfectly with buttery, creamy sauces, and here it's spiked with peppery watercress, a strong-tasting salad leaf that can hold its own against the intense flavour of griddled asparagus. It's a really simple dish, lifted by the browned butter.

BUTTER-POACHED BRILL AND ASPARAGUS WITH WATERCRESS SAUCE

Place a large, heavy-based saucepan over a medium heat. Add the butter and cook until it foams. Once foaming, reduce the heat and let the butter cook for another 10–15 minutes until it reaches a very dark brown colour and has a nutty aroma. It will be extremely hot. Remove the pan from the heat and allow to cool. When cool, strain through a muslin-lined sieve and discard the milk solids. Leave to one side.

To make the sauce, put the cream and stock in a small, heavy-based saucepan over a low heat and reduce by half. Transfer to a blender with the watercress and blend until smooth. Pass through a fine sieve and season.

Bring a large saucepan of salted water to the boil. Peel each asparagus spear and snap off the woody part of the stem. Blanch for 2 minutes, or until tender, then remove and refresh in a bowl of iced water. Drain and leave to dry on kitchen paper. When dry, coat each spear with a drizzle of rapeseed oil and scatter a generous pinch of salt over all of them. Heat a griddle pan over a high heat, add the asparagus spears and grill for 2–3 minutes, or until slightly charred.

In a medium, heavy-based saucepan over a low heat, bring the browned butter to a temperature of 55°C. Remove from the heat, add the fish and leave to cook gently in the residual heat of the butter for 15–20 minutes. Remove the fish from the butter and drain on kitchen paper.

Divide the asparagus among plates. Spoon the watercress sauce on to each plate and place the cooked fish on top. Finish with baby watercress and cornflowers.

SERVES 4

Butter-poached brill
500g unsalted butter
4 portions of brill, about 80g each

Griddled asparagus
20 spears of green asparagus
rapeseed oil
a pinch of salt

Watercress cream sauce
50ml double cream
100ml White Chicken Stock (see page 286)
150g watercress with stalks
a pinch of salt

baby watercress and cornflowers, to serve (optional)

The woodland behind Cartmel racecourse is a forager's paradise, and I love to go
down there to see what's growing in every season, and to find inspiration for new
dishes. In autumn you are hit by the earthy smell of mushrooms and aromatic
pine needles on the trees, and this dish comes from those foraging sessions. The
halibut is cooked in an oil made with pine needles to keep the fish moist and so
it can take on the subtle flavours of the infused oil. For the most intense flavours,
make the mushroom broth ahead and leave it overnight for the flavours to meld
together. The barigoule is a lovely, traditional Provencal method of preserving
fresh artichokes by braising them in a white-wine and vegetable broth.

HALIBUT AND ARTICHOKES IN MUSHROOM BROTH AND PINE OIL

To make the mushroom broth, warm the oil in a medium, heavy-based saucepan
over a low–medium heat, add the shallots and garlic and sweat for 5–6 minutes, or
until they are translucent, stirring regularly. Add the thyme and mushrooms and
cook for 10 minutes, stirring regularly. Deglaze with the Madeira and sherry vinegar
and reduce until nearly all the liquid has evaporated, then add 2 litres of water.
Bring to the boil, reduce the heat to a simmer and cook over a low heat for 2 hours.
Remove from the heat, cover with a lid and cool to room temperature. Infuse in the
fridge overnight. Strain through a fine sieve and season with salt. Leave to one side.

    To make the artichoke barigoule, put the grapeseed oil, white wine, vinegar,
bay leaves, stock, lemon juice and salt in a medium, heavy-based saucepan and
bring to the boil over a high heat. Reduce the heat to a simmer, add the prepared
artichokes and cover with a piece of greaseproof paper. Cook for 10–15 minutes,
or until the artichokes are tender. Remove the artichokes with a slotted spoon and
leave them to cool to room temperature on kitchen paper.

    Add the prepared globe artichokes to the barigoule cooking liquor and bring
to the boil. Reduce the heat to a simmer and cook for 30–35 minutes, or until the
artichokes are very tender. Remove the artichokes with a slotted spoon, discarding
the cooking liquor, and blitz in a blender with the double cream until smooth. Pass
through a fine sieve and season.

    For the halibut, put the pine needles and oil in a heavy-based saucepan and
cook over a very low heat. As soon as the pine needles begin to fizz and move,
remove the pan from the heat and allow to infuse and cool. Put the salt in 400ml
water in a bowl and whisk until dissolved. Submerge the halibut portions in the
brine for 5–8 minutes. Remove and dry on kitchen paper. Once cool, strain the oil
through a fine sieve and warm it to 55°C in a clean, heavy-based saucepan over a
low heat. Add the halibut to the warm oil and cook gently for 12–15 minutes.

    Fry the violet artichokes with the oil in a frying pan over medium heat for 4–5
minutes until golden brown. Divide among bowls with the warm artichoke purée.
Drain the fish from the oil and add to each serving. Drizzle with a little pine oil and
pour the mushroom broth into each bowl. Finish with sea beet leaves.

SERVES 4

Mushroom broth
2 tbsp sunflower oil
4 shallots, sliced
2 garlic cloves, sliced
4 sprigs of thyme
150g mixed dried mushrooms
250ml Madeira
2 tbsp sherry vinegar

Artichoke barigoule
100ml grapeseed oil
250ml white wine
2 tbsp white wine vinegar
2 bay leaves
500ml White Chicken Stock (see page 286)
juice of 1 lemon
1 tsp salt
8 violet artichokes, outer leaves removed
    and trimmed
1 tbsp sunflower oil

Globe artichoke purée
2 globe artichokes, outer leaves removed
    and trimmed
artichoke barigoule cooking liquor, see above
200ml double cream

Halibut in pine oil
150g pine needles
400ml sunflower oil
40g salt
4 portions of halibut, about 80g a portion

salt, for seasoning
sea beets, to serve

Also known as oyster plant, salsify is an unspectacular-looking root whose rough brown skin hides a creamy white flesh. After many trials and frustration at failure to grow this, we have finally succeeded in growing this in abundance at Cartmel, which is great as I love its versatility – both puréed and fried, it makes the perfect accompaniment to the meaty flesh of the spiced monkfish. Golden raspberries have the sweetest flavour as well as a sensational colour, so do seek them out for this.

FIVE-SPICED MONKFISH WITH GOLDEN RASPBERRY

To prepare the monkfish spice mixture, put the mint, citrus zests, liquorice stick and meadowsweet on a baking tray in an oven set to the lowest temperature possible for about 1 hour, or until they are dry. When dry, blitz to a powder in a blender or food processor. Leave to one side.

Wash and peel the salsify, cover with water combined with the lemon juice – the acidulated water will prevent oxidisation to stop the salsify turning brown. Thinly slice 600g of the salsify. Melt 50g of the butter in a medium, heavy-based saucepan over a medium heat, add the sliced salsify and sweat for 10–12 minutes, stirring regularly, until tender and soft. Add the milk and reduce by half. Remove from the heat and blitz until smooth in a blender, then pass the mixture through a fine sieve into a heatproof bowl, season with salt and leave to one side.

Cut the rest of the salsify into 4cm-long batons and dry them on kitchen paper. Warm the oil in a non-stick frying pan over a medium heat, add the remaining butter, reduce the heat and add the salsify batons. Cook for 8–10 minutes, keeping them moving around the pan to give them an even colour, until tender. Remove from the pan and drain on kitchen paper.

Blitz the raspberries in a blender until smooth and pass through a fine sieve into a bowl. Add the salt, sugar and vinegar, whisk together, and leave to one side.

To cook the monkfish, warm the oil in a non-stick frying pan over a medium heat. Dust the monkfish all over in the prepared spice, place in the frying pan and cook on each side for 4 minutes. Remove from the heat and leave the monkfish to finish cooking in the pan while it rests.

Spoon the salsify purée on plates. Dot the raspberry dressing around each plate and add the monkfish and roasted salsify.

SERVES 4

Monkfish
125g picked mint leaves
zest of ½ orange
zest of ½ lime
¼ liquorice stick
½ tsp meadowsweet powder
2 tbsp sunflower oil
8 portions of monkfish, about 40g each

Roasted salsify and purée
800g salsify
80g unsalted butter
200ml whole milk
1 tbsp sunflower oil

Golden raspberry dressing
100g golden raspberries
a pinch of salt
a pinch of sugar
2 tbsp raspberry vinegar

juice of ½ lemon
salt, for seasoning

This is a variation of a popular dish that we serve at L'Enclume. Hake is a really meaty fish that can be paired with so many different ingredients, but it's particularly good with stronger flavours. Here we've partnered it with chervil, which has a subtle anise flavour, in a creamy root purée to contrast with the crispy chicken skin. We grow Candisa cabbage at our farm because it is a very reliable, sweet-tasting cabbage which beautifully complements the hake here, but if you can't find this, just make sure you use a really fresh, crisp variety.

CHICK O HAKE WITH CHERVIL ROOT PURÉE

Scrape away any excess fat and flesh from the chicken skin. Cut out 4 portions, each twice the width and length of the fish pieces (because it will shrink during cooking). Neatly wrap the fish in the chicken skin and chill in the fridge.

Peel and thinly slice the chervil roots. Put them in a medium, heavy-based saucepan with the cream, milk and a pinch of salt. Cook over a medium heat for 20–25, minutes or until the chervil root is tender, stirring regularly. Transfer to a blender and blitz until smooth. Leave to one side.

To make the Champagne butter, warm the oil in a medium, heavy-based saucepan over a medium heat, add the onion and a pinch of salt and sweat for 5–6 minutes until translucent, stirring regularly. Add the herbs and the Champagne and reduce to a syrup. Add the stock and reduce by half, then add the cream and reduce by half again. Pass through a fine sieve into a clean saucepan and, using a hand-held blender, blend in the butter and lemon juice little by little until the sauce is light and foamy. Remove from the heat and leave to one side.

Blitz the oil and sea lettuce together in a blender on high speed for 5 minutes. Pass through a fine sieve and chill in the fridge.

To cook the fish, warm the oil in a non-stick frying pan over a medium heat. Place the wrapped fish in the pan, season with a pinch of salt and cook for 4–5 minutes on each side until evenly crisp and golden.

Put the cabbage in a small saucepan over a medium heat with 100ml water, the butter and a pinch of salt. Bring to the boil, reduce the heat and cook for 2–3 minutes until wilted.

Spoon a little chervil purée on each plate. Add the fish and cabbage, spoon the sauce over and around, split with the green oil and sprinkle with the spirulina powder.

SERVES 4

Chick o Hake
400g chicken skin, preferably from the
    crown
4 portions of hake loin, about 100g each
2 tbsp sunflower oil

Chervil root purée
350g chervil roots
150ml double cream
150ml whole milk

Champagne butter
2 tbsp sunflower oil
½ onion, diced
2 bay leaves
2 sprigs of thyme
250ml Champagne
250ml White Chicken Stock (see page 286)
150ml double cream
100g unsalted butter
juice of ¼ lemon

Seaweed oil
100ml sunflower oil
50g fresh sea lettuce

Candisa cabbage
1 light green cabbage, such as Candisa,
    broken down into individual leaves
50g unsalted butter

salt, for seasoning
spirulina powder, to serve

I love trout, and if I had to pick a favourite between this and salmon, this would win hands down, particularly the really fresh fish we get from the Bessy Beck trout farm in the Lake District. Blowtorching the trout not only gives it a nice charred look but also sears the flesh and gives it a caramelised flavour, which is perfect with the fresh vegetables and the thick, savoury and umami sauces. We grow a wide variety of courgettes on the farm, in different colours, shapes and sizes. Tromboncino is a favourite; it is a climbing and trailing courgette that is easy to grow and produces unusual and delicious twisting and curving fruits. If you grow these yourself, try to pick a flower, too.

TROUT AND TROMBONCINO COURGETTES WITH SAVOURY SAUCE

To make the savoury sauce, warm the oil in a medium, heavy-based saucepan over a low–medium heat, add the onion and sweat for 5–6 minutes, stirring regularly, until it becomes translucent. Add the tomato purée and sweat for a further 2 minutes, then add the remaining ingredients, bring to the boil and cook for 3–5 minutes. Remove from the heat, blend with a hand-held blender until smooth and pass through a fine sieve.

Warm the oil and butter in a non-stick frying pan over a medium heat, add the courgettes and fry for 3 minutes, or until golden.

Preheat the oven grill to high.

Brush the trout portions all over with oil and blowtorch all the flesh until charred and lightly torched. Place them on a baking tray and finishing cooking under the grill for a couple of minutes (or longer depending on the portion size).

Spoon the savoury sauce on to each plate, then add the warm trout and courgettes.

SERVES 4

Trout
4 portions of trout, skin removed, about 80g each
1 tbsp sunflower oil

Savoury sauce
2 tbsp rapeseed oil
½ white onion, sliced
2 tsp tomato purée
200g tinned plum tomatoes
25g light soft brown sugar
½ tsp salt
a pinch of chilli flakes
2 anchovies in oil, drained
20ml fermented mushroom juice (optional, see page 200)
1 tsp Worcestershire sauce

Tromboncino courgettes
2 tbsp sunflower oil
30g unsalted butter
8 Tromboncino courgettes (with flowers, if possible)
a pinch of salt

Turbot is not the most beautiful of fish, but it has a wonderfully delicate creamy-white flesh. It needs quick cooking to retain its texture, so don't skip the marinating step, as this helps the turbot to retain moisture during high-heat cooking and to absorb the flavours of the marinade. The subtle flavour of the fish works well with the caramelised cauliflower and savoury flavours of the fermented king oyster mushroom. Serve the mussels and creamy sauce on the side so that you can add as much or as little as you want.

MARINATED TURBOT AND MUSSELS WITH MISO PICKLE

Place the mushrooms, oil and salt in a sterilised 1-litre Kilner jar (see page 302) and mix well. Seal the jar with the lid and leave it in a cool, dry place away from direct sunlight for 2 weeks. After 2 weeks, remove the mushrooms from the jar and discard the juice that has come out of them (or use the recipe on page 198). Place the mushrooms in a clean jar or airtight container, seal and chill in the fridge.

To marinate the turbot, combine all the ingredients for the miso pickle in a container and submerge the fish in the mixture for 1 hour.

To make the cauliflower purée, melt the butter in a large, heavy-based saucepan over a low–medium heat, add the chopped cauliflower and cook gently for 30–35 minutes, stirring constantly so it caramelises slowly, until it turns a deep golden colour. Add the milk and cream to the pan and bring to the boil. Remove from the heat and blitz in a blender until smooth. Leave to one side.

Wash the mussels thoroughly under cold running water, removing all the beards and grit. Warm the oil in a large, heavy-based saucepan over a medium heat, add the shallots and garlic with a pinch of salt and cook, stirring regularly, for 5–6 minutes, or until the shallots are translucent. Add 300g of the cleaned mussels, the parsley stalks and white wine, cover the pan with foil and cook for another 10 minutes. Remove from the heat and strain the liquid through a fine sieve, discarding the solids. Transfer the stock to a clean small saucepan over a low heat and reduce by half. When reduced, add the butter and the cream and reduce to a sauce consistency. Season with a pinch of salt and add the lemon juice. Leave to one side.

To cook the remaining mussels, place a medium saucepan over a high heat. When the pan is extremely hot, add the mussels and 100ml water, cover immediately, cook and steam for 2 minutes, or until the mussels are all open (discard any that remain shut). Remove from the pan and while still warm, remove the meat from the shells and discard the shells.

Preheat the grill to high. Cook the marinated turbot on a tray under the grill for 1–2 minutes on each side until just cooked.

SERVES 4

Fermented king oyster
1kg king oyster mushrooms
2 tbsp sunflower oil
30g Maldon sea salt

Miso pickle
75ml sake
75ml mirin
225g white miso paste
110g caster sugar

Turbot
4 portions of turbot, about 80g each

Caramelised cauliflower purée
100g unsalted butter
1 large cauliflower, florets finely chopped
140ml whole milk
140ml double cream

Mussels and mussel sauce
500g live mussels
2 tbsp sunflower oil
3 shallots, sliced
2 garlic cloves, sliced
10 parsley stalks
200ml white wine
50g unsalted butter
200ml double cream
juice of ½ lemon

salt, for seasoning

While the fish is cooking, pan-fry the mushrooms in a frying pan over a medium-high heat with the oil for 4 minutes until deeply golden. Season with salt.

Serve the fish and the cauliflower purée on plates with the pan-fried fermented mushrooms, with the mussel sauce frothed up with a blender, if you like, and the mussels in separate bowls on the side.

This is a dish of many elements, some of which need a little planning ahead. But don't be put off, each one is important and they all complement each other, and they aren't difficult. Sole is a very delicate fish that needs other flavours around it, so the smoky, rich bone marrow adds meatiness, while the broccoli purée brings vibrant colour and simple freshness. Razor clams are not used much here in Britain, although they feature on a lot of menus in Europe; this is such a shame, because they are packed with flavour. Here we've made up for that with nothing going to waste, using both the meat and skirts of the clams.

SOLE FILLETS WITH SMOKED MARROWBONE AND RAZOR CLAM SAUCE

For the smoked bone marrow, put 500ml cold water and the salt in a container and stir until fully dissolved. Submerge the bone marrow in the brine and leave in the fridge for 24 hours.

Remove the bone marrow from the brine and dry on kitchen paper. Put the smoking chips in a nice even layer in a baking tray lined with foil. Sit a wire rack on top, one that is a similar size to the tray, making sure the wire isn't touching the chips. Put the bone marrow on the wire rack and cover the entire rack and tray with a tent of foil, so no smoke escapes. Sit the tray on the hob over a low heat for 10 minutes. Remove the covered tray from the heat and let the bone marrow smoke in the foil tent for 20 minutes, then place in the fridge while you prepare the rest of the dish.

To make the sauce, warm the oil in a large saucepan over a medium–high heat, add the shallots, garlic, thyme and salt and cook for 4–5 minutes until translucent, stirring regularly. Add the razor clams and stir again, so that they all evenly get the heat. Turn the heat up to high, add the vinegar and white wine and deglaze the pan. Bring to the boil then immediately strain through a colander over a bowl. Remove the razor clam meat from the shells, discarding the shells and thyme but keeping the skirts that you remove from the clam meat. Keep the clam meat in the fridge until you assemble the finished dish. Add the onions and garlic back to the pan along with the cooking juices and the razor clam skirts, making sure to remove the vein or sack beforehand. Add the cream and chicken stock and bring to the boil. Sift out the skirts, turn the heat down to a simmer and cook for about 15 minutes until the sauce has reduced by half. Once reduced, check the seasoning and add the lemon juice. Keep warm.

To make the broccoli purée, put 200ml water in a medium saucepan with the butter and salt and place over a high heat. Bring to the boil. Add the chopped broccoli to the boiling liquid and boil rapidly for 5 minutes, or until the broccoli has softened, then transfer to a blender and blitz until smooth. Pass through a fine sieve. Keep warm.

SERVES 4

Sole fillets
2 tbsp sunflower oil
8 fresh sole fillets
plain flour, for dusting
25g unsalted butter

Smoked bone marrow
150g bone marrow
50g table salt
wood smoking chips

Razor clam and sauce
2 tbsp sunflower oil
2 medium shallots, thinly sliced
2 garlic cloves, thinly sliced
3 sprigs of thyme
a pinch of salt
8 large live razor clams
1 tbsp white wine vinegar
100ml white wine
200ml double cream
160ml White Chicken Stock (see page 286)
juice of ½ lemon

Broccoli purée
55g unsalted butter
1 tsp salt
1 head of broccoli (300g), florets and stalk
    finely chopped

salt, for seasoning
Baby Pigeon leaves, to serve
Small bunch of chives, snipped, to serve

Warm the oil for the sole fillets in a non-stick frying pan, dust the sole fillets with flour and cook for 2–3 minutes on each side until lightly golden. For the last minute of cooking add the butter and the razor clam meat. Blitz the sauce with a hand-held blender until slightly frothy.

Divide the sole among plates, add a spoon of the warm broccoli purée, sauce, razor clams and thin slices of smoked bone marrow that have been warmed through the oven and finish with Baby Pigeon leaves and a scattering of snipped chives.

Scallops

I can't imagine a menu without scallops – they are quite simply my favourite shellfish. It's important for us to use the very best scallops we can, so we have ours sent down from Scotland, not least because they are hand-dived for in crystal-clear, non-polluted water and shipped down the same day, while still beautifully fresh. It's more expensive to buy these hand-caught scallops, but I prefer to do this than buy dredged scallops, as this method damages seabeds.

When buying scallops they should smell fresh like the sea and look firm, opaque and moist – we like to get them in their shells for freshness, and because we use these casings for plating as well as every part of the shellfish inside (see page 213). The orange (in the females) or grey-pink (males) corals attached to the main scallop are often discarded by many chefs, but don't, as they are both edible and delicious. The roes have a really robust flavour and cook faster than the white meat – they're particularly good quickly fried with lardons of bacon or pancetta.

Scallops can be steamed, fried or grilled, but however you cook them, do it gently and for the shortest time, otherwise their delicate flavour and texture will be spoiled. The trick to serving scallops is to make sure that you don't overpower them with strong flavourings. I prefer to cook them alongside small amounts of lemon zest or herbs, fresh vegetables, sharp fruits such as wild strawberries or gooseberries. Again, I love to cook them with my favourite flavouring, anise, which heightens the sweetness of scallops. Their meaty texture means they stand up well with the richly sulphurous flavours of garlic, and I love combining them with rhubarb and strawberries for a bit of sharp and sweet, as well as asparagus, which makes a heavenly combination. When you have really beautifully fresh scallops, lemon or vinegar is one of the greatest tools in a chef's toolbox, as they need little more than of drop of either to enhance their sweetness.

This looks beautiful on the plate with all the fresh vegetables against the creamy white smoked oysters. The secret is keeping the vibrant greens of the peas by briefly blanching them and plunging them into iced water. Peas and mint is another classic pairing, but we grow a lot of mint varieties and I find that calamint has a milder, more aromatic minty flavour than most, which gives the peas a subtle herby tinge. You can find calamint plants in most garden centres, and it's easy to grow a pot of it on your windowsill.

SMOKED SCALLOP WITH PEA MOUSSE

Put the smoking chips in a nice even layer in a baking tray lined with foil. Sit a wire rack on top, one that is a similar size to the tray, making sure the wire isn't touching the chips. Put the scallop meat on the wire rack and cover the entire rack and tray with a tent of foil, so no smoke escapes. Sit the tray on the hob over a low heat for 5 minutes. Remove from the heat and let the scallops smoke in the foil tent for 20 minutes.

To make the pea mousse, soak the gelatine in cold water for a few minutes until softened. Drain, squeeze out the excess water and leave the gelatine to one side. Bring a large saucepan of salted water to the boil and blanch the peas for 2 minutes. Drain and refresh in a bowl of iced water. Warm the stock in a small saucepan over a medium heat and melt the softened gelatine in it. Blitz the peas with the stock in a blender until smooth. Pass through a fine sieve. Whip the cream in a bowl until is aerated and holds soft peaks. Fold the cream through the pea mixture, season with salt and pour into an airtight container. Transfer to the fridge to set.

To make the calamint oil, bring a large saucepan of water to the boil and blanch the calamint leaves for 1 minute. Scoop them out with a slotted spoon and refresh in a bowl of iced water. Drain, squeeze out the excess water and blitz the calamint with the oil in a blender until smooth. Pass the herb oil through a muslin-lined sieve.

Dress the raw peas in a little of the calamint oil and salt and divide among small bowls. Put a smoked scallop on top of each serving, cover with a spoon of pea mousse and finish with a little more calamint oil and pea shoots and flowers.

SERVES 4, AS A STARTER

Smoked scallop
4 large hand-dived scallops, trimmed
    of roe
enough wood smoking chips to create a
    layer in the baking tray

Pea mousse
1 gelatine leaf
175g frozen peas
50ml Vegetable Stock (see page 286)
200ml double cream
½ tsp salt

Calamint oil
200g calamint leaves
100ml sunflower oil

raw peas, such as Peawee 65, pea shoots
    and flowers, to serve

Cauliflower and scallops are a suprisingly good combination. Slowly cooked until caramelised, the cauliflower florets become wonderfully tender and lose their characteristic strong cabbage-like flavour, so they don't overpower the naturally sweet, mild scallops. Strawberries make a lovely addition here; they enhance the sweetness of the other two main ingredients, but the verjus and spices in the stock add a little acidic kick too.

GRILLED SCALLOPS WITH CAULIFLOWER AND STRAWBERRY VINEGAR

Melt the butter for the purée in a medium, heavy-based saucepan over a medium heat, then add the cauliflower and sweat for 5–6 minutes, stirring regularly so it doesn't brown. When the cauliflower beings to soften, add the milk and cream and bring to the boil. Reduce to a simmer and cook util the cauliflower is soft and the liquid has almost completely evaporated, then remove from the heat and blitz in a blender until smooth. Pass through a fine sieve and season with salt. Leave to one side.

To make the strawberry vinegar, put the strawberries, wine, sugar and salt in a small, heavy-based saucepan with 40ml water and bring to the boil. As soon as it boils, remove the pan from the heat, cover and allow to cool for 20 minutes. Pass through a fine sieve and discard the solids, then pour the strawberry stock into a clean small saucepan and reduce by half over a low heat. While the liquid is reducing, heat the oil in another small, heavy-based saucepan, add the shallot and sweat over a low heat for 8–10 minutes, or until translucent. Deglaze with the verjus and add the strawberry stock and spices. Bring to the boil, reduce the heat and simmer for 3 minutes. Remove from the heat and allow to infuse and cool, then strain through a muslin-lined sieve.

To caramelise the cauliflower, cut each floret in half and place them cut side down in a cold non-stick frying pan (do this in two batches if necessary). Add the diced butter and salt. Cover the pan with foil and place over a low heat for 20 minutes, or until the florets are deeply golden on the cut side. Remove from the pan and transfer to kitchen paper.

Heat a small amount of oil in a non-stick frying pan over a high heat, add the scallops and fry them for 3 minutes until deeply caramelised on one side, then turn the scallops over, reduce the heat, add the knob of butter and cook for 1–2 minutes more. Once cooked, tear the scallops in half so you can see the natural ridges. Spoon the vinegar dressing on to each plate, followed by the warm purée, 3 scallop halves and the roasted cauliflower. Finish with the iceplant.

SERVES 4, AS A STARTER

6 large, hand-dived scallops with roes
sunflower oil, for frying
knob of unsalted butter

Cauliflower purée
25g unsalted butter
500g cauliflower, very thinly sliced
200ml whole milk
200ml double cream
salt, for seasoning

Strawberry vinegar dressing
150g strawberries
40ml white wine
2 tbsp caster sugar
a pinch of salt
1 tbsp sunflower oil
2 shallots, sliced
2 tbsp verjus
½ green cardamom pod
¼ cinnamon stick
1 tsp coriander seeds

Caramelised cauliflower florets
500g cauliflower, broken into large florets
200g unsalted butter, diced
a pinch of salt

iceplant, to serve

This recipe perfectly demonstrates our ethos: to use as much of the ingredient as we can. This dish showcases the whole scallop – meat, roe and skirt – so that none of the hero ingredient goes to waste. You can even use the shells as a dish! Serve the three plates together, to enjoy every element; the smoked flavours of the roe and the sweetness of the raw scallops, all washed down with sips of lightly scented bouillon.

RAW SCALLOPS WITH VINEGAR GEL, SCALLOP BOUILLON AND GOOSEBERRY TART WITH SCALLOP ROE

RAW SCALLOPS WITH VINEGAR GEL

To make the vinegar gel, put all the ingredients in a small heavy-based saucepan with 100ml water, bring to the boil over a high heat and boil for 1 minute. Remove from the heat, pour into a heatproof bowl and leave to set in the fridge. Transfer to a blender and blitz until smooth. then pass through a fine sieve and keep in the fridge until needed.

Carefully remove the scallops from their shells. Discard the shells (or keep them to use as a serving dish). Remove the scallop meat from the skirts and roes. Set the skirts and roes to one side for the next two recipes. Cut the scallop meat into 5mm dice and season with salt and a few drops of lemon juice. Thinly slice the radishes on a mandoline. Put the seasoned scallop meat in small serving bowls and cover with the thin radish slices and sea purslane leaves.

SCALLOP BOUILLON

Warm the oil in a heavy-based saucepan over a low heat, add the vegetables and sweat for 4–5 minutes, or until slightly softened, stirring regularly. Add the thyme and scallop skirts and cook for a further 2 minutes. Increase the heat to medium and deglaze the pan with the white wine. Reduce by half. Once reduced, add the fish stock and bring to the boil. Reduce the heat and simmer for 20 minutes. Pass the mixture through a muslin-lined sieve and season with salt and the lemon juice to taste.

Serve the warm bouillion in bowls with 3–4 sprigs of apple marigold.

SERVES 4, AS A STARTER

Raw scallops
4 large, hand-dived scallops
lemon juice, to taste
a pinch of salt
2 breakfast radishes
purslane leaves, to serve

Vinegar gel
100ml cider vinegar
a pinch of salt
2 tbsp caster sugar
1 level tsp agar agar

Scallop bouillon
2 tbsp sunflower oil
½ onion, diced
½ leek, sliced
2 garlic cloves, chopped
1 celery stick, chopped
1 sprig of thyme
4 scallop skirts, from the scallops above
50ml white wine
300ml Fish Stock (see page 287)
juice of ½ lemon

3–4 small sprigs of apple marigold, to serve
salt, for seasoning

GOOSEBERRY TART WITH SCALLOP ROE

Prepare the tart cases a day before serving. Combine the frozen gooseberries, oil, wine, salt and sugar in a heavy-based saucepan with 35ml water and bring to the boil, then cook for 3 minutes. When the gooseberries have softened and broken up, add the agar agar, blitz the mixture in a blender until smooth and pass it through a fine sieve. Spread the mixture as thinly as you can on a silicone mat and leave to dry in the oven for 3 hours at 60°C. After this stage, the mixture should have a leathery feel to it. Use a 6cm pastry cutter to cut the leather into 4 discs 1cm bigger than 4 small tart cases. Lightly grease the tart cases with oil or baking spray and line the cases with the discs. Put the tart cases in the oven for a further 24 hours at a reduced oven temperature of 50°C, or as low as your oven will go, for 24 hours to dehydrate and firm up.

Increase the oven temperature to 195°C/175°C Fan/Gas Mark 5. Bake the scallop roe in the oven on a baking tray for 15 minutes, or until firm. Remove and leave to cool, then dice and put in a food processor with the cream cheese, 10ml water and the lemon juice. Blitz until quite smooth then transfer to a bowl. Pass the smoked cod roe through a sieve and whisk it into the cream cheese mix. Once well mixed, gradually add the oil, whisking all the time, to create a mayonnaise consistency. Season with the salt. Put the mixture in a piping bag and reserve in the fridge.

Pipe the scallop roe into the tart cases and cover with freshly picked herbs and flowers.

Serve all three elements together to showcase the whole scallop.

Gooseberry tart
200g frozen gooseberries
25ml sunflower oil, plus extra for greasing
60ml white wine
a pinch of salt
40g caster sugar
½ tsp agar agar

Scallop roe
roe of 4 scallops, from the scallops above
100g cream cheese
juice of 1 lemon
50g smoked cod roe
100ml rapeseed oil
a pinch of salt

herbs and flowers, to serve

Scallops are a really popular ingredient in the restaurant and we are always trying to think of different ways to prepare them. This is a dish to impress your friends – the scallops are blended and whipped into a light mousse, which is gently poached while wrapped in little parcels of fresh, crisp, sprout top leaves, and served with a rich, smoky roe sauce. It's much simpler to make than it sounds, but looks so good!

SCALLOP MOUSSE WITH SMOKED ROE BUTTER SAUCE

Put the scallop meat straight from the fridge into a blender and blend until smooth. Transfer to a bowl and fold through the beaten eggs. Pass through a fine sieve. Add the cream to the mixture a little at a time, working it in with a spatula until it is all incorporated. Season with salt and put in the fridge to chill.

To make the sauce, warm the oil in a medium, heavy-based saucepan over a medium heat, add the onion and pinch of salt and sweat for 5–6 minutes until translucent, stirring regularly. Add the herbs to the pan along with the white wine and reduce to a syrup. When the wine has reduced, add the stock and reduce by half, then add the cream and reduce by half again. Pass through a fine sieve into a clean pan and use a hand-held blender to blitz in the butter and roe little by little until the sauce becomes light and foamy. Leave to one side.

Bring a large saucepan of salted water to the boil and blanch the sprout top leaves for 2 minutes. Scoop out and refresh in a bowl of iced water. Spread the leaves out flat on kitchen paper to dry. When dry, add a tablespoon of scallop mousse to the centre of each leaf, bringing the leaf up around the mousse to form a ball. Wrap all 20 balls individually in cling film.

Bring a medium pan of water to the boil and reduce to a simmer. Gently poach the scallop parcels in their cling film for 4–5 minutes.

Divide the sauce among bowls, then remove and unwrap the scallop parcels and add them to the warm sauce. Serve topped with the sea blite and sea campion.

SERVES 4, AS A STARTER

Scallop mousse
8 large scallops, meat only
3 eggs, beaten
150ml double cream

Smoked roe butter sauce
2 tbsp sunflower oil
½ onion, diced
a pinch of salt
2 bay leaves
2 sprigs of thyme
250ml white wine
350ml Fish Stock (see page 287)
250ml double cream
150g unsalted butter, diced
50g smoked cod roe

Sprout tops
20 large sprout-top leaves

salt, for seasoning
sea blite and sea campion, to serve

DAIRY

A combination of melt-in-the-mouth textures – from the delicate, airy and crispy chickpea wafers to the creamy, light goat's curd. Roasting the garlic mellows its flavours so it doesn't overwhelm the dish, but adds a sweet, caramelised hint. Dress it up with whatever edible flowers and herbs you have for a touch of colour.

CHICKPEA WAFER WITH GOAT'S CURD

To make the chickpea wafer, put the flour, salt and rosemary in a medium, heavy-based saucepan over a medium heat, add 150ml water and mix well. Cook for 4–5 minutes, stirring the mixture constantly, until it becomes very, very thick. When thickened, remove from the heat, spread teaspoons of the wafer mix on to a sheet of baking parchment to a thickness of about 5mm and let it cool to room temperature, cutting out 4cm oval shapes. Peel the wafers off the parchment when cool and deep-fry them in batches in a pan of oil heated to 180°C for 3–5 minutes, or until lightly golden, turning them regularly so they cook evenly. Remove with a slotted spoon and drain on kitchen paper. Leave to cool until ready to serve.

Preheat the oven to 200°C/180°C Fan/Gas Mark 6. Wrap the whole head of garlic in foil and bake it for about 40 minutes, or until the garlic is very soft to the touch. When cooked, remove the soft flesh from the garlic skins and add it to a blender along with the rest of the ingredients (except the oil). Blitz to combine, then gradually add the oil until the emulsion has a mayonnaise consistency.

Spread the goat's curd on to the crispy wafers, followed by the garlic emulsion. Decorate with the herbs and flowers.

SERVES 6, AS A STARTER

Chickpea wafer
80g gram flour
1 tsp salt
1 tbsp finely chopped rosemary needles
vegetable oil, for deep-frying

Garlic emulsion
1 head of garlic
2 egg yolks
1 tbsp made English mustard
1 tsp sherry vinegar
½ tsp Worcestershire sauce
juice of ½ lemon
a pinch of salt
125ml sunflower oil

50g fresh goat's curd
chive flowers, turnip tops, radish shoots,
    viola flowers, primrose flowers,
    nasturtium flowers, to serve

Whey is very much seen as a by-product of making yoghurt, but don't chuck it out – it is liquid gold. The versatility of this ingredient is beginning to be noted again, popping up in drinks and fermented food. We like to cook many ingredients in whey because it adds an acidity as well as a slight sweetness, and our pencil-thin home-grown Musselburgh leeks are perfect for this dish. As the whey reduces around the leeks here it caramelises and becomes sticky, and who doesn't like caramelised sticky onions?

LEEKS COOKED IN WHEY WITH BURNT CHIVE OIL

Roughly chop 20g of the chives and char them in a small dry frying pan over a high heat for 3–4 minutes until almost black, then add them to a blender along with the remaining raw chives and the oil. Blitz until smooth, pass through a fine sieve or muslin-lined sieve and chill as quickly as possible.

Put the leeks in a large, heavy-based frying pan and add enough whey to the pan to just cover them. Cook over a medium heat for 6–8 minutes until the whey has evaporated. Preheat a griddle pan while they are cooking, then transfer the leeks to the griddle pan and cook for 3 minutes on each side until charred on both sides.

Divide the leeks among plates, add a generous serving of the whey sauce and drizzle with the burnt chive oil. Finish with chive and leek flowers.

SERVES 4, AS A STARTER

Burnt chive oil
50g chives
150ml sunflower oil

Leeks cooked in whey
20 baby leeks, trimmed
1kg natural yoghurt, hung in muslin
    overnight to strain the whey from the
    curd (equals 300ml whey)

chive and leek flowers, to serve
Whey Sauce (see page 157)

Tunworth cheese

Tunworth is a staple ingredient of my kitchen, not just as a nod to its origins in my home county, but because it is a world-class cheese with a well-deserved international reputation. Produced from the milk of Ayrshire cows roaming the lush grazing of the Hampshire Downs, and named after a hamlet there, it is our own, very British, Camembert – a soft, white-rinded cheese that is reminiscent and as good as any French variation.

Tunworth was first produced around 2004 as a small-scale artisan product, but it is now a really popular and award-winning cheese. For me, Tunworth showcases how far we have come in this country as producers of cheese, and it's important to me to champion the best of British like this. Just as it was in the beginning, when only a few rounds were being made, Tunworth is still handmade, in fact, the whole process is done by hand, from the cutting to the ladling to the boxing up.

The finished cheese has a soft, thin and wrinkled rind, a rich and earthy mushroom fragrance, and a creamy texture with a long-lasting sweet, deep and nutty flavour. If you're serving it on a cheeseboard, it is best eaten when young but deliciously ripe – the centre of the cheese should just give under gentle pressure from your thumb – to retain its fresh dairy flavours. As it ages it becomes more pungent and earthy, relating more to mushrooms than truffles, and it works well with salty and fruity flavours. When pairing food with Tunworth, all elements should be highlighted equally, and go for flavours that will accentuate rather than overwhelm. However, don't be afraid to use a few fairly robust flavours, as Tunworth acts as an excellent foil to these, too.

Its uses are many, from being simply baked in its box and served with bread, cured meats, pickles and chutneys, to exploiting its creaminess in a sauce or in gratins, but it's also great for making ice cream.

Deep-fried cheese in breadcrumbs is always a winner, but crunchy coated Tunworth served with this mustard mayonnaise takes it up a notch, and these little bites are firm favourites at the restaurant. Don't worry if the mix seems very firm while you are making it, when it is deep-fried and warm you are left with oozing centres of melting cheese. Don't cook these for too long – if you over-fry them they will explode and you'll lose all that lovely gooey Tunworth.

TUNWORTH CROQUETTES

Soak the gelatine in cold water for a few minutes until softened. Drain, squeeze out the excess water and leave the gelatine to one side.

Warm the milk in a small, heavy-based saucepan over a low heat until simmering, then remove from the heat. Melt the butter in a separate small, heavy-based saucepan over a low heat, add the flour and mix well. Cook the flour and butter for 3–4 minutes until the roux leaves the sides of the pan clean. Gradually add the warm milk to the roux and beat until smooth and thick, then remove from the heat and add the cheese and softened gelatine. Stir until the cheese has melted and the gelatine dissolved, and season with salt. Transfer the mixture to a container or bowl and chill in the fridge. When cool and set, roll the mixture into small evenly-sized balls.

For the crumb, season the flour with salt and put it in a shallow dish. Put the beaten eggs in a second shallow dish and the breadcrumbs in a third. Roll and coat the croquettes first in the flour, then the egg and finally with a generous coating of the breadcrumbs. Return to the fridge to set for 10 minutes.

To make the mayonnaise, whisk together the egg yolks, mustard and sherry vinegar in a medium bowl. Keep whisking to emulsify while slowly adding the oils until you have a thick mayonnaise. Season with a pinch of salt.

Deep-fry the Tunworth croquettes in batches in a pan of oil heated to 180°C for 4 minutes, or until lightly golden. Remove with a slotted spoon, drain on kitchen paper and season with salt. Add small spoonfuls of mustard mayonnaise to each plate, top each one with a croquette and finish with mustard leaf.

SERVES 4, AS A STARTER

Tunworth croquettes
5 gelatine leaves
200ml whole milk
100g unsalted butter
100g plain flour
250g Tunworth cheese, grated

Crumb
75g plain flour
2 eggs, beaten
100g panko breadcrumbs

Mustard mayonnaise
2 egg yolks
50g English mustard
1 tsp sherry vinegar
140ml rapeseed oil
140ml sunflower oil

salt, for seasoning
vegetable oil, for deep-frying
mustard leaf, to serve

I have been doing variations of this dish for years – any excuse to use Tunworth! – mixing up the offal content by using lamb tongue or crispy duck gizzards, although here we've used braised duck hearts. The Tunworth cheese and potato purée is delicious enough on its own, but the addition of rich meats makes this dish one of my absolute favourites.

TUNWORTH POTATO PURÉE WITH DUCK HEARTS

Bring a saucepan of salted water to the boil over a medium heat, add the potatoes and cook for 8–10 minutes until the potatoes are soft and tender. Drain in a colander and leave them to air dry.

Put the cream and cheese in a small, heavy-based saucepan over a low heat and warm until the cheese has melted into the cream. Add the salt. Blitz the cooked potatoes and cheesy milk together in a blender, pass through a fine sieve and leave to one side.

To make the garlic oil, bring a large saucepan of water to the boil and blanch the parsley leaves for 1 minute. Scoop them out with a slotted spoon and refresh in a bowl of iced water. Drain, squeeze out the excess water and blitz the parsley and three-cornered garlic or chives with the oil in a blender until smooth. Pass the herb oil through a muslin-lined sieve and chill.

Season the duck hearts with the pinch of salt. Place a small, non-stick frying pan over a medium heat. When the pan is hot, add the oil and the duck hearts and cook for 3 minutes, moving the hearts around occasionally to give them a light colour all over, then add the butter to the pan. Baste the butter over the hearts for another minute to finish cooking. Remove the hearts from the pan and drain on kitchen paper. Heat the reduced stock in a small pan, then add the hearts to the warm stock.

Warm the Tunworth potato purée over a low heat in a small saucepan and divide it evenly among bowls. Carve the duck hearts in half after they have rested and place 3 halves on top of the potato purée. Finish with a drizzle of green garlic oil (leftover oil will keep in the fridge for 3 days) and the freshly chopped three-cornered garlic, leek scapes, garlic chives or chives.

SERVES 4, AS A STARTER

Tunworth potato purée
375g Ratte potatoes, peeled and cut into 2.5cm dice
225ml double cream
125g Tunworth cheese, rind on
2 tsp salt

Duck hearts
6 duck hearts, trimmed of membrane
a pinch of salt
1 tbsp sunflower oil
20g unsalted butter
80ml reduced Brown Chicken Stock (see page 286)

Three-cornered garlic oil
100g flat-leaf parsley leaves
50g raw three-cornered garlic or chives
150ml sunflower oil

2 tbsp finely chopped three-cornered garlic, leek scapes, garlic chives, or regular chives, to serve

This is a delicious and simple way to enjoy this fantastic British cheese. All it needs is a few sprigs of thyme for flavour and some hot crusty bread for dipping into the oozing melting cheese. This chutney is an extra indulgence, using the natural sweetness of apples and raisins alongside figs and flavoured with warming winter spices. This makes enough to enjoy with a cheeseboard or pâté another day, and I find I end up making a lot of it to use up the abundance of figs I have every year in my garden at Cartmel.

WHOLE BAKED TUNWORTH WITH FIG AND APPLE CHUTNEY

Preheat the oven to 200°C/180°C Fan/Gas Mark 6.

To make the chutney, put the juniper, coriander, cloves, cinnamon and star anise in a piece of muslin and tie it with string to form a bag. Put the bag in a large, heavy-based saucepan with all the remaining ingredients except the Calvados and diced apple. Slowly reduce over a low heat until you have a thick, jam-like consistency, stirring regularly so it does not catch on the bottom of the pan. Add the Calvados and reduce for 1–2 minutes to the same jam-like consistency. Add the diced apple and cook gently for 5–6 minutes until the apple is tender but still holds its shape and you have a thick chutney consistency. Remove from the heat, cool at room temperature then transfer to a container and chill in the fridge.

Make a few slits in the top of the whole cheese and poke the thyme sprigs into the slits. Put the Tunworth cheese, in its open box (the top of the box removed), in the oven and bake for 20 minutes until soft and gooey. Remove from the oven and serve immediately in the box with the chutney and hot crusty bread or bread crisps.

SERVES 4-6, AS A STARTER

250g Tunworth cheese in a box
a few sprigs of thyme

Fig and apple chutney
5 juniper berries
1 tsp coriander seeds
2 cloves
2 cinnamon sticks
2 star anise
400ml cider vinegar
200g Bramley apples, peeled and grated
300g demerara sugar
130g white onions, finely diced
100ml fresh apple juice (shop-bought is fine)
130g dried figs, roughly diced
60g golden raisins
1 tsp salt
20ml Calvados
1kg Granny Smith apples, peeled, cored and diced

hot crusty bread or toatsed bread crisps, to serve

For me, this dish has it all: my favourite cheese, my favourite mushrooms and the most dramatic of vegetables, the romanesco, featuring both as a new take on couscous and also added whole as a flourish. Topped off with crispy pancetta and red basil cress, this dish is a wonderful blend of textures and flavours.

TUNWORTH SAUCE WITH ROMANESCO COUSCOUS, CEP MUSHROOMS AND CRISPY PANCETTA

Preheat the oven to 180°C/160°C Fan/Gas Mark 4.

To make the cheese sauce, pour the milk into a small, heavy-based saucepan over a low heat and add the butter. When the liquid is warm and the butter has melted remove the pan from the heat. Add the cheese to the warm milk and stir until it melts into the sauce, returning the pan to a low heat if necessary. Season with the salt. Add the xanthan gum off the heat and blitz the sauce with a hand-held blender, then pass it through a fine sieve into another small saucepan for a smoother finish and set aside.

Lay the slices of pancetta out on a baking tray and cook them in the oven for about 20 minutes until crisp. Remove from the oven, allow to cool slightly, then carefully transfer to kitchen paper to drain. Allow to cool fully to become very crisp.

While the pancetta is in the oven, blitz the romanesco florets in the bowl of a food processor on the pulse setting until fine and crumbly like couscous, regularly using a spatula to encourage any romanesco from the edges of the bowl down into the bowl. Transfer to a bowl and set aside.

Warm the sunflower oil in a non-stick frying pan over a medium heat and when the oil is hot place the mushrooms in the pan cut side down, season them with the salt and cook for 3–4 minutes, or until lightly golden. Turn the mushrooms over and add the butter and thyme. Allow the butter to foam and baste the mushrooms for a further 2 minutes. Remove them from the pan with a slotted spoon and drain on a plate lined with kitchen paper.

Melt the butter for the romanesco in a medium, heavy-based saucepan over a high heat, then add the 'couscous' and cook for 2–3 minutes, stirring regularly to ensure the 'couscous' cooks evenly. Season with sea salt.

Divide the 'couscous' among plates, place 3 mushroom halves on top of each serving and top with the shards of crispy pancetta. I like to crumble them slightly. Warm the cheese sauce gently and spoon it around the plates. Finish with the cooked florets of romanesco and red basil cress.

SERVES 4

Tunworth cheese sauce
220ml whole milk
30g unsalted butter
270g Tunworth cheese (rind on), cut into
    small even-sized pieces
pinch of salt
½ tsp xanthan gum

Crispy pancetta
8 thin slices of pancetta

Romanesco couscous
2 large heads of romanesco, broken into
    florets (discard the stalk)
25g unsalted butter
a pinch of salt

Cep mushrooms
2 tbsp sunflower oil
6 medium cep mushrooms, cleaned and
    halved lengthways
a pinch of sea salt
1 tbsp unsalted butter
2 sprigs of thyme

small cooked romanesco florets and red
    basil cress, to serve

A sweet dish using a savoury ingredient, and while a cheese ice cream might not seem an obvious idea, this is a great way to finish a meal. This ice cream lends itself perfectly to serving with summer berries, in this case the Alpine strawberry, and the slight acidity of the verjus syrup cuts through the natural creaminess of a young Tunworth.

TUNWORTH ICE CREAM WITH STRAWBERRIES AND VERJUS SYRUP

Combine the milk, cream and cheese in a large, heavy-based saucepan. Cook over a low–medium heat until the cheese has melted, then remove from the heat.

In a separate heatproof bowl combine the egg yolks, sugar and salt. Pour the milk mixture over the egg yolks slowly, whisking constantly in order to prevent the eggs from scrambling. Once all incorporated, return to the pan and cook over low a low heat, stirring constantly, until the temperature of the mixture reaches 80°C (check with a thermometer). Strain the mixture through a fine sieve into a clean bowl, and leave it to cool, then chill in the fridge. Once chilled, churn in an ice-cream maker until frozen. Transfer to a freezerproof container and store in the freezer until required.

To make the verjus syrup, combine the verjus and sugar in a small, heavy-based saucepan, bring to the boil, then turn down the heat and simmer until the mixture has thickened and has a syrup consistency.

Spoon a pool of room-temperature verjus syrup into each bowl. Scoop the ice cream into the centre and put the Alpine strawberries around the ice cream.

SERVES 4

Tunworth ice cream
250ml whole milk
285ml double cream
140g Tunworth cheese, rind on
3 egg yolks
200g caster sugar
a pinch of salt

Verjus syrup
260ml verjus
40g caster sugar

strawberries, such as Alpine, to serve

A marriage of perfectly matched partners: blue cheese and pear. This is a rich, creamy and cheesy porridge unusually made with millet that has a sweet, fruity twist, while the addition of marrowbone lends it a luxurious richness. One of my favourite British blue cheeses is Stichelton; it's similar to Stilton, but as the makers were unable to call it this, instead they named it after an early form of the village name. It's a raw milk cheese with a soft and creamy texture, laced with blue veins, which is produced on the Welbeck Estate in Nottingham, and is beautiful cooked into this super-rich dish.

MILLET PUDDING WITH GRILLED PEAR AND MARROWBONE

Preheat the oven to 200°C/180°C Fan/Gas Mark 6.

Spread the millet, barley and oats out on separate baking trays and place in the oven for 10–20 minutes until lightly toasted. Remove from the oven and transfer them to a medium, heavy-based saucepan over a medium heat with the chicken stock. Cook for 5–10 minutes, stirring regularly, until tender and almost like porridge. Remove from the heat, season with salt and leave to one side in the pan.

To make the blue cheese butter, blitz all the ingredients in a food procesor until evenly combined, then transfer to an airtight container and put in the fridge to chill and firm up. When firm, cut the butter into small 1cm cubes.

To cook the pears, put the vinegar, sugar, salt and spices in a saucepan with 300ml water, bring to the boil, then add the pears. Reduce the heat to a simmer and cover the pears with a circle of greaseproof paper that fits inside the pan. Cook for 5–10 minutes until the pears are just tender. Remove from the heat and leave the pears to cool in the poaching liquid.

Preheat the grill. When the pears are cool, remove them from the poaching liquid and cook under the grill for 6–8 minutes until hot and starting to crisp.

Gently reheat the millet porridge over a low heat, adding a splash of water if necessary to loosen it. When warmed, gradually stir in the blue cheese butter over the heat to allow it to melt. Just before serving, fold in the lightly whipped cream and spoon into bowls. Add the grilled pear and top with fine gratings of the bone marrow.

SERVES 6, AS A STARTER

Millet porridge
80g millet flakes
30g barley flakes
30g porridge oats
500ml White Chicken Stock (see page 286)
a pinch of salt
25ml double cream, lightly whipped

Blue cheese butter
75g unsalted butter, softened
75g blue cheese, such as Stichelton or Cornish Blue
juice of ½ lemon
1 tsp Dijon mustard
1 tbsp ground almonds
a pinch of salt

Grilled pear
200ml chardonnay vinegar
100g caster sugar
a pinch of salt
2 cloves
2 star anise
½ cinnamon stick
3 ripe Conference or Comice pears, peeled (stalk kept intact), halved lengthways and cored

Smoked Bone Marrow (see page 202), frozen, to serve

Our take on a favourite pairing – beetroot and goat's cheese. We've swapped the latter for the creamy, fresh and slightly sour-tasting sheep's curd, which is the perfect foil for sweet, juicy roasted beets. Wheat berries make a delicious alternative to rice and other grains, but surprisingly have not reached the same heights of popularity of quinoa and bulgur wheat, although they are easily available. They are quite tough when raw and so require lengthy boiling, but if you soak them in cold water overnight first you can speed up the cooking time. When tender and combined with the curd on the plate they make a delicious sauce.

ROAST BEETROOT WITH SHEEP'S CURD AND WHEAT BERRIES

Preheat the oven to 200°C/180°C Fan/Gas Mark 6.

Gently scrub the beetroots clean and dry with kitchen paper. Place each beetroot in a square of foil big enough to enclose it, drizzle a little rapeseed over and season with salt. Wrap and encase each beetroot in the foil. Bake in the oven for 1–1½ hours until tender. Remove from the oven and, when cool enough to handle but still warm, trim and peel the beetroots. Keep warm.

Put the wheat berries and mushroom broth in a small, heavy-based saucepan over a medium to low heat and cook for 20 minutes, adding extra water if they need it, until tender. When tender, season with the salt, add the cheese, lemon and parsley and stir until the cheese has melted. It should end up having a consistency almost like risotto.

To make the beetroot glaze, simply combine all the ingredients in a small bowl.

To cook the oriental greens, bring 300ml water to the boil in a small, heavy-based saucepan with the butter and salt then emulsify with a hand-held blender over the heat. Increase the heat to medium, add the greens and blanch them for 30 seconds. Remove them from the butter emulsion, drain and serve immediately.

Spoon the warm wheat berries on to plates, add the warm roasted beetroot pieces and spoon around dots of the beetroot glaze. Finish with small spoonfuls of the sheep's curd and oriental greens.

SERVES 4, AS A STARTER

Roasted beetroots
4 long purple beetroots, such as Cylindra
rapeseed oil

Wheat berries
150g wheat berries, soaked overnight in
    cold water
300ml Mushroom Broth (see page 192)
a pinch of salt
50g smoked Cheddar cheese, grated
zest of 1 lemon
1 tbsp chopped flat-leaf parsley

Beetroot glaze
75g white miso paste
15ml mirin
40ml fresh beetroot juice (shop-bought
    is fine)

Oriental greens
80g mixed oriental greens, such as Hon
    Tsai Tai, Welcome and No 80
200g unsalted butter
a pinch of salt

salt, for seasoning
sheep's curd, to serve

These little puddings make a delicious bite, full of rich and decadent flavours. A sort of variation on a savoury bread and butter pudding, buttery croissants are layered with a rich and creamy truffle-flavoured custard and finished with a hit of black garlic purée. Gently pan-fried, the individual bites have a crisp exterior but a beautifully soft interior.

TRUFFLE PUDDING WITH BLACK GARLIC

Preheat the oven to 200°C/180°C Fan/Gas Mark 6. In a medium bowl, combine the cream, eggs, truffle oil and a pinch of salt. Mix well and leave to one side.

Grease a 900g (2lb) loaf tin with butter and line it with baking parchment. Layer the croissant slices in the tray, pouring a small amount of the truffle custard mixture over the slices between each layer along with a sprinkle of some of the Parmesan. Finish the top layer with the remaining Parmesan. Cover the tray with foil and bake for 15 minutes. Remove the foil and bake for a further 15 minutes. Remove from the oven and leave to cool, then transfer to the fridge, with a couple of tins on top of the pudding to weigh it down and flatten it. Keep it in the fridge until the custard has set.

Blitz the black garlic, chicken stock and a pinch of salt together in a blender until smooth. Pass through a fine sieve.

Cut the truffle pudding into six portions and warm through in a non-stick ovenproof frying pan over a medium heat until golden brown on both sides, then transfer to the oven for 5–8 minutes to warm through completely.

Place a portion of truffle pudding on each plate with the room-temperature black garlic purée and a thin slice of fresh truffle.

SERVES 6, AS A LIGHT BITE

250ml double cream

2 eggs

2 tbsp truffle oil

a pinch of salt

butter, for greasing

5 large croissants, slightly stale, cut
    lengthways into thin slices

40g Parmesan cheese, grated

2 heads of black garlic, skins removed
    (shop-bought or see page 90)

50ml White Chicken Stock (see page 286)

salt, for seasoning

fresh black truffle, to serve

Ice-cream sandwiches are a nostalgic treat and a delicious combination of crunchy and creamy textures. This is our version, made using buttermilk, which has a slightly sour taste and so makes a less rich ice cream. The gingerbread adds a lovely hit of flavour and crunch, complemented by the sticky sweetness of the whitecurrant jam and herby, floral aromas of the chervil purée. A winning combination.

FROZEN BUTTERMILK SANDWICH

Line a 1-litre terrine mould or loaf tin with a triple layer of cling film, twice the size of the tin.

To make the semi-freddo, separate the eggs and put the whites and yolks in different bowls. Whisk the whites with a hand-held electric whisk or in a stand mixer with 100g of the sugar for 5 minutes until the mixture forms stiff peaks. Leave to one side.

Beat the egg yolks with the remaining sugar until creamy and pale, then fold in the buttermilk. Lightly whip the cream until it forms soft peaks, and fold it through the yolk and buttermilk mix, then finally fold through the meringue. Pour the mixture into the lined terrine mould or loaf tin, cover with cling film and freeze for 6 hours.

Put the whitecurrants in a medium, heavy-based saucepan with 500ml water, bring to the boil, reduce the heat to a simmer and cook for 5 minutes until the berries are soft and have released their juices. Pass through a fine sieve, and for every litre of juice weigh out 1kg of caster sugar. Return to the pan and cook the juice and sugar together over a low heat for 15–20 minutes, stirring regularly, until the mixture has a jam consistency and has reached 105°C on a sugar thermometer. Remove from the heat, allow to cool and transfer to the fridge to chill until needed.

To make the purée, gently heat the sugar and 50ml water in a small saucepan over a low heat until the sugar has dissolved. Add the chervil and cook for 30 seconds–1 minute until slightly wilted then tip into a small blender and blitz until smooth. Add the xantham gum and chill in the fridge until ready to serve.

Preheat the oven to 120°C/100°C Fan/Gas Mark ¼. Cut the gingerbread into 20 thin slices. Dry in the oven for 10 minutes.

Spread a thin layer of chervil purée on one side of half the slices of dry gingerbread. Spread a thin layer of whitecurrant jam on one side of the other slices. Cut the semi-freddo into slices and sandwich each slice between two pieces of gingerbread. Serve immediately.

SERVES 10

Buttermilk semi-freddo
2 eggs
120g caster sugar
300ml buttermilk
150ml double cream

Whitecurrant jam
1kg whitecurrants
caster sugar (weigh after cooking the whitecurrants)

Chervil purée
50g caster sugar
30g chervil
½ tsp xanthan gum

Gingerbread (see page 252)

Greengages and buttermilk are fantastic together. These little plums start to ripen in August and September; when ripe they have a sweet, aromatic flesh that works really well with the mild flavour of creamy buttermilk. The custard isn't for the faint-hearted, as it's very creamy and rich, and very moreish! The custard base can be made in advance, then left in a bowl in the fridge overnight and baked the next day for ease.

BUTTERMILK CUSTARD WITH GREENGAGE COMPOTE

Preheat the oven to 65°C, or the lowest setting on your oven.

Start by making the aerated milk crisp. Put the milk and glucose in a small, heavy-based saucepan and warm to 80°C. Remove from the heat and create a froth by blitzing it with a hand-held blender. Spoon the froth on to a baking tray lined with baking parchment and dry out in the oven for 12 hours. Remove from the oven and leave to cool. Break the milk crisp into large shards and store in an airtight container.

In a bowl, fold together the egg yolks and caster sugar (do not whisk). Leave to one side.

Put the milk and buttermilk powder in a small, heavy-based saucepan over a low–medium heat, bring to the boil, and as soon as it has reached the boil remove from the heat and leave to cool for 10 minutes. Pour the milk on to the egg yolks and sugar, lightly whisk, then chill. Preheat the oven to 160°C/140°C Fan/Gas Mark 2. Divide the buttermilk custard mixture evenly among four heatproof bowls and cover the bowls with cling film. Bake in a bain marie (see page 302) in the oven for 30–35 minutes, or until the custard is just set, with a small wobble. Remove from the oven and allow to cool in the bain marie. When cool, transfer to the fridge to chill for 3 hours, or until fully set.

To make the greengage compote, put all the greengages and verjus in a medium, heavy-based saucepan over a low heat and stew until all the fruit has broken down and the juice has reduced, stirring regularly to make sure the compote does not catch on the pan. Once the fruit has broken down, pass through a sieve back into the pan and stir in the honey.

Divide the custard among bowls and top with a couple of buttermilk crisp shards and some warm greengage compote.

SERVES 4

_____

Aerated milk crisp
240ml whole milk
50g liquid glucose

Buttermilk custard
9 egg yolks
125g caster sugar
125g buttermilk powder
600ml whole milk

Greengage compote
500g ripe greengage plums, halved and
    stoned
30ml verjus
5 tbsp honey

FRUIT

These little bite-size tarts are a lovely way to finish a meal, and are particularly good around Christmas time, filling the kitchen with festive aromas as they bake. All the elements can be made in advance and assembled when needed, which is ideal if you've got guests popping in over the holidays. Keep the pastry in the freezer along with the ice cream, poach and caramelise the quince and store in the fridge until required.

QUINCE TART WITH GINGERBREAD ICE CREAM

Preheat the oven to 195°C/175°C Fan/Gas Mark 5, grease a 900g (2lb) loaf tin and line it with baking parchment.

To make the gingerbread, melt the butter and the molasses in a heavy-based saucepan over a medium heat. Once melted, remove from the heat and leave to one side. Mix the flour, caster sugar, baking powder, salt and lemon zest together in a large bowl. Blitz the milk, stem ginger, cinnamon, ground ginger and fresh ginger in a small food processor until smooth, then pass through a fine sieve. Beat the eggs in a bowl and mix with the ginger milk, then add the molasses mix. Whisk the wet ingredients into the dry ingredients little by little, until fully incorporated. Transfer the mixture to the prepared tin and bake for 50 minutes. Once cooked (a skewer inserted into the middle of the cake should come out clean), remove from the oven and leave to cool. Remove from the tin and cut into suitable size 125g pieces, wrap each piece in cling film and freeze.

To make the ice cream, bring the milk to the boil in a heavy-based saucepan over a medium heat. Combine the egg yolks, sugar and salt in a heatproof bowl. Gradually pour the hot milk into the yolk and sugar mixture, whisking constantly to prevent the eggs from scrambling. Return to the pan and cook over a low heat until the temperature of the mixture reaches 80°C (check with a thermometer), stirring constantly. Remove from the heat and add the fresh or defrosted from frozen gingerbread, then allow to cool. Blitz in a blender until smooth then churn in an ice-cream maker until frozen. Transfer the ice cream to a piping bag fitted with a star nozzle and keep in the freezer.

Recipe continues on the next page

MAKES 8

Gingerbread
80g unsalted butter
50g molasses
400g plain flour
250g caster sugar
1 tsp baking powder
a pinch of salt
zest of 1 lemon
50ml whole milk
80g preserved stem ginger (from a jar)
½ tsp ground cinnamon
1 tsp ground ginger
50g fresh ginger
2 eggs

Gingerbread ice cream
500ml whole milk
2 egg yolks
25g caster sugar
½ tsp salt
125g gingerbread, from recipe above, roughly broken into chunks

Pastry
270g plain flour, plus extra for dusting
150g unsalted butter, softened
75g soft light brown sugar
1 tsp salt
1 egg

While the ice cream is churning, make the tart bases. Mix the flour and the butter together by hand in a bowl until the mixture resembles breadcrumbs, then add the sugar, salt and egg and keep mixing until you have a smooth dough. Wrap the dough in cling film and put it in the fridge to rest for 1 hour. Once rested, dust a work surface with flour, unwrap the dough and roll it out to a thickness of 3mm. Cut to size with a cutter or upside-down small bowl to fit eight 4cm small tart tins. Line the tins with the pastry, pushing the pastry all the way down the sides, lightly prick the base of the tartlets and line them with greaseproof paper and a few baking beans. Bake blind for 8 minutes. Remove from the oven and allow to cool in the tins, then transfer to a wire rack to cool completely. Store in an airtight container.

Peel and cut the core away from the quince. In a small, heavy-based saucepan bring the wine and 200g of the sugar to the boil. Reduce the heat to low, add the quince and simmer for 18–20 minutes, or until the quince are just tender but still have a little bite. Remove from the heat and leave the quince to cool in the wine. Cut the cooled quince into 5mm dice. Make a caramel with the remaining sugar: heat the sugar in a heavy-based pan over a medium heat, without stirring, until it begins to melt, then start to stir and keep stirring until all the sugar crystals have dissolved. Cook for about 10 minutes until the sugar is a dark honey colour. Remove from the heat and add the butter, whisking constantly. Add the diced quince to the pan and cook for a further 30 seconds. Remove the caramelised quince from the pan and allow to cool.

Place a small amount of the quince in each tart case then pipe a rosette of ice cream on top to cover and serve immediately.

Poached quince
1 quince
350ml red wine
250g caster sugar
50g unsalted butter

This is a celebration of unusual fruits and herbs that we forage for around the farm and the local area. Meadowsweet flowers have an extraordinary honey almond scent that makes a wonderful flavouring for mousses and yoghurts. Here the creamy herby mousse is lifted with the little pineberries and a citrusy aromatic soup infused with freshly picked pineapple weed. If you've not come across them before, pineberries are beautiful little white strawberries with red seeds that are a cross between two alpine strawberries. The twist here is not just the colour but the flavour, as they have a distinct pineapple tang.

MEADOWSWEET MOUSSE WITH PINEAPPLE WEED

Start by making the mousse. In a medium, heavy-based saucepan, boil together the milk, salt and dried meadowsweet over a medium heat, and once boiling, remove from the heat. Mix the honey and egg yolks together in a heatproof bowl. Soak the gelatine in cold water for a few minutes until softened. Drain, squeeze out the excess water and leave the gelatine to one side. When the milk has boiled, gradually pour it on to the egg yolk and honey mixture and mix well. Return the mixture back to the pan along with the gelatine and cook over a low heat for a further 5 minutes, stirring constantly. Strain through a fine sieve into a heatproof bowl set over ice and gradually whisk in the sheep's yoghurt. Whip the cream in a separate bowl to soft peaks. When the yoghurt mix is cool, fold through the semi-whipped cream. Transfer the mousse mixture to a plastic container and keep in the fridge until needed.

To make the pineapple weed soup, bring the milk and lemon zest to the boil in a medium, heavy-based saucepan over a medium heat. Remove from the heat, add the pineapple weed buds and allow to infuse at room temperature for 3 hours. Pass through a muslin-lined sieve. Combine the yolks and sugar in a bowl, pour over the infused milk and mix well. Return to a heavy-based saucepan and cook over a low–medium heat, stirring occasionally, until the mixture reaches 80°C (check with a thermometer). Pass through a muslin-lined sieve once more and chill in the fridge to thicken.

When ready to serve, scoop out a serving of mousse and place in the middle of the plate. Drizzle the soup around it and garnish with the pineberries and a few fronds of bronze fennel.

SERVES 4

————

Meadowsweet yoghurt mousse
125ml whole milk
a pinch of salt
10g dried meadowsweet
50g honey
3 egg yolks
2 gelatine leaves
125g sheep's yoghurt (not hung)
160ml double cream

Pineapple weed soup
1 litre whole milk
zest of 1 lemon
80g pineapple weed
3 egg yolks
75g caster sugar

To serve
Fresh pineberries
Bronze fennel fronds

POACHED RHUBARB WITH BROWN BUTTER ICE CREAM

To make the apple crisps, put the sugar in a small saucepan with 50ml water over a low heat and warm gently until the sugar has dissolved. Remove from the heat and leave to cool. Slice the apple as thinly as possible using a mandoline – try and keep the natural apple shape (leave them intact: skin on and core in). Dip the apple slices into the cooled sugar syrup to cover then lay them flat on a baking sheet lined with baking parchment. Dry the apple slices in the oven at 55°C, or as low as the oven will go, for 12 hours. Remove, leave to cool completely and store in an airtight container.

To make the brown butter ice cream, put the butter in a medium, heavy-based saucepan over a medium heat and cook for 10–15 minutes until the melted butter is dark brown and has a nutty aroma. Remove from the heat and allow to cool (the butter will be extremely hot, so be very careful). When cool, strain through a muslin-lined sieve and discard the solids. Transfer to the fridge.

Put the milk in a small, heavy-based saucepan, bring to the boil then remove from the heat. Combine the egg yolks and sugar in a heatproof bowl and gradually pour the milk over the eggs, whisking constantly. Return to the pan and cook over a low heat, stirring constantly, until the temperature of the mixture reaches 80°C (check with a thermometer). Remove from the heat and, using a hand-held blender, gradually blend the cooled brown butter into the ice cream mixture. Leave to cool completely, then churn in an ice-cream maker until frozen. Transfer to a freezerproof container and store in the freezer until required.

To poach the rhubarb, put the sugar, grenadine, citrus peels and vanilla pod in a medium, heavy-based saucepan over a medium heat with 500ml water and bring to the boil, then reduce the heat to a simmer and cook for 4 minutes. Remove from the heat, add the rhubarb stalks and allow to cool in the liquor.

To make the sorrel syrup, put the sugar and 200ml water in a container and freeze until slushy. Transfer the ice to a blender, add the fresh sorel and blitz. While blending, add the xanthan to thicken. Pass through a fine sieve and chill.

Divide the ice cream among dishes, cut the rhubarb into smaller pieces and arrange them on the plates, adding some poaching liquor too. Drizzle over the sorrel syrup and add an apple crisp to each serving. Serve immediately.

SERVES 4

Apple crisps
50g caster sugar
1 Granny Smith apple

Brown butter ice cream
100g unsalted butter
400ml whole milk
4 egg yolks
90g caster sugar

Poached rhubarb
400g caster sugar
50ml grenadine
peel of 1 orange
peel of 1 lemon
½ vanilla pod
4 pink rhubarb stalks, cut into 5cm batons

Sorrel syrup
30g caster sugar
45g large sorrel leaves
½ tsp xanthan gum

Although originally a Canadian variety, the Harrow sweet pear grows well in Britain, producing good crops of really juicy, sweet fruit with a lovely smooth, yellow skin tinged with a pinky red blush. They taste as good as they look, and although they are fantastic when really ripe and juicy, for poaching purposes they are best cooked while still firm. Cobnuts are in season at the same time; related to the hazelnut, they are a delicacy that originated in Kent, and their lovely sweet flavour is delicious in these airy little crisps. Drizzled with rosehip syrup, this is the flavours of autumn in a bowl.

POACHED PEARS WITH ROSEHIP AND COBNUT CRUMB

To make the ice cream, soak the gelatine in cold water for a few minutes until softened. Drain, squeeze out the excess water and leave the gelatine to one side. Combine the yolks and sugar in a heatproof bowl. Put the cream cheese and milk in a medium, heavy-based saucepan over a medium heat and bring to the boil, then remove from the heat and slowly pour the mixture over the yolks, whisking constantly to prevent the eggs from scrambling. Once all incorporated, return to the pan and cook, stirring constantly, over a high heat until the temperature of the mixture reaches 80°C (check with a thermometer). Remove from the heat and stir in the gelatine. Strain the mixture through a fine sieve into a clean bowl and leave it to cool, then chill in the fridge. Once chilled, churn in an ice-cream maker until frozen. Transfer to a freezerproof container and store in the freezer until required.

To poach the pears, put 350ml water in a saucepan with the sugar, wine and lemon juice. Bring to the boil, add the pears and cover with a circle of greaseproof paper that fits inside the pan. Reduce the heat to a simmer and cook for 5–10 minutes until just tender. Remove from the heat and leave the pears to cool in the liquid, then chill in the fridge. When cool, strain off and freeze the poaching liquid for another recipe.

Line a baking tray with baking parchment. To make the cobnut crumb, put the glucose and caster sugar in a small, heavy-based saucepan over a medium heat with 1 tablespoon of water, bring to the boil and make a light caramel, without stirring – the temperature on a sugar thermometer should reach 165–170°C. Add the cobnuts, remove the pan from the heat and pour the mixture on to the lined baking tray, spreading the nuts evenly, and leave to cool. Bake the bread dice in the oven at 180°C/160°C Fan/Gas Mark 4 for 6–8 minutes until crisp, then remove and leave to cool. Smash the cobnut praline into small pieces using the end of a rolling pin and mix with the crisp bread cubes in a bowl. Add the icing sugar and cornflour and mix well. Fold through the egg and melted butter. Spread out on a baking tray lined with baking parchment, in an even layer and bake at 180°C/160°C Fan/Gas Mark 4 for 20 minutes until lightly golden. Remove from the oven, cool, then blitz in a blender to a coarse crumb.

Cut the poached pears into quarters or chunks and divide among bowls. Add a scoop of ice cream, sprinkle with cobnut crumb and drizzle with rosehip syrup.

SERVES 4

—————

Sweet cheese ice cream
1 gelatine leaf
4 egg yolks
100g caster sugar
225g cream cheese
300ml whole milk

Poached pears
250g caster sugar
250ml dry white wine
juice of 1 lemon
4 sweet Harrow or other pears, peeled, halved lengthways and cored

Cobnut crumb
1 tbsp liquid glucose
50g caster sugar
30g cobnuts
3 slices of white bread, cut into small dice
30g icing sugar
40g cornflour
½ egg, beaten
45g unsalted butter, melted

Rosehip syrup
see Tomato Bone Marrow recipe (page 34)

A really simple mousse – and a dessert that celebrates local apples at their best – the granita is a great way to use up a glut at harvest time. Apple marigold is a real find for flavouring, and I would not have known about this herb's existence if we didn't grow our own produce. It smells of anise, with notes of hay, and has a spicy warmth with notes, of course, of apple. I absolutely love this herb, so I like to add leaves as a garnish so that each appley mouthful enhances the flavours of the granita and the cider mousse.

APPLE GRANITA WITH CIDER MOUSSE

Mix the apple juice with the lemon juice to keep it from turning brown. Soak the gelatine in cold water for a few minutes until softened. Drain, squeeze out the excess water and leave the gelatine to one side. Pour half of the juice into a small, heavy-based saucepan over a low heat and reduce by half. Add the gelatine while the pan is still over the heat, stir until dissolved, then pour back into the remaining apple juice. Transfer the mixture to a freezerproof container and freeze for 4 hours until frozen solid.

To make the cider mousse, soak the gelatine in cold water for a few minutes until softened. Drain, squeeze out the excess water and leave the gelatine to one side. Put the cider, egg yolks, lemon juice and sugar in a heatproof bowl and place it over a pan of simmering water, making sure the bottom of the bowl does not touch the water. Whisk constantly over the heat for 15–20 minutes to incorporate air into the mixture until it is thick and aerated. Add the gelatine and incorporate well, then remove from the heat and chill in the fridge for 10 minutes. Whip the cream until it forms soft peaks. Fold through the chilled, almost-set mousse, transfer to an airtight container and chill in the fridge for 4–5 hours until set.

Scrape the granita with a fork, to form small, fine ice crystals. Place three spoonfuls of mousse on each plate and fill the gaps between each spoonful with granita. Top each mound of mousse with apple marigold leaves and serve immediately.

SERVES 4

Apple granita
500ml fresh apple juice, such as Cox or
    Braeburn
juice of ½ lemon
1 gelatine leaf

Cider mousse
1½ gelatine leaves
50ml medium cider
4 egg yolks
juice of ½ lemon
100g caster sugar
340ml double cream

apple marigold leaves, to serve

Artichoke might seem an unusual ingredient for an ice cream, but try it, it really works. The earthy, malty flavours of the sweetened artichokes infuse the cream and are balanced by the nutty walnut crumb, rich buttery butterscotch and sweet and sour cherries.

To the north of Cartmel in spring we can find wild cherries in a good season; British cherries are renowned for being sweeter than foreign imports, and these wild fruits have a superior flavour.

MACERATED CHERRIES WITH ARTICHOKE ICE CREAM AND BUTTERSCOTCH SAUCE

To make the ice cream, melt the butter in a large, heavy-based saucepan over a medium heat, add the grated artichokes and cook for 15–20 minutes, stirring, until golden brown. Remove from the pan and strain off the butter. In another heavy-based saucepan bring the milk, cream and milk powder to the boil, then remove from the heat and blitz with the artichokes in a blender until smooth. Pass through a fine sieve. Return the artichoke milk to a heavy-based saucepan and whisk in the egg yolks and caster sugar then cook over a low heat, stirring constantly, until the temperature of the mixture reaches 80°C (check with a thermometer). Remove from the heat, leave to cool and chill in the fridge. Once chilled, churn in an ice-cream maker until frozen. Transfer to a freezerproof container and store in the freezer until required.

Preheat the oven to 180°C/160°C Fan/Gas Mark 4 and line a baking tray with baking parchment.

To make the walnut crumb, put the caster sugar and glucose in a small, heavy-based saucepan over a medium heat with 1 tablespoon of water, bring to the boil and heat to 170–180°C on a sugar thermometer until the mixture turns into a light caramel. Add the walnut halves, remove the pan from the heat and pour the mixture out on to the lined baking tray. Spread the nuts out evenly and leave to cool. Bake the bread dice in the oven on another baking tray for 6–8 minutes until crisp, then remove from the oven and leave to cool. Smash the walnut praline into small pieces using the end of a rolling pin and mix them with the crisp bread cubes in a bowl. Add the icing sugar and cornflour and mix well. Fold through the beaten egg and melted butter. Transfer to a lined baking tray, spread out into an even layer and bake in the oven for 20 minutes until lightly golden. Remove from the oven, leave to cool then blitz in a blender to a coarse crumble.

To make the butterscotch sauce, melt the butter with half of the sugar over a low heat in a medium, heavy-based saucepan. Once melted, add the cream, bring to the boil and boil for 4 minutes, then remove from the heat.

SERVES 4

Artichoke ice cream
100g unsalted butter
200g Jerusalem artichokes, washed and grated
300ml whole milk
100ml double cream
15g milk powder
4 egg yolks
50g caster sugar

Walnut crumb
50g caster sugar
1 tbsp liquid glucose
30g walnut halves
3 thin slices of white bread, cut into small dice
30g icing sugar
40g cornflour
½ egg, beaten
45g unsalted butter, melted

Butterscotch sauce
110g unsalted butter
70g caster sugar
130ml double cream

In a separate small, heavy-based saucepan make a dark caramel by cooking the remaining sugar, without stirring, until the temperature on a sugar thermometer reaches 180–200°C, then remove from the heat and slowly add the warm cream, whisking constantly. Leave to one side until it reaches room temperature.

Put the cherries in a bowl. Sprinkle over the sugar, add the vanilla, pepper and cinnamon, stir and leave to macerate at room temperature for 30 minutes.

Place a spoonful of ice cream on each plate, add the cherries, drizzle with the butterscotch sauce and sprinkle each serving with the walnut crumb.

Macerated cherries
500g fresh cherries, stoned
30g caster sugar
¼ vanilla pod, seeds scraped
a pinch of freshly ground black pepper
¼ cinnamon stick

Once a really popular British fruit, gooseberries don't seem to be as widely used as they once were, which is a shame as they are very versatile. This may be in part due to the fact that gooseberries can be quite tart, but if you choose slightly under-ripe fruits and cook them with a little sugar they are very tasty and sweet. The creamy, sharp mousse here is beautifully complemented by the sweet crunch of honeycomb and the refreshing, palate-cleansing granita, and all the elements can be prepared in advance, making assembly really easy.

GOOSEBERRY MOUSSE WITH HONEYCOMB AND BUTTERMILK GRANITA

To make the gooseberry mousse, start by making the purée. Put the frozen gooseberries, sugar and 150ml water in a medium, heavy-based saucepan. Cook for 10 minutes over a medium–high heat, or until the berries are soft, then remove from the heat and blitz in a blender until smooth.

Soak the gelatine for the mousse in cold water for a few minutes until softened. Drain, squeeze out the excess water and leave the gelatine to one side. Put the gooseberry purée, egg yolks and sugar in a heatproof bowl and place the bowl over a pan of simmering water, making sure the bottom of the bowl is not touching the water. Whisk constantly for 30–40 minutes to incorporate air into the mix until thick and aerated. Add the soaked gelatine to the bowl over the pan of simmering water, and incorporate well using a spatula, then chill the mixture in the fridge for 10 minutes. Whisk the cream in a bowl to form soft peaks, then fold it through the chilled, almost-set mousse. Transfer the mousse to an airtight container and put in the fridge to chill for 4–5 hours until fully set.

To make the granita, put the sugar in a small saucepan with 150ml water and bring to the boil, then remove from the heat and stir in the gelatine until melted. Add all the remaining ingredients and blitz together using a hand-held blender. Transfer the mixture to a freezeable container and freeze for 4 hours until solid. Scrape with a fork to form small ice crystals and return to the freezer.

Line a baking tray with baking parchment. To make the honeycomb, put the honey, sugar, glucose and 20ml water in a small, heavy-based saucepan over a medium heat. Cook the mixture without stirring until it reaches 160°C on a sugar thermometer, then remove the pan from the heat and whisk in the bicarbonate of soda. Pour the honeycomb into the lined tray and allow to cool. When cool, break into small pieces.

Divide the mousse among plates, break up the granita crystals again with a fork and add them to each serving, then top with a piece of honeycomb.

SERVES 4

Gooseberry purée
500g frozen gooseberries
150g caster sugar

Mousse
4 gelatine leaves
300g gooseberry purée, as above
4 egg yolks
125g caster sugar
250ml whipping cream

Buttermilk granita
150g caster sugar
1 gelatine leaf
200ml buttermilk
juice of ½ lemon

Honeycomb
35g honey
85g caster sugar
30g liquid glucose
10g bicarbonate of soda

Aniseed is one of my favourite flavours, which I use across many of my dishes, and of course it lends itself so well to desserts. This rich, creamy liquorice custard is the perfect foil for the sharp, acidic tang of the sea buckthorn. Although we don't grow mangoes, this fruit helps to soften the powerful flavour of these tiny orange berries which appear in summer on plants along the west coast of Cumbria and even now along some roadsides. Picking them can be challenging because of their sharp thorns, but you only need a few of them to feel their kick! If you can't get the berries, you can buy the juice, freshly pressed.

LIQUORICE CUSTARD WITH ICED SEA BUCKTHORN

In a small, heavy-based saucepan over a low heat, warm the Pontefract cakes, along with 150ml water until the cakes have melted (don't let it boil) and the mixture is thick and glossy. Add the cream, stir well and heat through to make a smooth, evenly coloured mixture.

Meanwhile, in a bowl, fold together the egg yolks and caster sugar (do not whisk). Pour the cream mixture on to the egg yolks and sugar, mixing thoroughly with a rubber spatula or wooden spoon.

Preheat the oven to 160°C/140°C Fan/Gas Mark 2. Divide the custard mixture evenly between six small heatproof bowls and cover each bowl with a double layer of cling film. Place into a deep-sided roasting tray and pour boiling water into the roasting dish until it reaches halfway up the sides of the bowls.

Bake for 15-20 minutes, or until the custard has a small wobble. Remove from the oven, remove the cling film and allow to cool in the bain marie. When cool, transfer to the fridge to chill for 2 hours, or until fully set.

To make the sea buckthorn granita, start with the syrup. Put the sugar in a heavy-based saucepan with 300ml water and bring to the boil, stirring gently until the sugar has fully dissolved. Remove from the heat and allow to cool. When cool, add the sea buckthorn juice.

Blitz all the granita ingredients together in a blender. Transfer the mixture to a freezerproof container and freeze for 4 hours until solid. Scrape the top with a fork before serving, to form small, fine ice crystals.

Remove the set custards from the fridge, cover with the sea buckthorn granita, top with fresh loganberries and serve immediately.

SERVES 6

Liquorice custard
200g Pontefract cakes
400ml double cream
5 egg yolks
50g caster sugar

Sea buckthorn granita

Syrup:
100g caster sugar
500ml sea buckthorn juice

Granita base:
40g mango flesh, blitzed to a purée in a
    blender
80ml cooled Earl Grey tea
600ml sea buckthorn syrup, from recipe
    above
90g natural yoghurt
juice of 1 lemon
½ tsp xanthan gum

fresh loganberries, to serve

Blackcurrants are abundant around the farm, they grow easily and don't need much attention, popping up all over the bushes in the height of summer as bright little deep, red-black jewels. They have to be pulled off the plants as strings to prevent damaging the skins and to preserve the flavoursome juice, and they need to be used quickly, within a few days of harvesting, or they shrivel or go mouldy. They can be used in so many different ways, and this dish offers a few ideas in one!

FROZEN BLACKCURRANT MOUSSE

First, make the blackcurrant purée. Put the currants and sugar in a small heavy-based saucepan over a low heat and bring to the boil. Reduce the heat and simmer for 7–8 minutes until the currants have broken down. Remove from the heat and cool, then blitz to a smooth purée in a blender. Pass through a fine sieve and keep in the fridge until needed. Preheat the oven to its lowest possible temperature.

To make the meringues, put the sugar and glucose in a small, heavy-based saucepan with 20ml water and boil until it reaches 170–180°C on a sugar thermometer and becomes thick and syrupy. While it is boiling and reducing, put the egg whites in a stand mixer fitted with the whisk attachment and whisk until stiff and fluffy. Pour the hot sugar mix into the egg whites with the mixer running in a steady stream down the sides of the bowl, and whisk until the mixture reaches room temperature. Transfer the meringue mixture to a bowl and gently fold in the blackcurrant purée until it's fully incorporated. Spread the meringue on to a baking sheet lined with baking parchment to a thickness of 5mm and dust with the juniper powder. Dehydrate in the oven overnight or for 12 hours, then break into shards and store in an airtight container until needed.

To make the mousse, put the egg yolks in a stand mixer fitted with the whisk attachment and whisk until light and airy. Put the sugar in a small, heavy-based saucepan with 125ml water and bring to the boil. Boil for 5 minutes until thickened, then slowly pour it into the yolks, whisking constantly. Keep whisking until the bottom of the bowl cools to room temperature. Meanwhile, whip the cream in a bowl to soft peaks. Transfer the yolk mixture to a separate bowl and gently fold in the blackcurrant purée and crème de cassis. When fully incorporated, fold in the semi-whipped cream. Add the mixture to four half-sphere silicone moulds and freeze for 8 hours. If you do not have silicone moulds, pour the hot jelly mix into a cling film-lined baking tray and allow to set the same way, but you will have to turn the mousse out and cut to the desired size using a knife.

Preheat the oven to 200°C/180°C Fan/Gas Mark 6. To make the malto, blitz the blackcurrants to a fine powder in a blender. Roast the hazelnuts on a baking sheet lined with baking parchment for 10–12 minutes, or until deeply golden. Leave to cool, then add the hazelnuts to the blender with the blackcurrant powder and blitz again. Put the

SERVES 4

Blackcurrant purée
1kg fresh or frozen blackcurrants
160g caster sugar

Blackcurrant and juniper meringues
70g caster sugar
1 tbsp liquid glucose
1½ egg whites
50g blackcurrant purée, as above
15 juniper berries, ground to a fine powder

Frozen blackcurrant mousse
4 egg yolks
125g caster sugar
500ml double cream
250g blackcurrant purée, as above
2 tbsp crème de cassis

Blackcurrant and hazelnut malto
20g freeze-dried blackcurrants
50g hazelnuts
75g maltodextrin
20ml hazelnut oil
10g caster sugar
¼ tsp salt

Blackcurrant and anise sauce
150g caster sugar
10 star anise
100g blackcurrant purée, as above
juice of ½ lemon

malto in a bowl, add the powdered fruit and nut mixture and whisk well. Slowly pour in the oil, whisking constantly, and whisk until combined. Season with sugar and salt.

To make the blackcurrant and anise sauce, put 300ml water in a small, heavy-based saucepan with the sugar and star anise and bring to the boil over a medium heat, then reduce the heat to a simmer and reduce by half. When reduced, strain the syrup to remove the star anise and mix in the blackcurrant purée and lemon juice. Allow to cool.

Unmould the mousse on to plates by briefly plunging the moulds into warm water to release them. Arrange a few meringue shards around the mousse and scatter around the blackcurrant and hazelnut malto. Drizzle the blackcurrant and anise sauce around each serving to finish.

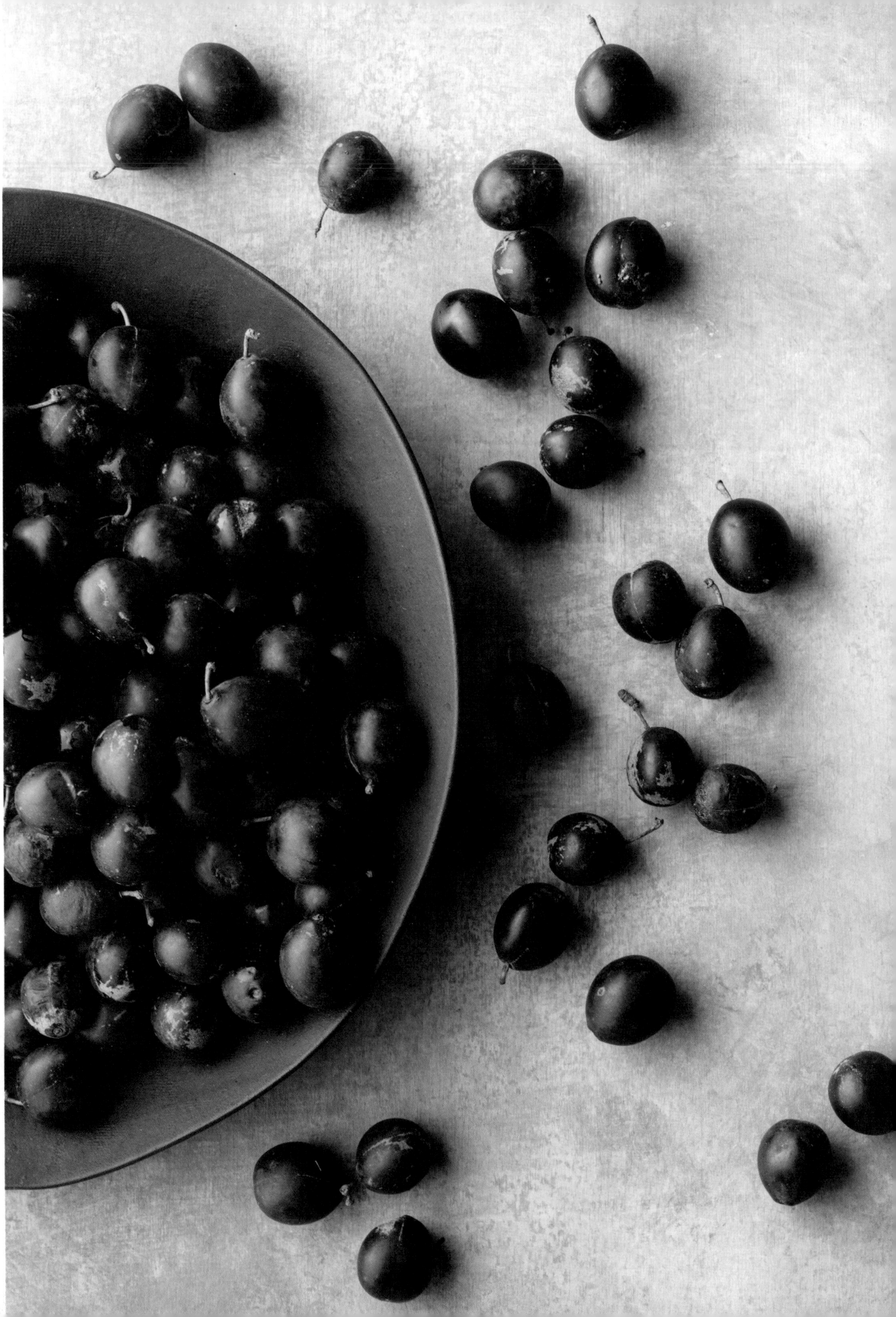

Damsons

The really intensely flavoured purple fruits grown in the Lake District are world famous, as the valleys act as the perfect microclimate for growing them. Damsons are a smaller subspecies of the better-known plum, and although for a while they were not as popular, they are finally getting a well-deserved comeback and are much more widely available, once they are in season between late August and October. Aside from their fantastic flavour, I like to use these local fruits because they are yet another connection to our surroundings, as we forage for them in the wild, and also grow them in the orchards at Our Farm.

Damsons are a small fruit with dark blue-black skin and a strong, sour flavour, much richer, darker and stronger than that of plums. The taste of these juicy fruits is amazing, but not when raw; it is when they are cooked that they come alive and have a remarkable depth of flavour. The wild varieties are really tart, and are often better used in preserves with other flavourings; we use them in combination with an array of other ingredients and spices, such as spiced damson sauce, damson and cinnamon jam, damson and onion relish, damson, lime and coriander chutney and even a spicy damson ketchup.

They are such a versatile fruit that they complement both sweet and savoury dishes. They are great for making an infused vinegar, used to add a tang to meat casseroles, and delicious cooked into a glaze for lamb chops or to top pork pies. You can subdue their plummyness in a dessert topped with crispy crumble or batter, or stew them up to serve as a sweet sauce with cakes or meringue. They are also delicious blended into fools, ice creams and sorbets.

I'm also partial to using these little fruits to make wine or flavour spirits – a chilled glass of damson gin is a real favourite.

This cake is extremely light, and dotted through with dark-coloured damsons. Here the tart fruits are not sweetened before being added to the cake batter, so they have a sharper flavour, but this balanced by the goat's milk jam, which adds the right amount of sweetness. Serve this simply with some fresh raspberries, picked from autumn-fruiting canes at the height of their season.

DAMSON CAKE

Preheat the oven to 180°C/160°C Fan/Gas Mark 4, grease a 250g (9oz) loaf tin and line it with baking parchment.

Cut the damson halves in half again then set aside.

Put the the icing sugar, ground almonds, baking powder and eggs in a stand mixer fitted with the whisk attachment and whisk on high speed for 10 minutes. Melt the butter in a small, heavy-based saucepan over a low heat. Gradually pour the melted butter into the cake batter, whisking constantly. Once the butter is fully incorporated, transfer the batter to a bowl and gently fold in the sifted flour. Put the cake batter in the lined loaf tin and sprinkle over the chopped damsons – these will sink through the cake when cooking. Bake in the oven for 30 minutes, and check it is cooked through by poking it with a skewer and seeing if it comes out clean. Remove from the oven and let stand for 10 minutes before turning the cake out of the tin to cool on a wire rack.

While the cake is cooling make the milk jam. Put the sugar and 50ml water in a small, heavy-based saucepan over a medium heat and make a dark caramel by boiling it until it reaches 170–180°C on a sugar thermometer and becomes thick. Once the caramel has formed, very gradually pour in the milk, stirring (the liquid will boil rapidly). Once all the milk has been added, stir well to dissolve the caramel again. Cook over a low heat for 20–25 minutes until the mixture has thickened, almost to the consistency of condensed milk. Transfer to a bowl, leave to cool, then chill in the fridge (it will thicken further).

Serve slices of the cake with some of the goat's milk jam and a few fresh raspberries.

SERVES 4–6

Damson cake
60g unsalted butter, plus extra for greasing
100g damsons, halved and stoned
75g icing sugar
50g ground almonds
½ tsp baking powder
2 eggs
20g plain flour, sifted

Goat's milk jam
100g caster sugar
300ml goat's milk

fresh raspberries, to serve

Who can resist a warm chocolate pudding with an oozing fruity filling? Damsons and dark chocolate are particularly good partners, as both share sweet and slightly tart flavours, which mellow on cooking. The damson filling is so easy to make and has to be frozen in little cubes before adding to the chocolate mix, so you can make a more and have a stash of this in the freezer to whip up into this deliciously decadent dessert any time you like. Serve piping hot and watch the beautiful damson jam spill out over your spoon as you break them open.

DAMSON CHOCOLATE FONDANT

Brush six dariole or pudding moulds evenly with softened butter. Place on a baking tray and chill the moulds for 10 minutes in the fridge until the butter has set. Once set, brush them again with softened butter and dust the insides with the cocoa powder, tapping out any excess powder that hasn't stuck. Chill the moulds again until required.

To make the damson filling, put the damsons and 100ml water in a medium, heavy-based saucepan and bring to the boil over a medium heat. Reduce the heat to a simmer and cook the fruit for 10–12 minutes. Strain the cooked damsons through a fine sieve into a clean, heavy-based saucepan, pushing as much of the pulp as you can through the sieve using the back of a spoon or ladle. Discard the damson stones. Add the sugar to the damson juice and cook over a low–medium heat for 15–20 minutes until the mixture has the consistency of jam. Remove from the heat and allow to cool slightly. Divide the damson mixture between six holes in a 20ml ice-cube tray and transfer to the freezer until hard.

While the damson filling is freezing, melt the butter and chocolate together in a heatproof bowl set over a pan of simmering water (make sure the bottom of the bowl doesn't touch the water), stirring regularly. While the chocolate is melting, whisk the whole eggs, egg yolks and sugar in a stand mixer fitted with the whisk attachment on high speed until pale, light, fluffy and quadrupled in size. Transfer the mixture to a bowl and gently fold the melted butter and chocolate mixture through the eggs. Once fully incorporated, sift in the flour and fold through again.

Put the fondant mixture in the fridge for 10 minutes and preheat the oven to 180°C/160°C Fan/Gas Mark 4.

Keeping the moulds on the tray, pour 50–60g of the chilled fondant mixture into the bottom of each chilled mould, gently add 1 frozen damson cube and cover each cube with 50–60g of fondant mixture. Bake the fondants for 12–13 minutes, then remove from the oven and allow to sit in the mould for 2 minutes before turning out on to plates. Serve immediately, dusting with cocoa powder.

SERVES 6

Damson filling
300g damsons
2 heaped tbsp caster sugar

Chocolate fondant
250g unsalted butter, plus extra softened
    butter for greasing
3 tbsp cocoa powder, plus extra for
    dusting
250g dark chocolate (60% cocoa solids),
    broken into pieces
5 eggs, plus 5 egg yolks
125g caster sugar
100g plain flour

Crab apples are the ancestors of our modern apples, but they aren't as popular because of their small size and flavour when raw – they are pretty sour and tart. However, their appley notes increase on cooking, and any sharpness can be balanced out with a little added sugar. Cooked with seasonal damsons, this combination of classic British orchard fruits makes a lovely contrast to the rich and intense flavour of the stout ice cream and the crunchy, nutty granola.

STOUT ICE CREAM WITH DAMSON AND CRAB APPLES

To make the damson vinegar syrup, prick the damsons all over with a sharp pin and transfer to a clean 1.5-litre Kilner jar. Pour over the vinegar and leave the damsons to steep in the vinegar for 10 days. Strain into a medium, heavy-based saucepan, add the sugar and reduce to a syrup. Remove from the heat and allow to cool at room temperature.

To make the stout ice cream, put the cream and Guinness in a medium, heavy-based saucepan over a low–medium heat and bring to the boil, then remove from the heat. Whisk together the egg yolks and sugar in a heatproof bowl to combine. Slowly pour the hot cream over the egg yolks, whisking constantly to prevent the eggs from scrambling. Once all incorporated, return to the pan and cook over a low heat until the temperature of the mixture reaches 82°C (check with a thermometer). Strain the mixture through a fine sieve into a clean bowl and leave it to cool, then chill in the fridge. Once chilled, churn in an ice-cream maker until frozen. Transfer to a freezerproof container and store in the freezer until required.

To make the oatmeal granola crumble, preheat the oven to 180°C/160°C Fan/Gas Mark 4. Put the demerara sugar, sunflower oil, honey and butter in a small saucepan over a low heat and heat until the sugar has fully dissolved. Mix the dry ingredients in a bowl and pour in the melted sugar mixture. Mix well so that everything is fully combined, then transfer to a baking tray lined with baking parchment, spread out evenly and bake in the oven for 15 minutes, or until golden, stirring it at regular 5-minute intervals. When golden, remove from the oven and leave to cool (leave the oven on). When cool enough to touch but still warm, break the granola into smaller pieces.

To bake the crab apples, melt the butter in a large frying pan over a high heat. When the butter is foaming add the apples, stir well and cook for 4–5 minutes until golden. Transfer the apples to a baking tray and toss with the sugar and caraway. Bake in the oven for 6–8 minutes until starting to burst out of their skins.

Divide the components among bowls: start with baked crab apples, then the oatmeal granola crumble, and finish with a scoop of ice cream and a drizzle of damson vinegar syrup.

SERVES 4

Damson vinegar syrup
900g damsons
1 litre red wine vinegar
700g caster sugar

Stout ice cream
375ml double cream
90ml Guinness
4 egg yolks
50g caster sugar

Oatmeal granola crumble
50g demerara sugar
20ml sunflower oil
60g honey
30g unsalted butter
30g desiccated coconut
20g flaked almonds
50g porridge oats
30g shelled pistachios, roughly chopped
a small pinch of salt

Baked crab apples
50g unsalted butter
400g crab apples
70g caster sugar
1 tsp ground caraway

Damsons have a pretty short season; once they ripen, they start to fall from the trees as fast as you pick them. This sorbet is a fantastic way to preserve the fruit to eat later. The beautiful burnt meringue shards add a smart finish to this dessert if you want to serve this to friends, and the creamy cheesecake sauce takes the edge off the sharp fruits. Keep the sorbet in the freezer and it's ready to serve whenever you want it.

DAMSON SORBET WITH BURNT MERINGUE AND SALTED ALMONDS

Start by making the damson sorbet. Put the whole damsons and 500ml water in a small, heavy-based saucepan and bring to the boil over a medium heat. Reduce the heat to a simmer and cook the fruit for 10 minutes, or until the damsons have burst and almost stewed. Remove from the heat and strain through a fine sieve into a heatproof bowl, pushing as much pulp through the sieve as you can using the back of a spoon or ladle. Discard the damson stones and set the damson juice aside. Soak the gelatine in cold water for a few minutes until softened. Drain, squeeze out the excess water and stir the gelatine into the warm damson juice until dissolved. Meanwhile, put the sugar, glucose and 200ml water in a medium, heavy-based saucepan over a high heat. Bring to the boil and boil for 1 minute, then remove from the heat and add to the damson juice and stir well. Leave to cool, then chill in the fridge for 1 hour. Once chilled, churn in an ice-cream maker until frozen. Transfer to a freezerproof container and store in the freezer until required.

To make the meringue, preheat the oven to 120°C/100°C Fan/Gas Mark ¼ and line a baking sheet with a silicone mat. Make sure your utensils are grease-free and clean otherwise the egg whites won't whip up. Put the egg whites in a bowl and whisk until lightly and fluffy using an electric whisk. Add the icing sugar a teaspoon at a time, whisking continuously, to create a glossy meringue. Once all the sugar has been added, stop whisking. Spread the meringue on to the lined baking sheet to a thickness of about 2mm, place in the oven and cook for 3–4 hours. Remove from the oven and allow to cool to room temperature.

To make the salted almonds, put the sugar in a small, heavy-based saucepan with the almonds and 250ml water over a medium heat and bring to the boil, then reduce the heat and simmer for 10 minutes until the mixture becomes sticky and is losing its colour. Strain the almonds from the liquid and allow to cool slightly on a plate, then deep-fry the nuts in a pan of oil heated to 180°C for 2–3 minutes, or until deeply golden. Remove from the hot oil with a slotted spoon, transfer to a plate lined with kitchen paper and season lightly with salt. Allow to cool. Once cooled, put some of the nuts in a sandwich bag and break them up by bashing them lightly with a rolling pin, leaving a few whole to decorate.

SERVES 4–6

Damson sorbet
500g damsons
6 gelatine leaves
100g caster sugar
1 tbsp liquid glucose

Burnt meringue
3 egg whites
60g icing sugar

Salted almonds
200g caster sugar
30 blanched almonds
vegetable oil, for deep-frying
a pinch of salt

Cheesecake sauce
50g ricotta
20g caster sugar
50g fromage frais
½ vanilla pod, split lengthways and seeds
    scraped out

To make the cheesecake sauce, whisk the ricotta and sugar together in a bowl until the sugar has dissolved. Fold through the fromage frais and vanilla seeds.

To char the meringue, break and snap away large shards of meringue (it should be very fragile) and gently blowtorch the shards to add a light burnt effect.

Serve a couple of scoops of sorbet on each plate with shards of charred meringue, drops of the cheesecake sauce and salted almonds scattered around.

Pâte de fruit is made from fruits cooked with sugar and pectin, which is set in moulds or cut into bite-sized treats. Originally this was used as a method of preserving the flesh of fruits, but that doesn't do this delicious jelly justice. The hibiscus sugar adds a wonderfully aromatic crunch which contrasts with the soft texture of the pâte de fruit. This recipe makes about 25–30 jellies that can be served as a petit four to impress friends as the dinner finale.

DAMSON PÂTE DE FRUIT

Start by making the damson purée. Put the damsons and 150ml water in a medium, heavy-based saucepan and bring to the boil over a medium heat. Reduce the heat to a simmer and cook the fruit for 10–12 minutes until the damsons have burst and almost stewed, then strain the cooked damsons through a fine sieve into another medium, heavy-based saucepan, pushing as much of the pulp as you can through the sieve using the back of a spoon or ladle. Discard the damson stones.

Stir the pectin and 35g of the caster sugar in a bowl to evenly disperse the pectin. Whisk this into the damson purée. Put the fruit purée back over a medium heat, add the remaining sugar and glucose and whisk well. Cook the mixture, whisking constantly, until it reaches 108°C on a sugar thermometer.

Once the temperature has been reached, divide the hot jelly mixture between 25–30 x 15ml silicone half-sphere moulds and allow to set at room temperature for about 1 hour. Transfer to the fridge and allow to chill for a further 2 hours.

Alternatively, if you do not have silicone moulds pour the hot jelly mix into a cling film-lined baking tray and allow to set the same way, but you will have to turn the jelly out and cut to the desired size using a knife.

To make the hibiscus sugar, blitz the hibiscus and the sugar cubes together in a small blender. Transfer to a small bowl and fold through the granulated sugar.

Toss the set jellies in the hibiscus sugar before serving.

MAKES 25-30 JELLIES

Damson purée
500g damsons

Pâte de fruit
18g powdered pectin
335g caster sugar
375g damson purée (above)
90g liquid glucose

Hibiscus sugar
10g dried hibiscus
5 white sugar cubes
1 tbsp granulated sugar

Poaching the damsons and making the shiso granita couldn't be simpler; the only challenge comes with making the accompanying puffed rice, but do give it a go, as the sweet crunch really makes this dish. Damsons have a flavour that can really stand up against other strong flavours, but also blends beautifully in the right combination. Shiso – or perilla – is a member of the mint family, and the leaves have notes of cinnamon and cumin, so when combined with ginger the granita adds a refreshing note to the poached fruit.

POACHED DAMSONS WITH ICED SHISO

To make the granita, put the sugar in a medium, heavy-based saucepan with 250ml water and bring to the boil. While it's heating up, roughly slice the shiso leaves. Once the water and sugar mixture has come to the boil, remove it from the heat and add the shiso leaves, ginger, pared lemon peel and juice. Stir well and leave to infuse and cool for 30 minutes, then strain through a fine sieve into a freezerproof container. Place in the freezer for 4–5 hours until frozen solid.

While the granita is in the freezer, poach the damsons. Put the sugar, honey, overripe plums and lemon juice in a medium, heavy-based saucepan with 200ml water. Place over a medium heat and bring to the boil, then reduce the heat and simmer for 10–15 minutes until the plums are just holding their shape. Pass the liquid through a fine sieve into a small, heavy-based saucepan and discard the solids. Bring to the boil again, then remove from the heat and allow to cool for 5 minutes. Add the damsons to the poaching liquid and leave to gently poach in the residual heat. When completely cool, transfer to the fridge to chill.

Heat the oil for the puffed rice in a small, heavy-based saucepan over a low–medium heat until it reaches 220°C, then reduce the heat to low. Using a metal slotted spoon, add the rice in batches to the hot oil and stir gently. Be extremely careful as the oil is very hot. If the oil is at the correct temperature it should take no longer than 15 seconds for the rice to puff and rise to the top of the oil. Using the slotted spoon, remove the puffed grains of rice from the oil and allow to drain and cool on kitchen paper for a couple of minutes. Once cool, transfer the rice to a small bowl and add the maltodextrin and icing sugar. Mix well.

Divide the chilled poached damsons evenly among bowls, along with some of the chilled poaching liquor. Remove the granita from the freezer and scrape the surface with a fork to create ice crystals. Spoon the ice crystals over the damsons to cover, then sprinkle over the sweetened puffed rice to add crunch. Finish with micro perilla leaves.

SERVES 4–6

Shiso granita
30g caster sugar
30g shiso leaves
small knob of fresh ginger (about 8g),
    sliced
juice and peel of 1 lemon

Poached damsons
500g caster sugar
125g honey
200g overripe plums, such as Victoria,
    halved and stoned
juice of ½ lemon
300–400g damsons, halved and stoned

Puffed rice
400ml sunflower oil
2 tbsp black wild rice
1 tbsp maltodextrin
1 tbsp icing sugar

micro perilla shoots, to serve

STOCKS

VEGETABLE STOCK

3 onions, finely chopped
2 celery sticks, finely chopped
2 carrots, finely chopped
1 fennel bulb, finely chopped
1 leek, finely chopped
1 head of garlic, halved
15g chervil
15g tarragon
15g flat-leaf parsley

Put all the vegetables and the garlic halves in a large, heavy-based saucepan with 4 litres of water. Bring to the boil over a medium heat, then reduce the heat and simmer for 30 minutes. Take off the heat, add the herbs and leave to cool, then chill and infuse in the fridge overnight. The following day, strain it through a muslin-lined sieve. Keep the stock covered in the fridge and use within 3–4 days, or freeze and use within 3 months.

BROWN CHICKEN STOCK

3kg chicken wings

Preheat the oven to 200°C/180°C Fan/Gas Mark 6. Roughly chop the chicken wings, put them in a roasting tin and roast in the oven for 35–40 minutes until deeply golden brown. Discard any fat and put the wings in a large, heavy-based saucepan with 5 litres of water. Bring to the boil over a medium heat, then reduce the heat and simmer for 2–3 hours, skimming occasionally. Remove from the heat and leave to cool. Strain through a muslin-lined sieve into a clean container. Keep the stock covered in the fridge and use within 3–4 days, or freeze and use within 3 months. For an intense chicken sauce, reduce the stock in a saucepan over a low–medium heat, skimming it regularly to discard any fats that rise to the top, until it has reached a glossy sauce consistency.

WHITE CHICKEN STOCK

3kg chicken wings

Roughly chop the chicken wings and put them in a large, heavy-based saucepan with 5 litres of water. Bring to the boil over a medium heat, then reduce the heat and simmer for 2–3 hours, skimming occasionally. Remove from the heat and leave to cool, the strain through a muslin-lined sieve. Keep the stock covered in the fridge and use within 3–4 days, or freeze and use within 3 months.

HAM STOCK

2 ham hocks
2 onions, roughly chopped
2 carrots, roughly chopped
1 leek, roughly chopped
2 celery sticks, roughly chopped
1 head of garlic, halved
5 sprigs of thyme
2 bay leaves
1 tsp black peppercorns
1 tsp fennel seeds
1 tsp coriander seeds
15g flat-leaf parsley, leaves and stalks
15g tarragon, leaves and stalks

Rinse the ham hocks under cold running water for 5 minutes. Put the vegetables, garlic, thyme, bay, peppercorns, fennel seeds and coriander seeds in a large, heavy-based saucepan along with the ham hocks and cover with 5 litres of water. Bring to the boil over a medium heat, then reduce the heat and simmer for 3 hours Remove from the heat, add the parsley and tarragon and leave to infuse for 30 minutes. Strain through a muslin-lined sieve. Keep the stock covered in the fridge and use within 3–4 days, or freeze and use within 3 months.

BEEF STOCK

2kg diced key chain of beef
2kg minced flank steak
2 tbsp sunflower oil
3 onions, sliced
100g shiitake mushrooms, sliced
1 star anise
1 bay leaf
3 sprigs of thyme
7 litres White Chicken Stock (see opposite)

Preheat the oven to 200°C/180°C Fan/Gas Mark 6.
Roast the two cuts of meats in separate roasting tins in
the oven for 25–30 minutes until browned. Warm the oil
in a large, heavy-based saucepan over a medium heat,
add the onions and caramelise for 10–15 minutes. Add the
mushrooms, star anise and herbs and cook for a further
2 minutes. Add the roast beef to the pan, cover with the
chicken stock and bring to the boil. Reduce the heat and
simmer for 3 hours, skimming occasionally. Remove from
the heat and allow to cool, then strain through a muslin-
lined sieve. Keep the stock covered in the fridge and use
within 3–4 days, or freeze and use within 3 months.

For an intense beef sauce, reduce the stock in a saucepan
over a low–medium heat, skimming it regularly to discard
any fats that rise to the top, until it has reached a glossy
sauce consistency.

FISH STOCK

2 fennel bulbs, roughly chopped
4 shallots, roughly chopped
½ head of garlic
2 tbsp sunflower oil
1 tsp coriander seeds
1 tsp white peppercorns
1 star anise
200ml white wine
2kg flat fish bones (halibut, turbot, brill), roughly chopped
10g chervil
10g flat-leaf parsley, leaves and stalks
1 lemon, sliced

Warm the oil in a large, heavy-based saucepan over a
medium heat, add the vegetables and garlic and cook,
stirring regularly, for 5–6 minutes, or until the shallot is
translucent (you do not want to brown the vegetables). Add
the spices and the wine, cook until the wine has almost
completely evaporated, then add the fish bones and
3 litres of water. Bring to the boil over a medium heat, then
reduce the heat and simmer for 20 minutes, skimming off
any scum that rises to the top. Remove from the heat and
add the chervil, parsley and lemon. Allow to infuse for
30 minutes, then strain through a muslin-lined sieve. Keep
the stock covered in the fridge and use within 3–4 days, or
freeze and use within 3 months.

GLOSSARY
OF
PLANTS
AND
FLOWERS

1. WILD ROCKET

2. NASTURTIUM LEAVES

3. DIANTHUS

4. OXALIS SORREL FLOWER

5. BABY RED CHARD

6. CHOI SHOOTS

7. ANISE HYSSOP

8. TURNIP LEAVES

9. BRASSICA FLOWERS

10. FENNEL

11. SWEET CICELY

12. BABY CUCUMBERS

13. BORAGE

14. GREEN MUSTARD FRILL

15. CORNFLOWER

16. WILD CHERVIL

17. GARLIC CHIVES

18. FRISEE LETTUCE

19. KALE FLOWERS

1. WILD ROCKET

Warm peppery, pleasantly pungent flavour, the flowers have a faint orangey aroma. Use raw in salads or as a garnish.

2. NASTURTIUM LEAVES

Agreeable peppery cress-like taste, refreshing flavour. Use raw in salads or as a garnish.

3. DIANTHUS

Use flowers for their attractive appearance, colour and their gentle clove-like, nutmeg flavour.

4. OXALIS SORREL FLOWER

Packed with vitamins, this little flower adds a citrus tang to dishes.

5. BABY RED CHARD

Elegant salad leaf with good flavour for use in salads or as a garnish.

6. CHOI SHOOTS

These micro shoots have a sweet and succulent brassica flavour and are great raw in salads.

7. ANISE HYSSOP

Both the flowers and leaves of this herb have a subtle anise flavour. The purple flowers make a lovely garnish. Commonly used in teas and summer drinks.

8. TURNIP LEAVES

Grown as baby shoots, these leaves have a milder flavour than the sometimes overpowering taste of mature turnips.

9. BRASSICA FLOWERS

Appearing in winter, these flowers have a lovely broccoli flavour.

10. FENNEL

These little yellow flowers have a potent anise flavour – lovely as a garnish, or in soups or desserts. Drying produces fennel pollen.

11. SWEET CICELY

Leaves and flowers have a delightful anise flavour; they can also be used as a natural sweetener (see page 47). A herb for many uses.

12. BABY CUCUMBERS

These tiny flowers give a spectacular splash of colour as well as a delicate cucumbery flavour.

13. BORAGE

Beautiful blue flowers with a faint cucumber flavour, cool and fresh-tasting with a slight hint of saltiness. Great in salads, as a garnish as well as in sorbets and soups. Looks good floating on a jug of Pimm's!

14. GREEN MUSTARD FRILL

These little leaves add a mustard and horseradish taste to dishes. Use as a garnish or in salads.

15. CORNFLOWER

Delicate, frilly flowers have a sweet to spicy flavour, a little like cloves. Use as a colourful garnish.

16. WILD CHERVIL

Lightly anise, with a herby flavour. Fantastic in vinaigrettes, butter and cream sauces and with fish, poultry or vegetables. If using it in cooking, add it as late as possible to preserve its flavour.

17. GARLIC CHIVES

These look like ordinary chives but have a delicate garlic and onion flavour. Good in soups, dressings, salads, sauces and as a garnish.

18. FRISEE LETTUCE

The inside yellow leaves add delicious crunch and a slightly bitter, peppery flavour.

19. KALE FLOWERS

These tiny yellow flowers are sweet and have a brassica flavour. Lovely as a garnish or lightly fried.

20. WILD CHIVE FLOWER

The attractive pink/purple flower heads add colour to a plate. Great in salads or omelettes, with a light onion taste.

21. RED ORACHE

These pretty, arrow-shaped leaves have a spinach-like flavour, so are great alongside pungent, stronger-tasting leaves. They are an attractive red addition to the salad bowl.

22. COURGETTE FLOWER

These mildly courgette-flavoured flowers can add colour and crunch while raw, or be stuffed and fried.

23. RADISH SHOOTS

Tender, succulent little shoots with a mild radish flavour that are lovely lightly sautéed or in salads.

24. CALENDULA

Calendula have a distinctive muskiness with light citrus notes similar to coriander. The daisy-like flowers add a vibrant colour to salads but also cooked dishes, as saffron would. The petals can be used dried or picked and scattered fresh.

25. BURGUNDY OXALIS

An attractive, red, cultivated alternative to wood sorrel but with many of the same characteristics. Oxalic acid is the source of its flavour; it's good in salads or as a garnish for both savoury dishes and desserts.

26. RED DRAGON MUSTARD FRILL

Pretty, frilly salad leaves with a mild and a fiery mustard flavour. Good as a garnish or scattered through a salad.

27. PINEAPPLE WEED

As the name suggests, this delicate, chamomile-looking herb has a mild pineapple flavour which is perfect for salads, desserts and teas. Also good for flavouring stock, syrups and jellies.

28. ICE PLANT

These quirky-looking sprigs look like they have tiny little ice droplets stuck to them, hence the name. They add a sparkle to dishes but also have a tangy, succulent, juicy taste.

29. RADISH FLOWERS

These pretty little purple or sometimes white flowers have a subtle pepper flavour, a bit like the radish itself. Lovely in butters, creams, salads and as a garnish.

30. MIZUNA CRESS

These little glossy serrated leaves look great but also have a peppery flavour similar to rocket.

31. TAGETES FLOWER

These citrus flavoured flowers look lovely but can also be used instead of saffron to infuse cooked dishes with a light colour.

32. VIOLA

Not just pretty garnishes, these cheery little flowers have a mild grassy and slightly herby flavour.

33. PINEAPPLE MINT

The small, light green leaves have a tropical fruit flavour, with a tinge of mint. Great for drinks, fruit desserts and salads.

34. NASTURTIUM FLOWER

Not only do these have a strong peppery flavour, they also add fantastic colour to dishes. Flower buds and seeds make great 'capers' when pickled.

35. RED AMARANTH

The bright red, intensely coloured leaves make these a lovely addition to a plate, but they also have a pea-like flavour and high nutritional value.

20. WILD CHIVE
FLOWER

21. RED ORACHE

22. COURGETTE FLOWER

23. RADISH SHOOTS

24. CALENDULA

25. BURGUNDY
OXALIS

26. RED DRAGON
MUSTARD FRILL

27. PINEAPPLE
WEED

28. ICE PLANT

29. RADISH
    FLOWERS

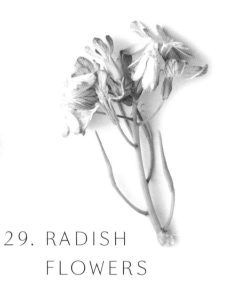

31. TAGETES FLOWER

30. MIZUNA CRESS

32. VIOLA

34. NASTURTIUM
    FLOWER

35. RED AMARANTH

33. PINEAPPLE
    MINT

INDEX

COOK'S NOTES

GENERAL NOTES

- All eggs are medium, free-range and organic, unless otherwise stated.
- All vegetables are medium unless otherwise stated.
- All spoon measures are level unless otherwise stated.

TECHNIQUES

- Blanching involves immersing an ingredient into boiling water for just a minute or two, to soften it slightly but not cook it fully, thus helping it to retain its colour and freshness.
- In the restaurant, we blitz our sauces in a blender to a very fine purée, then pass them through a fine sieve for a really smooth texture. This additional step is, of course, optional: if you don't pass the sauce through a sieve the sauce will have the same flavour but a rougher texture.
- To sterilise glass jars or bottles, remove the lids (and any rubber seals) if they are not heatproof, and either run them through a hot dishwasher cycle or wash them in hot soapy water, rinse and leave to dry in a hot oven for 20 minutes. Wash the lids and seals separately if necessary. Fill the jars or bottles while they are still warm and seal immediately.
- To home-smoke foods, put a nice even layer of smoking woodchips in a large baking tray lined with foil. Sit a wire rack on top, one that is a similar size to the baking tray, making sure the wire rack isn't touching the chips. Put the meat or fish on the rack and cover the entire rack and tray with a tent of foil, so no smoke escapes. Sit the tray on the hob over a medium–low heat for 10 minutes. Remove the covered tray from the heat and allow the meat to smoke in the foil tent for 30 minutes. Make sure you open a window to prevent smoke build-up in your kitchen, or alternatively, you can use your homemade smoker on a barbecue outdoors.
- To separate curds and whey, tip the yoghurt into a muslin bag or cheesecloth, tie the cloth to a cupboard door, hang over a bowl and leave for 3–4 hours at room temperature or in the fridge if you have room. The whey will drip into the bowl below. Refrigerate in two containers once separated until needed.

EQUIPMENT

- A bain marie consists of a heatproof dish or pan placed over or in another pan of warm water, to allow the contents of the dish or pan to cook, warm through or melt gently. If the bain marie is over the hob, the heatproof dish or pan shouldn't touch the water, but if it's in the oven, the dish or pan should sit in the pan of water.

UNUSUAL INGREDIENTS

Maltodextrin
This is available in many forms but we use it as a highly refined powder; when mixed with moist ingredients, such as fat, it absorbs them and so thickens the powder. However, when the powder hits your mouth the maltodextrin dissolves, leaving behind only the fat or flavouring. It has a naturally sweet taste, which means it can be used to add sweetness without sugar.

Land seaweed (Salsola soda)
Also known as agretti or roscano in Italy, where it is much used, these fine, grass-like fronds have a flavour that is a little like spinach. It grows easily from seed and is delicious in salads, dry-fried or served as a garnish.

Agar agar
Available in powder or flakes, when boiled with liquids it sets into a jelly. Derived from red algae, it is a good vegetarian substitute for gelatine in ice cream, sauces and gels.

Xanthan gum
Mostly known as a magic ingredient in gluten-free baking to bind flours, it is useful for emulsifying and thickening dressings and sauces. Similar to cornflour in texture, we use this white powder to stabilise foams, gels and emulsions and prevent them splitting.

Kuzu starch
The starch made from Kuzu – also known as wild or Jaapanese arrowroot – is excellent as a thickener to produce really smooth soups and sauces, or can be dusted over vegetables, fish or meat before frying for a light, crispy crunch. You can add the powder straight to dishes or make a paste before adding to sauces.

Dashi
Mostly used as the base for a broth, this Japanese ingredient makes clear, thin stocks that have a salty, umami flavour. Fresh dashi can be made using dried kombu seaweed and dried bonito flakes, which are simmered to infuse the flavours, but you can also buy good-quality granules.

Dried kombu

Another umami ingredient, this edible kelp seaweed is packed with vitamins and minerals and makes healthy and delicious stocks, or the dehydrated strips can be boiled with beans to make them more digestible.

Summer savory

The little green-grey leaves of this herb have a really pungent flavour and only need to be used in small quantities. Summer savory has a piquant, peppery bite and is delicious with meat, oily fish and vegetables, and in particular with beans.

Bonito flakes

These paper-thin flakes are made by drying and fermenting tuna and then smoking them to produce an intense umami flavour. A pinch goes a long way, and can be added to dashi, other stocks or used as a garnish on light dishes.

Meadowsweet powder/dried meadowsweet

Meadowsweet is a perennial herb that grows in damp meadows. Its extraordinary honey almond scent is delicious in light puddings, vinegars, wines and dressings, and even in jams, and its flavour is well preserved when the whole plant is dried.

Sea buckthorn

This native shrub tends to be found happily growing along coastlines, and if you can get past its prickly spines you can crop its jewel-like orange berries. They have a fantastic sharp, acidic tang which is very potent, and just as powerful health benefits. You can buy buckthorn berries already juiced. A little goes a long way.

ABOUT SIMON ROGAN

Over the past 25 years Simon has developed a distinctive and inventive cooking style, underpinned by his passion for working with the best possible ingredients.

Building a culinary destination in Cartmel in the southern Lake District, Simon opened L'Enclume in 2002 followed by Rogan & Co in 2008. Developing his commitment to the area, Simon has been running his own farm just outside Cartmel since 2009.

L'Enclume currently holds 5 AA Rosettes and 2 Michelin stars and was named *Good Food Guide*'s number-one restaurant from 2014–2017. In 2018 it retained its 10/10 score and was awarded second place. Rogan & Co holds 3 AA Rosettes and offers guests a more casual dining experience, while retaining the unparalleled precision and creativity of Simon's famed culinary style.

Simon opened Aulis London in October 2017 – by day an experimental development kitchen and by night an intimate eight-seater chef's table. He opened Roganic in Marylebone in January 2018 after achieving cult status as a pop-up between 2011–2013.

ACKNOWLEDGEMENTS

A big thank you to all the following for making this book become a reality. Everyone involved made my first book a joy to work on.

The team at HarperCollins: Grace Cheetham, James Empringham, Isabel Hayman-Brown and Katya Shipster.

Cristian Barnett for his amazing photography skills and patience and his assistant Chris Horwood.

Nicole Herft and Rosie MacKean for the food styling and endless laughs.

Helena Caldon for help with writing and editing – I know it has been tough at times but we got there in the end.

Harry Guy, for his tireless work on this book and for putting up with me!

My long-serving team behind me in Cartmel village at L'Enclume and Rogan & Co, and the London team at Roganic.

Dan Cox at Crocadon Farm, not just for his service over many years but for still being on the team, still supporting the cause and sorting some of the artisan ingredients you see here in this book.

Sean and Clare of Good Earth growers for their endless support over the years and inspiring us with their ethos and huge array of beautiful produce.

My other half in anything and everything, the single most important person, solely responsible for where I am today, my driving force and the smart, logical half of our partnership, thank you my darling Penny.

And to Mark Veyrat, for his innovative use of wild herbs and flowers in cooking that inspired me and set me on the path that I've followed with my restaurants.